"Finally! I've been hoping and pr
years. With insight and clarity, I
theological truth that can revolutionize the churches understanding and ....
tion of singleness. This book is a gift to God's people, and the impact could be
nothing less than incredible. Read it and rejoice!"

> **Steve Brown,** radio broadcaster, Key Life Network;
> Emeritus Professor of Preaching, Reformed Theological Seminary

"Immensely helpful! Amidst extremes of celibacy versus marriage in Christian
traditions on the one hand and today's proliferation of sexual noncommitment
on the other, Danylak gives us a thorough-going biblical theology of singleness.
He unfolds themes of marriage and singleness from both Old Testament and New
Testament with essential, delightful applications for all of us."

> **J. Scott Horrell,** Professor of Theological Studies,
> Dallas Theological Seminary

"Barry Danylak's book on singleness is now the most thorough and helpful book
on the subject. He treats directly the main difficulty in grasping the new covenant
view—the strong Old Testament emphasis on procreation and its importance for
establishing and carrying forward the old-covenant people. The change in the
nature of the blessing of God for the human race that comes with the new covenant is the key new perspective for understanding Christian singleness, a perspective too often missed in discussions of singleness and voluntary celibacy in
the Christian life. Danylak's careful exegesis sustains his overarching view well."

> **Stephen B. Clark,** Director of Research (retired), National Secretariat of
> the Cursillo Movement; author, *Building Christian Communities*

"Barry Danylak not only presents a deeply penetrating study of the New
Testament teaching on singleness but also shows how this teaching fits the entire
storyline of the Bible. Far from being a book just for single people, *Redeeming
Singleness* demonstrates how marriage and the single life give a complementary
witness to the gospel in the modern world. This is a hugely important and timely
book for all Christians."

> **Daniel Keating,** Associate Professor of Theology, Sacred Heart
> Major Seminary

"Barry Danylak's work has been a great help to me in understanding the distinctive role of singleness in God's new-covenant people. His writing provides a clear framework of biblical theology, which I found deeply valuable for drawing together the intuitions I had about the meaning of singleness. There is much that the church as a whole, and not just single people, can learn from this."

Lydia Jaeger, Academic Dean, Institut Biblique de Nogent-sur-Marne

"I like the way Danylak methodically and progressively turns over pieces of the biblical jigsaw and assembles them to reveal a thoughtful perspective on marriage and procreation. From the New Testament he firmly grasps the nettle of exegetically difficult passages, and with reference to the cultural influences brings a redemptive perspective to singleness for the contemporary world."

John D. Wilson, Missiologist and mentor (Southeast Asia), World Team

Redeeming Singleness

How the Storyline of Scripture Affirms the Single Life

Barry Danylak

Foreword by John Piper

WHEATON, ILLINOIS

Redeeming Singleness: How the Storyline of Scripture Affirms the Single Life

Copyright © 2010 by Barry Nicholas Danylak

Published by Crossway
      1300 Crescent Street
      Wheaton, Illinois 60187

Cover design: Amy Bristow

Cover photo: Getty Images

First printing 2010

Printed in the United States of America

Unless otherwise indicated, Scripture quotations are from the ESV® Bible (*The Holy Bible, English Standard Version®*), copyright © 2001 by Crossway. Used by permission. All rights reserved.

Scripture quotations marked AT are the author's translation.

Scripture quotations marked NASB are from *The New American Standard Bible®*. Copyright © The Lockman Foundation 1960, 1962, 1963, 1968, 1971, 1972, 1973, 1975, 1977, 1995. Used by permission.

Scripture quotations marked NET are from *The NET Bible®* copyright © 2003 by Biblical Studies Press, L.L.C. www.netbible.com. All rights reserved. Quoted by permission.

Scripture references marked NIV are taken from the Holy Bible, New International Version®. Copyright © 1973, 1978, 1984 Biblica. Used by permission of Zondervan. All rights reserved. The "NIV" and "New International Version" trademarks are registered in the United States Patent and Trademark Office by Biblica. Use of either trademark requires the permission of Biblica.

Scripture references marked NLT are from *The Holy Bible, New Living Translation*, copyright © 1996, 2004. Used by permission of Tyndale House Publishers, Inc., Wheaton, Ill., 60189. All rights reserved.

Scripture references marked RSV are from *The Revised Standard Version*. Copyright © 1946, 1952, 1971, 1973 by the Division of Christian Education of the National Council of the Churches of Christ in the U.S.A.

All emphases in Scripture quotations have been added by the author.

Trade paperback ISBN: 978-1-4335-0588-1
PDF ISBN: 978-1-4335-0589-8
Mobipocket ISBN: 978-1-4335-0590-4
ePub ISBN: 978-1-4335-2286-4

Library of Congress Cataloging-in-Publication Data
Danylak, Barry.
Redeeming singleness : how the storyline of Scripture affirms the
single life / Barry Danylak ; foreword by John Piper.
    p. cm.
  Includes bibliographical references and index.
  ISBN 978-1-4335-0588-1 (tpb)
    1. Celibacy—Biblical teaching. 2. Single people—Religious life—
Biblical teaching. I. Title.
BS680.S5D36   2010
220.8'306732—dc22   2010006579

Crossway is a publishing ministry of Good News Publishers.

VP		19	18	17	16	15	14	13	12	11	10
14	13	12	11	10	9	8	7	6	5	4	3	2	1

To
my parents,
Walter and Marjorie Danylak,
who begat me in Christ

Contents

List of Abbreviations

AB	Anchor Bible
BA	Biblical Archaeologist
CBQ	Catholic Biblical Quarterly
CTR	Criswell Theological Review
HR	History of Religions
Int	Interpretation
ISBE	International Standard Bible Encyclopedia
ITC	International Theological Commentary
JAOS	Journal of the American Oriental Society
JBL	Journal of Biblical Literature
JETS	Journal of the Evangelical Theological Society
JR	Journal of Religion
JSNT	Journal for the Study of the New Testament
JSOT	Journal for the Study of the Old Testament
LCL	Loeb Classical Library
NAC	New American Commentary
NICNT	New International Commentary on the New Testament
NICOT	The New International Commentary on the Old Testament
NIDOTTE	New International Dictionary of Old Testament Theology and Exegesis
NIGTC	New International Greek Testament Commentary
NTS	New Testament Studies
OCD	Oxford Classical Dictionary
OTL	Old Testament Library
ResQ	Restoration Quarterly
RevExp	Review and Expositor
ScrHier	Scripta hierosolymitana
SP	Sacra pagina
TDNT	Theological Dictionary of the New Testament
TDOT	Theological Dictionary of the Old Testament
TLOT	Theological Lexicon of the Old Testament
TynBul	Tyndale Bulletin
USQR	Union Seminary Quarterly Review
VT	Vetus Testamentum
WBC	Word Biblical Commentary
ZAW	Zeitschrift für die alttestamentliche Wissenschaft
ZNW	Zeitschrift für die neutestamentliche Wissenschaft und die Kunde der älteren Kirche

List of Figures and Tables

Foreword

by John Piper

The greatest, wisest, most fully human person who has ever lived never married—Jesus Christ. His greatest apostle never married and was thankful for his singleness. Jesus himself said that in the age to come we do not marry. And he added that the age to come had already broken into this world.

Therefore, the presence of single people in the church not only "attests the sufficiency of Christ for the reception of God's covenantal blessings in the new covenant," as Danylak has written, but also reminds us "that the spiritual age has already been inaugurated in Christ and awaits imminent consummation."

When I met Barry Danylak at Tyndale House in Cambridge, England, in the summer of 2006, I was amazed at the research he was doing on a biblical theology of singleness. Not only was the scope of it unprecedented, but the theological and practical insights struck me as biblically compelling and practically urgent. I don't know of anyone else who has ever provided the extent of biblical reflection on singleness that Barry has provided for us here.

Both marriage and singleness demand the most serious and solid biblical insight. These are realities that affect every area of our life and thought. We cannot settle for superficial pep talks. Our lives cry out for significance, and significance comes from seeing ourselves the way God sees us—including our singleness. My guess is that virtually every single who reads this book will finish with a sense of wonder at who they are and how little they knew about this gift and calling.

Barry is keenly aware of the progress of redemptive history and its stunning implications for the single life. Early in that history, marriage and physical children were fundamental to the blessings of the Mosaic covenant, but they are not fundamental to the new covenant the way they were then. And what is beautiful about the way Barry develops this historical flow is that the glory of Jesus Christ is exalted above all things.

Barry elevates but does not absolutize the calling of the single life. Its greatness lies, he says, in this: "It is a visible reminder that the kingdom of God points to a reality which stands beyond worldly preoccupations of marriage, family, and career." Indeed. And that greater reality is the all-satisfying, everlasting friendship of Jesus himself in the new heavens and the new earth. Marriage and singleness will be transcended, and Christ himself will make those categories obsolete in the joy of his presence. A life of joyful singleness witnesses to this.

—John Piper
Pastor for Preaching and Vision
Bethlehem Baptist Church

Introduction

This book is not like many others you will pick up about a Christian perspective of singleness. It does not focus on the personal experience of singleness, or on cultural analysis of the phenomenon of singleness in the contemporary church. Nor is it a conventional presentation of the biblical teaching on the subject, or an attempt to glean from exemplary models of single people from Scripture or church history. This book is also not a how-to manual either for living the single life well or for most expediently relieving oneself of the status. There are many other well-written books that focus on all these areas. The starting point for this book is to reflect on the purpose of biblical affirmation of the single life by exploring how singleness itself fits into God's larger purpose of redeeming a people for his glory. The fruit of such reflection will contribute toward constructing a *biblical theology* of singleness.

One must confess in this modern age that to claim that a book is a "theology" of anything is tantamount to playing with fire, and perhaps it is even the kiss of death for any author wishing to attract interested readers. For many Christians theology connotes that which is boring and obscure and divides well-meaning people over distinctions without a difference. Why then would a theology of singleness be even remotely helpful? The answer is that theology provides a degree of logic and coherence for understanding our faith. It is theology that provides the handles for us to make sense of both *what* we believe as Christians and *why* we believe it. So our purpose here is to explore the logic and coherency of *why* the Christian Scriptures affirm singleness as good in a created world in which sexual partnerships and marriage are the pervasive norm for human beings.

The payoff of such an endeavor is that such theological grounding gives rootedness and dimensionality to living as biblically principled people. Just as prudent theological reflection on the nature and attributes of God (e.g., his omnipotence, omnipresence, sovereignty, etc.) might revolutionize how we approach God in prayer, so too, prudent theological reflection on a comparatively minor biblical topic—singleness—can revitalize how we think and approach living as the family of God in the modern world. Moreover, biblical theological reflection is especially fruitful on topics such as marriage and singleness because at the surface level the cultural bridge between our modern world and the biblical world can be very great.[1]

The aim of such a biblical theology of singleness is not to provide an apologetic for singleness as an attempt to biblically persuade anyone either to marry or to remain single. Nevertheless, theological reflection can give an added degree of excitement and richness to living a life singly for the kingdom of God. Likewise the whole church can benefit through such theological reflection, whether we are married, single, divorced, or widowed, since greater clarity in understanding any one part of the body of Christ simultaneously brings greater clarity in understanding the whole.

Christianity versus Judaism, Islam, and Mormonism

One might wonder why singleness should have any theological significance at all. In our modern Western culture, the decision to marry or not to marry is largely viewed as a personal lifestyle choice without any particular ethical or theological implications. For many, the decision to marry is inextricably linked to encountering or not encountering a suitable partner; it is not seen as a conscious *a priori* choice apart from potential partners. Why then should we expect any fruit at all in exploring the unmarried state as especially *theologically* significant?

The first clue is the observation that the affirmation of singleness as a lifestyle commitment is somewhat *distinctive* to New Testament Christianity. This is most visible when comparing the view of celibate singleness within Christianity with Christianity's closest monotheistic siblings: Judaism, Islam, and Mormonism. In regard to marriage and family values, all four "sibling" faiths have much in common. Adherents of all see themselves as champions of "family values"; all look to the creation accounts of Genesis 1 and 2 as normative for understanding the institution of marriage as fundamentally good and part of the designed order of creation; conversely, all uniformly condemn the practice of adultery and fornication at least in part on the teaching of the Pentateuch. Yet on the question of maintaining a life of celibate singleness, Christianity is strikingly different from the other three. Rabbinic Judaism viewed procreation and, by implication, marriage as a divine commandment on the basis of the creation mandate in Genesis 1:28 to "be fruitful and multiply."[2] A negative disposition toward a life of celibacy persists in modern Judaism. The citation for "celibacy" in *The New Encyclopedia of Judaism* begins bluntly: "Marriage is a commandment in Jewish tradition and celibacy is deplored." The Koran similarly encourages the single person to marry, and Mohammed himself apparently condemned the practice of celibacy as "exceeding the law of God."[3] Celibate singleness is also explicitly rejected in Mormonism, where undergoing the rite of *celestial marriage* in the temple is necessary to achieve exaltation in the highest heaven in the hereafter, whereby human beings become gods and increase their posterity eternally.[4]

Thus while Christianity is similar to its Judeo-Christian siblings in its sexual ethics and value for family, it is notably different from its siblings in its affirmation of singleness as a *gift* and valued lifestyle within the life of the believing community. This difference, as we shall see, is more than simply an enlightened relegation of the marriage decision to the realm of individual choice but relates to something fundamentally distinct within Christianity itself—namely, the atoning work of Jesus Christ.

The Emerging Culture of Non-marriage: The Data Speaks

There are also powerful cultural forces at work in the twenty-first century that compel the need for clarifying theological reflection on the question of singleness. This is evidenced dramatically in demographic trends of the past generation. The two graphs below show that since the mid-twentieth century the percentage of married adults has been on a steady decline from (in the U.S.) over two-thirds of the overall adult population in 1960 to less than 55 percent by 2009 (Fig. 1.1).[5] In England and Wales the trend has been even more severe, where the percentage of married adults has dropped from over two-thirds of the population in 1971 to less than 50 percent by 2007, and is projected to drop to only 41 percent by 2031 (Fig. 1.2).[6] The increase in the never-married single population as indicated in both graphs is a major factor (along with the notable increase in divorced population), and a major factor in this is the rise of cohabitation as an acceptable lifestyle. But the demographic reality is that the world the church is trying to reach in England and Wales is now *in the majority* an unmarried world, and the trend in the United States is not far behind. Whether or not we like it, we now find ourselves more and more living amidst an unmarried society.

Figure 1.1: Marital Status Trend: United States

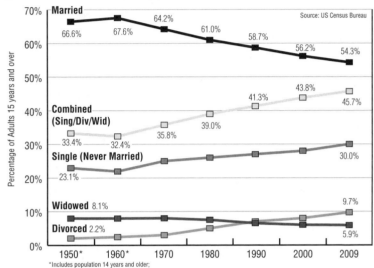

Figure 1.2: Marital Status Trend: England and Wales

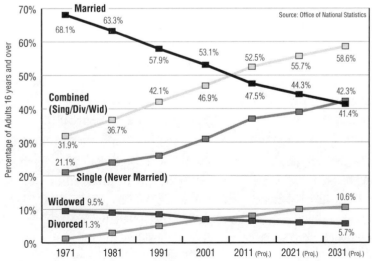

While unmarried adults are becoming dominant outside the church, a recent study by George Barna suggests they are significantly under-represented in nearly every facet of church life.[7] While on a typical week slightly more than half of married Americans attend a church service, only about one of every three single (adult) Americans attends.[8] Presence at a service is much more likely among widowed singles than among divorced or never-married adults.[9] Though 23 percent of married adults additionally attend a Sunday school class, only 15 percent of single adults attend. Although singles might have more discretionary leisure time for church-related activities, fewer than one in five regularly volunteer at church, attend a Sunday school class, or participate in a small group. On the other hand, singles are 50 percent more likely to volunteer their services to a nonprofit charitable group during a typical week than to offer themselves to the ministry of their church.[10]

Single adults are also less financially committed to their respective churches, with never-married adults contributing in an average year less than a quarter of what their married counterparts contribute.[11] Similarly, they are half as likely to serve in leadership capacities within the church.[12] The trend is the same in every category. Single people are less involved in the life of the church than their married counterparts. And while most single American adults think of themselves as Christian, Barna's research demonstrates a remarkably tepid level of commitment among them. The composite message of data is clear: the future life and vitality of the evangelical faith will require greater engagement with single adults both inside and outside the walls of the local church.

Understanding Biblical Teaching on Singleness

While only a minority of adults remain single their entire lives, we all begin our lives single, and the majority of us also will exit this life single. Also, most married people are close to people who are unmarried, whether not-yet-married children or friends or divorced or widowed friends and family members. Even those who are healthy and happily married will typically on occasion find themselves reflecting on the possibility of losing their mate to disease or accident and the prospect of living life alone again. The tendency for such reflection generally increases with age as the potential becomes greater. The apostle Paul also hints that there is a constructive dimension to keeping the temporality of marriage in view, when he admonishes that even those who have wives should be as if they had none (1 Cor. 7:29). Indeed there is health and vitality in keeping an appropriately loose grip on all aspects of our temporal life as a way to acknowledge that all the material bestowments we have are good gifts from God but temporary in their duration.

But in exploring biblical teaching on the subject of singleness, one inevitably encounters a couple of immediate difficulties. First, all questions relating to marriage, singleness, divorce, and procreation of children are heavily conditioned by culture, and the culture of the biblical world is considerably different from our modern context. Moreover, the "biblical" world itself was far from culturally monolithic. The customs and cultural expectations of Moabite Ruth and her Jewish fiancé Boaz of early Israel were a far cry from the Greco-Roman urban world of first-century Corinth. The concerns of the ancient Israelites with the institution of levirate marriage, for example, are entirely foreign to our modern experience, while the modern question of homosexual marriage would have seemed utterly absurd to the ancients. Since the reasons and purposes for *why* people married then are not always precisely equivalent to the modern world, fully appreciating the biblical teaching on marriage and singleness also requires some attention to the world of the original writers and readers of the biblical text. This task is not insurmountable, nor can we afford to ignore or underestimate it.

Moreover a number of the biblical texts that speak to the subject are exegetically difficult. What did Jesus mean when he spoke of making oneself a eunuch "for the sake of the kingdom of heaven" in Matthew 19:12? Though the figure of the eunuch was generally negative in the Old Testament and they were banned from access to the temple,[13] Jesus appears to speak of them positively. The statement in 1 Corinthians 7:1b (NASB), "*it is good* for a man not to touch a woman," is especially perplexing. On the one hand the language recalls the language of Genesis 2:18, "It is *not* good that the man should be alone" and would thus be a surprising assertion for Paul to make given his Jewish heritage. But nor does it seem to be a logical assertion of the Corinthians, who from evidence elsewhere in the letter appear to be anything but celibates. A close reading of *both* biblical Testaments reveals a curious dichotomy. While in much of the Old Testament we find a generally negative disposition toward one who is single and unmarried, in the New Testament the view we find is much more positive. Given that the New Testament authors generally affirm Old Testament ethical principles on sexuality and family, it is curious that New Testament authors deviate from the Old Testament on this particular point.

The Approach of This Book

Taken at face value both the eunuch statement of Jesus' in Matthew 19:12 and the "it is good" statement of Paul in 1 Corinthians 7:1b appear to conflict with the creation story affirmation of Genesis 2:18, "It is not good that the man should be alone." How these texts are best reconciled is the task of theologians. Some might opt to let the clearer texts interpret the less clear or to look for an appropriately qualified overarching principle that seems to reconcile the apparent differences. The approach taken here is a *diachronic* biblical-theological approach, by which we mean one that acknowledges the theological development that occurs through the progressive stages of biblical revelation. What is often depicted and described at first by means of illustrations, metaphors, allusions, and prophecies is often seen more clearly in a richer, more fully orbed form in subsequent phases of biblical revelation.

We can simplify our task by identifying a few major stages of biblical revelation. The most obvious division in the biblical canon is the separation between the Old and New Testaments. The word *testament* is an English derivation from the Latin *testamentum*, which is the common translation of the Greek word *diathēkē*, which means "covenant."[14] Thus, from its name the Old Testament is primarily an account of the old covenant that God established with the nation of Israel, while the New Testament is primarily an account of the new covenant God later established with the church.

Within the Old Testament we may identify a further distinction between the ideal embodied by the Old Testament covenants, which include the Abrahamic covenant, the Sinaitic covenant, and the Davidic covenant, and the resulting failure of the nation of Israel to keep the

Sinaitic covenant, as recorded in the prophetic books. The prophets stand in a critical juncture. They pronounce judgment upon the nation for its failure to live according to the stipulations of the covenant. But, at the same time, they offer a picture of expectant hope, anticipating a coming messiah and a new covenant.

The New Testament represents a new stage of biblical revelation in two important and related respects. First, the New Testament authors wrote from a post-resurrection perspective. They had witnessed the fulfillment of the ages in the life, death, and resurrection of Jesus. But they also had the benefit of the illuminating insight of the Holy Spirit. In the Gospel of John, Jesus tells his disciples, "When the Spirit of truth comes, he will guide you into all the truth" (John 16:13). Luke records in the Emmaus road experience that the two walking with Jesus had their eyes "opened" when they recognized Jesus (Luke 24:31). The same Greek word for *opened* (*dianoigō*) is used by Luke in the very next verse to describe how Jesus opened the Scriptures to them, explaining from Moses through the Prophets all the Scriptures concerning himself.

The writers of the New Testament thus had the benefit of all the early writings of the Old Testament, the prophets and their prophecies, the life and testimonies of Jesus, and the theological illumination of the Holy Spirit. Writing from the perspective of their distinct vantage point, they were in a position to provide a theological capstone upon the whole storyline of biblical history.

The Structure of This Book

The book is divided into six chapters that explore the issue of singleness, mindful of the progressive stages of biblical revelation we have just examined. The primary benefit of this approach is that the topic can be seen to fit within the developing flow of the biblical storyline and the primary theological point of that storyline, namely, God's plan to reconcile a people unto himself for the sake of his glory. That plan centers upon the life, death, and resurrection of Jesus Christ by which God retains his justice in reconciling a people unto himself. A secondary benefit to taking this approach is that some of the apparent dissonances between the view of singleness in the Old Testament and the view in the New Testament can be much more readily reconciled when they are seen within the developing biblical-theological storyline.

Chapter 1 begins where the biblical canon begins, examining the importance of marriage and procreation within the pre-history of the old covenant, namely in the accounts of creation and the patriarchs. The next chapter focuses on the place and importance of marriage and procreation within the Sinaitic and Davidic covenants and how they were lived out in the nation of ancient Israel. Chapter 3 examines the new hope given to singles and those without children amidst the prophets' expectant hope of a new work of God. Chapter 4 jumps to the end of the story and considers what is fundamentally different in the new covenant, as described by the apostle Paul, and its implications for singleness and marriage in the church age. Chapter 5 considers Jesus' teaching on birth, singleness, and family as described by the Gospel writers. The final chapter concludes with an examination of the topic of marriage and singleness given by Paul in 1 Corinthians 7—a capstone discussion of singleness as a spiritual gift for the Corinthian church.

This is one biblical topic for which it is crucial to get to the *end* of the biblical story, i.e., the post-resurrection perspective of the New Testament writers, in order to most fully appreciate the beginning of the story in the Old Testament. So I urge readers not to stop the journey too soon and thereby miss the full sense of how things develop. One key to good biblical theology is always to keep the parts in proper perspective to the whole, and that is also my desire in this biblical treatment of singleness.

1

Begetting from the Beginning

*Procreation, Marriage, and the
Blessing of God to the World*

When I have occasion to speak before various church groups on questions of singleness and marriage, I often begin the discussion by asking, "Can anyone tell me what is the first commandment in the Bible?" After some momentary blank stares, generally one or two individuals are brave enough to assert themselves and faithfully quote Matthew 22:37, "You shall love the Lord your God with all your heart and with all your soul and with all your mind."

"Ah, yes," I respond, "you have faithfully cited the *first and greatest* commandment. But I actually only asked for the *first* commandment in the Bible, as in the first one we would find if we began reading it from page 1."

At this point I encounter more quizzical stares. After all, most Christians do not pay much attention to the order of biblical commandments, and even when we do, we struggle to agree on what constitutes a bona fide command.

If I were addressing a circle of Orthodox Jews, my audience would probably not have been tricked by the question. They would likely have known of the work of the twelfth-century Jewish sage Maimonides, who codified all 613 commandments of the Torah. The first of these 613 to appear chronologically in the Old Testament is the commandment, "Be fruitful and multiply," in Genesis 1:28.

Once the answer is given, it seems painfully obvious. So I press the audience with a further question: "And to whom was this commandment *first* given?" If there is silence a second time, it is because the question appears too obvious to answer. Once again the question is a bit of a trick, because the commission to "be fruitful and multiply" is first given in Genesis 1:22 on the fifth day of creation, to the sea creatures and the birds, when God says, "Be fruitful and multiply and fill the waters in the seas, and let birds multiply on the earth." The mandate is given again by God to human beings on the sixth day: "Be fruitful and multiply and fill the earth and subdue it and have dominion over the fish of the sea and over the birds of the heavens and over every living thing that moves on the earth" (Gen. 1:28).

In the Beginning . . .

The First Commandment

Reflecting upon this double occurrence in Genesis 1 of the mandate, "Be fruitful and multiply," is instructive. It underscores that reproducing oneself is a fundamental and natural task, commissioned by God not only for human beings but for the whole created order. The procreative mandate is given even *before* human beings are created. It is woven into the very fabric of the created order that God fashioned before human beings were on the earth. What differentiates human beings from the rest of the animal kingdom is not found in the reproductive commission but in the distinctive that they were created in the *image of God* and have an additional mandate to subdue the earth and have dominion over it.

Jewish tradition, from the rabbinic interpreters of the New Testament era onward, has not questioned interpreting "be fruitful and multiply" as a divine command of the Torah. The Jewish Mishnah makes it explicit: "No man may abstain from keeping the law, 'Be fruitful and multiply,' unless he already has children."[1] The rabbis were explicit that the duty of procreation falls on the man and not the woman.

Some of my Protestant friends, on the other hand, have questioned the presumption that "mandate" need be understood as a commandment at all. Is it not rather a divine blessing? Genesis 1:28 makes the association between *begetting* and *blessing* explicit:

> God blessed them. And God said to them, "Be fruitful and multiply
> and fill the earth and subdue it and have dominion over the fish of the

sea and over the birds of the heavens and over every living thing that moves on the earth."

The imperative to "be fruitful and multiply" expected of the first human beings goes hand-in-hand with the act of God's blessing them. Procreation requires that a human act be carried out, but the results of the human act are efficacious only through divine provision. We already have perhaps a hint of the forthcoming drama found later in Genesis where the offspring of the covenantal blessing arises not simply through the human procreative act but as a result of God's supernatural act of provision.

While the act of being fruitful and multiplying is thus a divine-human act, in actuality the Hebrew author sometimes stresses one aspect more than the other. By examining whether blessing is mentioned in the immediate context of the reference, and by looking at the subject and form of the verb, we can get a relatively good sense of where the dominant emphasis is being applied. Table 1.1 provides a list of all the occurrences of the couplet in the Old Testament (it never appears at all in the New Testament). Of the twelve Old Testament references to being fruitful and multiplying, only five are clear imperatives upon humans or creatures (bolded in the table). It is given as an imperative to human beings only in three instances: to the first human beings, Adam and Eve; to Noah and his family; and to Jacob. At first it might seem surprising that it was given to Jacob and not also to Abraham, Isaac, Jacob's sons, or Israel as a nation. But it does make some sense when we consider that Adam was the progenitor of the human race, Noah was a second Adam, and Jacob was the immediate progenitor of the nation of Israel.[2] Each of the three was father to a human race of critical importance.

From the table it seems surprising that the mandate is given twice to Noah, and in the second instance it is issued without the blessing. However, as Genesis 9:1–7 forms a single text unit, the command, as given in verse 7, may be nothing more than an emphatic reiteration of verse 1. Maimonides cites Genesis 1:28, 9:1, and 9:6–7 as proof-texts for including "be fruitful and multiply" among the commandments of the Torah.[3] Whether Maimonides was correct to include it among the divine commands for *all* human beings is debatable. What we can conclude from the creation account is that procreation is part of the pattern of the created order, it is associated with God's blessing, and it was an explicit divine commandment given to Adam, Noah, and Jacob.

Table 1.1: Occurrences of "Be Fruitful and Multiply"
in the Old Testament

Text	Referent	God's Blessing Stated in Context?	Subject of Verb	Verb Form	Emphasized Action
Gen. 1:22	sea creatures and birds	yes	Sea creatures and birds	imperative-plural	divine and animal
Gen. 1:28	the first humans (Adam and Eve)	yes	the first humans (Adam and Eve)	imperative-plural	divine and human
Gen. 8:17	animals	no	animals	indicative-plural	animal
Gen. 9:1	Noah	yes	Noah	imperative-plural	divine and human
Gen. 9:7	Noah	no	Noah	imperative-plural	human
Gen. 17:20	Ishmael	yes	God	causative-indicative-singular	divine
Gen. 28:3	Jacob	yes	God	causative-indicative-singular	divine
Gen. 35:11	Jacob	yes	Jacob	imperative-singular	divine and human
Gen. 48:4	Jacob	yes	God	causative-indicative-singular	divine
Lev. 26:9	Israel	no	God	causative-indicative-singular	divine
Jer. 23:3	remnant	no	remnant	indicative-plural	human
Ezek. 36:11	post-exilic Israel	no	God and Israel	indicative-plural	divine and human

The Provision of Marriage

While marriage is not explicitly mentioned early in the creation account, it is certainly implied in the concluding clauses of Genesis 1:27: "In the image of God he created him; *male* and *female* he created them." The biblical etiology (an account of something's origin) of marriage as a divinely sanctioned human institution does not appear until the final scene of the creation account in Genesis 2:18–24. In this latter episode we find no mention at all of procreation as the basis for marriage; rather, here the motivation for the account is the initial observation by the Lord God that "it is not good that the man should be alone; I will make him a helper fit for him" (Gen. 2:18).

With this initial pronouncement God puts Adam to sleep, takes his rib from him, and creates Eve. The didactic function of the episode is made clear in the concluding pronouncement in 2:24: "Therefore a man shall leave his father and his mother and hold fast to his wife, and they shall become one flesh." So while an implied purpose for marriage in the creation account is to enable fulfillment of the divine mandate to "be fruitful and multiply," the explicit purpose the account gives is for companionship and assistance.

Here we see emerging a seminal theology of marriage. The wife serves both as relational companion and as provider of material assistance to the husband. The husband in turn functions in a complementary role for the wife. The separation of the two incidents perhaps serves to highlight the author's point that marriage was intended to provide *more* than the mere need to procreate legitimate heirs; it was also the foundation of the new institution of relational support in the human family unit.

In Jesus' discussion with the Pharisees about divorce, he cites as the basis for marriage Genesis 1:27, "*male* and *female* he created them," which he conjoins with the conclusion in 2:24, "*Therefore* a man shall leave his father and his mother and hold fast to his wife, and they shall become one flesh."[4] In the context of Genesis 2, the "therefore" of verse 24 follows from the man's condition of first being alone (v. 18) and subsequently receiving the woman as "flesh of my flesh" (v. 23). Jesus, however, links the conclusion not to the man's need for companionship but rather to God's ordained pattern of creation as constituting them "male and female."

Maimonides also lists "taking a wife" through contractual arrangement among his 613 commandments of the Torah but cites a casuistic legal precept in Deuteronomy 22:13–15 rather than Genesis 2 as the basis of the commandment.[5] Maimonides' understanding of marriage as a commandment of the Torah would have resonated with the earlier rabbinic tradition, which presumed marriage to be a requirement as the means to fulfill one's lifelong procreative duty to "be fruitful and multiply," illustrated well in the second-century rabbinic tractate ʾAbot R. Nathan:

Marry a wife when you are young, and marry a wife when you are old, beget children when you are young, and beget children when you are old. Do not say, "I shall not get married," but get married and produce sons and daughters and so increase procreation in the world. *"For you do not know which will prosper, the one or the other, or perhaps both of them will survive, and they shall both turn out well. In the morning sow your seed and in the evening keep it up"* (Eccles. 11:6).[6]

The presumed close tie between marriage and procreation was a common concept in the ancient world. Prescribing them as codified legal mandates was also common, beyond mere Jewish interpretations of the Old Testament. The idea of state-instituted laws requiring marriage was also common amongst Greco-Roman political theorists. In Plato's later discussion of political theory, given in his *Laws*, for example, he recognizes that the foundational building block of any political state lies in the partnership of marriage. Thus, it follows that the state's first legal enactment should be the institution of laws requiring a man to marry.[7] Plato was not alone, for, as we shall see later, similar ideas were common to other ancient writers.

In exploring the close connection between marriage and procreation in the ancient world, we begin to see clearly the distinctive view of marriage given in the Genesis account. First, we are struck by the immediate prominence of God's blessing on the whole created order through procreation. Marriage is acknowledged implicitly from the very beginning in God's creation of humans as *male* and *female*. Marriage thus provides the means to accomplish God's initial blessed mandate to human beings to "be fruitful and multiply." But in providing a secondary account of the institution of marriage at the end of the creation story, the biblical author emphasizes that marriage has been ordained by God to be more than just a provision for procreation; it is also the means for companionship and support through a couple's unity in forming a new family unit.

Offspring and the Fall

Having already seen the prominence of procreation within the creation account, it is not surprising to find that *offspring* emerges as a recurring theological motif through the development of biblical history. The

Hebrew term used for *offspring* is the word *zera'*, which can be translated into English as "offspring" or "seed" or other words, depending on the context. Just as the English word *seed* can refer botanically to the *seed* sown by a farmer, the *semen* of a male animal, a single physical *offspring* of a human or animal, or the aggregate *descendants* of a human being, so too a similar range of usage applies in the Hebrew. Although the once ubiquitous King James Version nearly always translated *zera'* as "seed," modern translations tend to translate the term into a range of contextually specific English equivalents such as "seed," "semen," "offspring," "children," "lineage," or "descendants."

Even before the narrative moves out of Eden, we encounter the importance of offspring in the account of the fall. The text of Genesis 3 portrays three separate culpable agents. The Serpent deceived Eve with a lie. Eve listened to the Serpent, disobeying God. Adam listened to Eve, disobeying God. In God's pronouncement of judgment upon the Serpent, two references to offspring occur:

> I will put enmity between you and the woman, and between your offspring and her offspring; he shall bruise your head, and you shall bruise his heel. (Gen. 3:15)

The judgment upon the Serpent is that there will be constant enmity between his offspring and the woman's offspring. At one level, we could have here a biblical etiology of why snakes bite men, and why men try to kill snakes. But as Gordon Wenham points out, this is a judgment against the Serpent, not the woman.[8] The serpent is at a tactical disadvantage. Moreover, a wound to the head is more likely to be fatal than a wound to the heel. Likewise, a personified speaking serpent in the account suggests that it represents more than a suborder of reptiles but rather the personified power of evil hostile to the plans and purposes of God.

In short, the enmity between two sets of offspring points to the future continued struggle between human beings (the offspring of the woman) and the personified forces of evil in Satan and his cohorts. Whereas the forces of evil will inflict harm upon the offspring of Eve, the offspring of Eve will eventually fatally crush the forces of evil.

Patristic authors from Justin and Irenaeus onward have regarded

Genesis 3:15 as the *protoevangelium*, the first Old Testament prophecy of Christ.[9] The patristic authors employ the ambiguity between the collective offspring and a singular offspring in making the assertion. Paul tells the Roman church, "The God of peace will soon crush Satan under your feet" (Rom. 16:20). If this is an allusion to Genesis 3:15, it suggests an image of God crushing Satan through his people, i.e., the church. So perhaps there is a sense in which both a particular and an aggregate sense of *seed* are simultaneously in view.

Another Offspring

The next reference to *offspring* in Genesis occurs in Genesis 4:25 as part of Eve's response when she bears her third son, Seth. The dominant storyline of Genesis 4 concerns the contrast between Abel's acceptable sacrifice and Cain's unacceptable sacrifice, Cain's accountability before God for his subsequent murder of Abel, and the portrayal of how Cain's violent disposition is subsequently passed down through his progeny, as represented by the figure of Lamech. From the foundation of human history we can observe two distinct lines of progeny coming from Adam and Eve—one represented by Cain marked by violence, which was eventually destroyed in the flood, and the other represented by Abel and Seth, which was marked by obedience, sacrificial death, and new life.

While the traditional contrast of the chapter is between Cain and Abel with Seth only mentioned in the concluding two verses, when we look at the description of the birth accounts it is Cain and Seth that form the interesting parallel, while there is only passing mention of the birth of Abel. The births are described as follows:

> . . . and she conceived and bore Cain, saying, "I have gotten a man with the help of the LORD." (Gen. 4:1)

> . . . and she bore a son and called his name Seth, for she said, "God has appointed for me another offspring instead of Abel, for Cain killed him." (Gen. 4:25)

In each case Eve bears a son, names him, and makes a declaration to the Lord commemorating the occasion; but in two instances the subject, verb, and object are different. In the first instance the act of producing a child is Eve's. Eve "gets" for herself a "man" with the "help" of the Lord. To commemorate her act, she names her son Cain, meaning "possession," a wordplay on the Hebrew verb *qanah* meaning "get."

In the second instance God is the subject and Eve is the indirect object. This time Eve acknowledges that *God* appointed another offspring. She names this son Seth, meaning "substitute," which is also an apparent wordplay on the Hebrew verb *shith* for "placing" or "appointing." The contrast in the type of birth is expressed in the names of Eve's sons. Cain is the result of Eve's own act of getting a man, whereas Seth is God's provision of an appointed offspring. In her effort, Eve bears sinful progeny of violence and ultimate death. But God provides through her another offspring that ultimately brings life and hope.

The theme of offspring as a special provision of God is a recurring one throughout the book of Genesis. It is a theme that reinforces a fundamental difference between the God of the Old Testament and fertility deities popular among Israel's ancient Near Eastern neighbors.[10] Unlike the gods of other Semitic traditions, the God of Israel has no female consort and is not worshiped by means of cultic prostitution. Most importantly, the God of Israel is not *manipulated* by human beings as in the case of other fertility-oriented religions, where, through the worship and sacrifices of human beings, the gods were stimulated to replenish the earth. But from the first generation of humankind, Genesis emphasizes by contrast that it is God *alone* who provides the appointed offspring.

The vocabulary distinction between Eve's bearing Cain as a "man" and God's providing Seth as "another offspring" also hints that, as in Genesis 3:15, messianic implications are in view. These messianic overtones in the provision of Seth were recognized within the Jewish interpretive tradition even prior to the New Testament era.[11] In the book of *Jubilees*, for example, it is Adam rather than Eve that names Seth and comments on his birth:

> He [Adam] named him Seth because he said, "The LORD has raised up another seed for us upon the earth in place of Abel because Cain killed him." (*Jub.* 4:7)[12]

At least three changes in vocabulary underscore that messianic overtones are in view. The child is not merely provided by the Lord but he is one "raised up" by the Lord. He is a child provided by God not just to Eve but "for us," with Adam rather than Eve as prominent. The child is placed by the Lord "upon the earth," ostensibly to complete a mission.

The other messianic hint is in the term "another offspring" or "another seed." As in English the Hebrew word for "another" (*'akher*) used here can connote the sense of "subsequent" or "following," but it can also carry the nuance of "other" or "different" (e.g., Lev. 27:20; Ps. 109:8). A later Jewish midrashic commentary thus concluded:

> And what was that "other child" [that would arise from another source to which she made reference]? It was the king-messiah.[13]

Though the Jewish interpreters could see that the modifier "another" might imply something more significant than simply that God provided a "subsequent" offspring, the particular nature of the different offspring provided by God is here unspecified. The full nature of that special character is to be fully revealed only in the course of the developing storyline of the biblical text.

Abraham and His Offspring

We turn next to the substance and content of God's covenant blessing to Abraham. Whereas the history of the human race begins with Adam, the history of God's chosen people begins with the figure of Abraham. Abraham is thus a pivotal figure in the whole of biblical history and theology. The central drama of the book of Genesis is the narrative account of God establishing his covenant with Abraham and confirming it with his descendants. God's covenant with Abraham is a unilateral promissory covenant—a commitment of how God *will* bless Abraham and his descendants. And, not surprisingly, the provision of offspring features prominently both in the narrative drama of the story of Abraham and in the substance of the covenantal promises. To see this effectively and to explore the implications requires a careful examination of the substance of covenantal promises that God gives to Abraham as they unfold in the narrative. This occurs not on a single occasion but through a series of episodes during the course of his sojourn in Canaan as God develops and tests his faith.

Abraham's Call: Genesis 12:1–9

The account of the Abraham narrative opens with God's call to Abraham to go to a new land, followed by a series of promissory statements:

> Now the LORD said to Abram, "Go from your country and your kindred and your father's house to the land that I will show you. And I will make of you a great nation, and I will bless you and make your name great, so that you will be a blessing. I will bless those who bless you, and him who dishonors you I will curse, and in you all the families of the earth shall be blessed." (Gen. 12:1–3)

Abraham's act of faith in following God's command to *go* is all the more significant when we consider a number of factors. First, in leaving his father's family in Haran, he relinquished his claim to his family inheritance—the move effectively severed him from his familial homestead in Haran. In Genesis 11:30 the text makes explicit that Sarah was barren and had no child. Thus, Abraham must follow God and go, devoid of both the security of his existing family and the future security of children. Moreover, he must go without having any indication as to where God is taking him—he must follow God to an unknown destination that God has yet to reveal.

It is on the occasion of God's initial command to Abraham to go that God gives some of the initial promises of the covenant, all of which, in one form or another, are dimensions of God's blessing to Abraham. Five promises are articulated in 12:2–3:

1) Abraham's progeny will become a great nation;
2) Abraham will be blessed;
3) Abraham will be blessed through having a great name;
4) Those who bless Abraham will be blessed; conversely those who curse him will be cursed; and
5) All the families of the earth will be blessed in Abraham.

Two elements are featured prominently in this list. The very first promise God gives to Abraham essentially concerns progeny. God does not just promise a son to care for Abraham in his old age and inherit his estate, but he promises to make Abraham into a great nation. The second element that features prominently is blessing.

We see in the next four promises a concentric movement of blessing from Abraham himself, to his progeny, who will be the ones to remember his name and make it great, to his neighbors around whom he lives and interacts, to ultimately all the families of the earth. The implication of these two elements in tandem is that they relate to one another. Abraham will have progeny through which the world will be blessed by God. What this passage demonstrates so vividly is that from the very beginning of God's covenant with Abraham, progeny and blessing are at the core.

In 12:4–9 the narrative depicts Abraham's journey of obedience to God's command to go, and at the oak of Moreh we find an additional promise:

> Then the LORD appeared to Abram and said, "To your offspring I will give this land." (v. 7)

Here we have the first appearance of the key word *offspring* in the Abrahamic narrative. The noun *offspring* is singular—as is typical in its appearance in Genesis—with the implication that it refers to a collective plural. This promise in some sense serves to bracket the first promise God gave in verse 2. God *will* make Abraham's progeny into a nation, and here God *will* give his progeny the land. The consequence of this will be the pouring out of a concentric series of God's blessings, beginning with Abraham, through which the entire world *will* be blessed. Surprising is that in this initial promise of land, God grants it to Abraham's offspring rather than to Abraham himself—the emphasis is on a future rather than present fulfillment.[14]

Indeed, despite Abraham's faithful obedience in following God's command to go, to relocate to Canaan, there is little in the text to indicate that the land was particularly hospitable to Abraham's arrival. He immediately encounters Canaanites already dwelling in the land and is forced to maintain a nomadic lifestyle, ending up in the even less hospitable Negev. Abraham then encounters a famine in the land (v. 10) that forces him again to leave the land to go down to Egypt for food.

The Granting of the Land: Genesis 13:14-18

After Abraham's sojourn in Egypt he again returns to Bethel with his livestock and household together with the livestock and household of Lot. After the limitations of the land force Abraham and Lot to move their households apart, the LORD again speaks to Abraham:

> The LORD said to Abram, after Lot had separated from him, "Lift up your eyes and look from the place where you are, northward and southward and eastward and westward, for all the land that you see I will give to you and to your offspring forever. I will make your offspring as the dust of the earth, so that if one can count the dust of the earth, your offspring also can be counted. Arise, walk through the length and the breadth of the land, for I will give it to you. (Gen. 13:14–17)

Genesis speaks of how both men acquire land, but there is an observable contrast in how they do so. Lot "lifts up his eyes" (v. 10) and sees the fertile Jordan valley in the east and chooses it for himself. With the same idiom, God commands Abraham to "lift up his eyes" and grants to him and his offspring the land in every direction.[15] The tension in the lack of land provides a backdrop for another episode of the renewing of the covenant promises. The focus on this occasion is upon the magnitude of Abraham's offspring (as "dust of the earth") and the magnitude of the land ("all the land you see"). While this time the promised grant is given to both Abraham and his offspring, it is still yet a future grant—with the implication that it will be given to Abraham through his offspring.

The Covenant Established: Genesis 15:1-21

Claus Westermann rightly declared that Genesis 15 stands at the center of the external structure of the Abraham narratives and is regarded in the history of exegesis as the very heart of the Abraham story. It is here that God's covenant with Abraham and Abraham's faith appear in the kernel form of what the Bible says about him.[16] And here again we find God's promises declared to Abraham center on the dual poles of offspring and land. As most commentators have observed, the structure of the chapter follows a repeated parallel pattern (15:1–6 and 15:7–21) of dialog between God and Abraham that builds upon these two fundamental promises. A sketch of the parallels is outlined in Table 1.2.

Table 1.2: The Parallel Structure of Genesis 15:1–6 and 15:7–2

The Lord's Declaration	15:1	"Fear not, Abram, I am your shield; your reward shall be very great."	15:7	"I am the LORD who brought you out from Ur of the Chaldeans to give you this land to possess."
Abraham's Objection	15:2–3	"O Lord GOD, what will you give me, for I continue childless, and the heir of my house is Eliezer of Damascus? . . . Behold, you have given me no **offspring**, and a member of my household will be my heir."	15:8	"O Lord GOD, how am I to know that I shall possess it?"
The Lord's Act			15:9–18a	"On that day the LORD made a covenant with Abram."
The Lord's Promise	15:4–5	"This man shall not be your heir; your very own son shall be your heir. . . . Look toward heaven, and number the stars, if you are able to number them. . . . So shall your **offspring** be."	15:18b–21	"To your **offspring** I give this land, from the river of Egypt to the great river, the river Euphrates."
Abraham's Act	15:6	"He believed the LORD, and he counted it to him as righteousness."		

These two sections of Genesis 15 are instructive both in their parallel and nonparallel elements. At a basic level, we can observe three parallel elements in the dialogs: (1) each begins with God making a declaration about himself; (2) each is followed by an objection raised by Abraham; and (3) the objection is followed by a re-articulation of the fundamental promise in line with what God had given previously.

The first sub-episode concludes with Abraham's response of faith that has no parallel in the second sub-episode, while the second sub-episode includes an act of the Lord that finds no parallel in the first.

The inclusion of these additional actions by Abraham and God are not incidental but will prove to be the climactic events of the whole Abrahamic narrative. It is with this episode that we get for the first time an inside glimpse of the drama of Abraham's struggle of faith in his response to God.

The first dialog arises in the context of Abraham's defeat of Chedorlaomer and the kings aligned with him and Abraham's rejection of the subsequent offer of the battle plunder by the king of Sodom (Genesis 14). Genesis 15 opens with God's declaration to Abraham in a vision. Abraham need not fear possible reprisals by Chedorlaomer and his allies because God is his shield, and unlike the tarnished booty offered by the king of Sodom, God's reward to Abraham will be very great.

From the mere circumstances of the narrative Abraham's objection is surprising. God had just promised him protection and reward and had given him a marvelous victory in battle. It seems odd that Abraham takes the moment to raise a concern about being childless.

Abraham's objection shows so clearly that the provision of physical offspring was at the focal point of *everything* that mattered to him. The promises of the covenant—innumerable offspring, becoming a great nation, having a great name, being a blessing to the world, and the future acquisition of the land—all depended on Abraham's having physical progeny. But Abraham had no son and no progeny and a barren wife with no apparent prospects for children. All God's promises depended on the one thing God had not provided—a son and an heir. The means and method by which God would provide the offspring to Abraham is the central drama of the Abrahamic narrative.

It is also somewhat remarkable that when the Lord does respond in Genesis 15:4–5, he provides no greater assurance than his word. God simply states explicitly what Abraham desired evidence for materially—that God would indeed provide him his own son as his heir. It was divine affirmation of the fundamentally obvious truth—that everything depended on the provision of offspring that only God could provide.

God then reiterates to Abraham his promise that he shall have innumerable offspring, this time comparing his offspring to the stars of the sky. God was standing by his previous promise, and Abraham needed to respond in faith. In Romans 4:19 Paul describes the reality of human doubts that directly confronted Abraham's faith at that moment—namely, that, being one hundred years old, his own body was as good as dead, and his wife had been barren her entire life. It is at this very moment in the Abrahamic narrative (Gen. 15:6) that Abraham's climactic act of faith occurs: "He believed the LORD, and he counted it to him as righteousness." And it is this particular moment that becomes the pivotal event that Paul refers to in Romans 4 as the evidence that Abraham himself was justified by faith and not by works.

Important to see in this text is that the specific object of Abraham's faith that is being commended is the promised *offspring*. The faith of Abraham that Paul commends in Romans 4 is not a vague sort of trust that God would provide for Abraham's personal well-being and general welfare. Rather, the issue of faith for Abraham *is* the promised offspring. So, while on one hand, in the Abraham narrative we find promises of innumerable offspring and progeny as a mark of God's bountiful blessing to Abraham, on the other hand we soon find the whole drama of the narrative focused upon the provision of a particular divinely promised offspring.

The second dialog, in Genesis 15:7–21, has elements of the same pattern. This time God gives Abraham tangible confirmation of the land promise in the formalization of the covenant. The original meaning of the Hebrew term *covenant* (*berith*) connotes the notion of "imposition," "liability," or "obligation."[17] The term is used on a number of occasions in the Old and New Testaments to designate a binding commitment of some nature between God and human beings, chief among them being the covenant with Noah (Gen. 9:9–16), the Abrahamic covenant (Gen. 15:18), the Sinaitic covenant with Israel (Ex. 19:5–6; Deut. 4:13), the Davidic covenant (2 Chron. 13:5), and the new covenant mentioned by Jeremiah and in the New Testament (Jer. 31:31–34; Luke 22:20; 1 Cor. 11:25).

Scholars have categorized these covenants into two different types: the obligatory type reflected in the covenant at Sinai that God made with the nation of Israel, and the promissory type reflected in the Abrahamic and Davidic covenants.[18] These in turn resemble (respectively) in their forms two different types of judicial documents known in the Mesopotamian world from the middle of the second millennium BC—the political *treaty* constituting primarily an obligation of vassal to the suzerain or lord, and the *grant* constituting an obligation of the master to the servant. The former served mainly to protect the rights of the master, while the latter served mainly to protect the rights of the servant.[19] The grant type of treaty was generally of the form of royal grants bestowed upon individuals who excelled in loyally serving their masters.[20] The proclamation of the grant of land in 15:18–21 is styled according to the prevalent pattern of judicial grants given by a lord to a faithful servant as a permanent endowment to an individual and his descendants.[21]

What appears to us to be a somewhat obscure pattern of events would have had profound and immediate significance to Abraham. His act of faith in trusting in God's word alone for the promised offspring in the first sub-dialog results, in turn, in the second sub-dialog with God's act of granting the covenant as a sign of his commendation of Abraham's act of faith. This granting of covenant formalizes the promises that God had previously given to Abraham through a ritualistic covenant oath whereby the precise terms of the grant are specified. In this case, the land of ten named nations is given to Abraham and his descendants for perpetuity.

The Covenant Confirmed: Genesis 16–18

With true dramatic irony, we find that immediately following the high point of the whole Abrahamic narrative, when Abraham expresses his unswerving faith to the word of God alone, the narrative gives the account of how Abraham and Sarah proceed with their own work-around plan to circumvent the apparent shortfall in divine initiative.

In these chapters we see the tension between human initiative and divine provision expressed in the contrast between the births of Abraham's two sons, in the midst of which the covenant is again expressed and confirmed with poignant clarity and power not yet seen in the Abrahamic narrative. The drama that unfolds between the births of Abraham's two sons centers on the nature of the respective births of the two boys and bears some direct similarities with the contrast we observed with Eve in the births of Cain and Seth. Just as for Eve the birth of Cain was a tribute to her own accomplishment, while Seth's birth was a testimony to God's provision, so also Ishmael's birth comes as a consequence of human intervention, while the birth of Isaac comes strictly by means of God's supernatural intervention.

As the narrative unfolds in Genesis 16, we find Sarah initiating the action—directing Abraham to take her maidservant Hagar to bear children on her behalf, since "the LORD has prevented me from bearing children" (v. 2). The pattern of interaction suggests another parallel with Adam and Eve, this time with the account of the fall into sin in Genesis 3.[22] In both cases the wife takes initiative to which the husband acquiesces. Abraham "listened to the voice of Sarai" (v. 2) in the same way that Adam "listened to the voice" of Eve and was judged because of it (3:17). And as Adam passively received and ate the fruit his wife gave him, so too Abraham willingly takes Hagar, whom Sarah gives him, and lies with her. Just as Adam and Eve chose to act on their human inclinations instead of fully trusting in God's word, so too here Abraham and Sarah take initiative based on their own judgment of the situation instead of completely trusting God to provide fully in accordance with his promise.

Sarah's action was a culturally appropriate option for a barren woman who wished to have children. Since servants were considered property, Sarah's maid could be used for, among other household services, bearing children as a surrogate mother on behalf of her mistress. The same right is later exercised by Rachel and Leah with their servants Bilhah and Zilpah, who similarly bear sons to Jacob on behalf of their mistresses (Gen. 30:3–13). The birth of Ishmael is thus the result of Sarah's taking her own initiative to produce a son when God did not otherwise provide. Just as Eve gets herself a man in producing Cain, so too Sarah gets a son for herself through using her maidservant. Thus, the primary sin in view here is Sarah and Abraham's attempt to usurp divine provision by means of human intervention.

The contrast with the expression of divine initiative in Genesis 17 could not be more dramatic despite the fact that it does not come until thirteen years after Ishmael's birth. God comes to Abraham as "God Almighty" or "El Shaddai," an Old Testament name for God that first occurs here probably for the purpose of confirming God's power to produce supernatural offspring.[23] Gordon Wenham notes that although the etymology of the epithet *Shaddai* is obscure, it is always used in connection with promises of descendants: "Shaddai evokes the idea that God is able to make the barren fertile and to fulfill his promises."[24] Moreover, if God's name makes it patently clear that he alone is fully capable of giving Abraham offspring, the delay in God's response until Abraham is nearly one hundred years old also serves to reinforce the reality that *only* divine intervention will accomplish the result.[25] God again appears, saying:

> "I am God Almighty; walk before me, and be blameless, that I may make my covenant between me and you, and may multiply you greatly." Then Abram fell on his face. And God said to him, "Behold, my covenant is with you, and you shall be the father of a multitude of nations. No longer shall your name be called Abram, but your name shall be Abraham, for I have made you the father of a multitude of nations. I will make you exceedingly fruitful, and I will make you into nations, and kings shall come from you. And I will establish my covenant between me and you and your offspring after you throughout their generations for an everlasting covenant, to be God to you and to your offspring after you. And I will give to you and to your offspring after you the land of your sojournings, all the land of Canaan, for an everlasting possession, and I will be their God." (Gen. 17:1b–8)

God begins by making it unmistakably clear that *he* (alone) is the one who both makes the covenant and provides Abraham his multitudinous offspring. The verb *multiply* (*ravah*) in 17:2 and "make fruitful" (*parah*) in 17:6 are the same verbs used earlier in Genesis in the command, "Be fruitful and multiply," given to the birds and the fish (1:22), Adam and Eve (1:28), and Noah (9:1, 7). This might seem to imply that Abraham also inherits the Adamic mandate, in the same way that Noah did, to be fruitful and multiply and fill the earth with his offspring. But the conspicuous lack of imperative here belies an important distinction between Abraham and Adam and Noah. Adam and Noah are given the mandate to fill the earth through their procreative efforts. Abraham, by contrast, is told that his multitudinous offspring will be the result of God's covenantal provision. It occurs despite Abraham's misguided human effort (i.e., in siring Ishmael) rather than through it.

Here again we have the two major covenant promises articulated, the promise of many offspring and the promise of land for Abraham and his offspring. The offspring promise, however, is articulated with three points, a trifold repetition that emphasizes even more strongly that:

1) Abraham will be exceedingly fruitful (17:6)
2) Abraham will be the father of many nations (17:4, 6)
3) Abraham will be the father of kings (17:6).

Likewise the land promise is also reiterated here, this time explicitly as an "everlasting possession." God also assures Abraham that he will be his God and the God of his offspring in the land. Here is where Abraham's name is changed from Abram to Abraham. *Abram* means "exalted father," and *Abraham* sounds like the Hebrew word for "father of a multitude."[26] God's changing Abram's name at this moment of the covenant reaffirmation is another dramatic reinforcement of the main point. Just as God has full control over Abraham's inner constitution to provide him with offspring, so too he exercises his full authority over Abraham's outer constitution by renaming him in keeping with his divinely sanctioned mission.

After God gives the *sign* of the covenant in circumcision, the narration moves to two sequential episodes that announce, first to Abraham in 17:15–21 then to Sarah in 18:1–15, that Sarah will bear the appointed offspring. In hearing the news, both Abraham and Sarah react similarly— they laugh in disbelief. These passages add a final reinforcement to the dramatic irony in the difference between the births of Abraham's two sons. Just as *both* Sarah and Abraham were complicit in preempting God's plan with their own initiative, so *both* are incredulous in the act of God to provide a son through Sarah. Their response underscores the fundamental point: the appointed offspring comes strictly by divine provision; it comes not in any way through the effort of Abraham and Sarah, but despite their efforts. It comes rather through their unbelieving laughter, as reinforced in Isaac's name, meaning "laughter." Abraham even goes so far as to argue with God, "Oh that Ishmael might live before you!" (17:18).

Thus despite Abraham's commended expression of faith in Genesis 15:6, he himself can take no credit for the divinely provided offspring and readily betrays his ignorance concerning the plan of God in its provision. Sarah's response of laughter followed by the response, "Shall I indeed bear a child, now that I am old?" prompts the response from the Lord, "Is *anything* too hard for the LORD?" (18:13–14). Yet again the fundamental difference in the two births is reinforced: Ishmael was the result of human initiative, but Isaac was the provision of divine initiative.

The Testing of Abraham: Genesis 22:1–19

A final confirmation of the covenant occurs in response to Abraham's faithfulness in the narrative of the sacrifice of Isaac. The sacrifice of Isaac meant for Abraham much more than just the loss of his son—it was the loss of everything he had been promised in the covenant. The event again underscores the recurring theme of divine provision throughout the Abrahamic narrative, and Abraham responds by sacrificing a trapped ram and calling the place, "The LORD will provide" (22:14). In the aftermath of the sacrifice, Abraham is again met by an angel who declares:

> By myself I have sworn, declares the LORD, because you have done this and have not withheld your son, your only son, I will surely bless you, and I will surely multiply your offspring as the stars of heaven and as the sand that is on the seashore. And your offspring shall possess the gate of his enemies, and in your offspring shall all the nations of the earth be blessed, because you have obeyed my voice. (Gen. 22:16–18)

While this final confirmation of the covenant promises ties together the essential threads of promises given earlier, there is a degree of escalation in each of the four promises here (see Table 1.3).

In Genesis 12:2 God promises Abraham, "I will bless you," but in Genesis 22:17 the first verb of the promise is repeated for emphasis, which, translated into English, reads, "I will surely bless you."[27]

In 17:2 God commands Abraham to walk before him and be blameless, that he "may multiply" Abraham greatly. The second promise in Genesis 22:17 is stated in response to Abraham's obedience, and the verb is again emphatic: "I will surely multiply your offspring as the stars of heaven and as the sand that is on the seashore."[28] God previously used the metaphor of dust (in 13:16) and stars (15:5) for Abraham's many offspring, but here he compares them to *both* the stars in the sky and the sand on the seashore, the latter of which appears here for the first time.

The third promise is slightly more cryptic: "Your offspring shall possess the gate of [their] enemies." To possess the gate of one's enemies connotes having control over the city with the enemy having been subdued. Whereas the earlier promises only mention God giving land (Gen. 12:3; 13:5; 15:18–21; 17:8) without mention of what is to happen to the existing population resident on the land, the promise in 22:17 clarifies that God will give the land to Abraham's offspring by means of giving them victory over their enemies.

Table 1.3: The Promises as Given in Chapter 22
Compared with Earlier Promises

Text	Promise	Text	Promise
Gen. 12:2	I will bless you.	Gen. 22:17	I will *surely* bless you.
Gen. 17:2	I am God Almighty; walk before me, and be blameless, that I may make my covenant between me and you, and may multiply you greatly.	Gen. 22:17	I will *surely* multiply your offspring as the stars of heaven and as the sand that is on the seashore.
Gen. 15:5	Look toward heaven, and number the stars, if you are able to number them. . . . So shall your offspring be.		
Gen. 12:7	To your offspring I will give this land.	Gen. 22:17	Your offspring shall possess the gate of his enemies.
Gen. 12:3	In you all the families of the earth shall be blessed.	Gen. 22:18	In your offspring shall all the nations of the earth be blessed.
Gen. 12:3	In you all the families of the earth shall be blessed.	Gen. 22:18	In your offspring shall all the nations of the earth be blessed.

The final promise in Genesis 22:18 differs from the earlier rendition in 12:3 in two respects. Whereas in 12:3 it is all the "families" or "clans" in the world who are blessed, the language in 22:18 elevates the designation to all the "nations" of the world who are blessed. And whereas Abraham mediates blessing to all the families of the earth, it is Abraham's singular "offspring" that mediates blessing to all the nations of the earth. These verses once again are examples in which the grammar is ambiguous regarding whether the term *offspring* is to be read as a collective noun or as referencing a single individual (e.g., "Your offspring shall possess the gate of his enemies"). The possibility that these verses are intended to foreshadow messianic fulfillment cannot be ruled out.

The Contexts of the Covenant: Summary and Observations

The covenant that God made with Abraham was not a one-time event. Rather, it developed through a series of encounters that Abraham had with God as he walked the journey of faith and trust in God. Through a series of five successive episodes, God progressively revealed his covenantal promises to Abraham, and we can summarize their significance with a few observations.

Table 1.4: God's Promises in His Covenant to Abraham

Episode	Text	Promise	Recipient
Abraham's call	Gen. 12:2	Progeny to become a great nation	Abraham
	Gen. 12:2	Blessing	Abraham
	Gen. 12:2	A great and blessed name	Abraham
	Gen. 12:3	Blessing	Abraham's allies
	Gen. 12:3	Blessing	The families of the earth
	Gen. 12:7	Land	Abraham's offspring
The granting of the land	Gen. 13:15	Land	Abraham and Abraham's offspring
	Gen. 13:16	Offspring as dust of the earth	Abraham
	Gen. 13:17	Land	Abraham
The covenant established	Gen. 15:5	Offspring as stars of the sky	Abraham
	Gen. 15:18–21	Land	Abraham's offspring
The covenant confirmed	Gen. 17:4	Father of a multitude of nations	Abraham
	Gen. 17:6	Exceeding fruitfulness	Abraham
	Gen. 17:6	Kings shall come from descendants	Abraham
	Gen. 17:8	Land as everlasting possession	Abraham and Abraham's offspring
	Gen. 17:8	The Lord as their God	Abraham's offspring
The testing of Abraham	Gen. 22:17	Great blessing	Abraham
	Gen. 22:17	Offspring as stars of sky and sand of seashore	Abraham
	Gen. 22:17	Possessing the gate of one's enemies	Abraham's offspring
	Gen. 22:18	Blessing	All the nations of the earth

1) *There is progression in the content of what God reveals to Abraham*

through the course of the episodes (see Table 1.4). In the first episode God promises Abraham progeny and that Abraham will be a blessing to the world. In the second God gives Abraham the land. In the third God gives Abraham his covenant. In the fourth God confirms the covenant with the sign of circumcision. And in the final episode the promises are escalated in response to Abraham's obedience. Despite the progression in degree of content and formalization, there is a striking commonality across the five episodes in the fundamental content of what God promises to Abraham. Each of the five sections mentions in some form the same two fundamental items: *offspring* and *land*. These are understood in the temporal-physical sense: physical progeny and a physical land grant.

2) *All the promises in the covenant ultimately depend on the single promise of abundant offspring.* While the land is given to Abraham in the second episode, it is only to Abraham's offspring that God promises the conquest of the land with the eradication of the existing residents (Gen. 22:17). The promise of a "great name" (12:2) in Semitic cultures comes through being remembered and venerated by one's descendants. Likewise, the other promises of nations and kings and the means by which Abraham is to be a blessing to the world also depend on offspring. Over the course of five episodes offspring are promised twelve different times (12:7; 13:15, 16 (2x); 15:5, 18; 17:7 (2x), 8; 22:17 (2x), 18), and the innumerability of Abraham's offspring is compared with three different metaphors: dust (13:16), stars (15:5; 22:17), and sand (22:17).

3) *The promise of innumerable offspring depends, in turn, completely on the provision of God's singular offspring to Abraham.* The narrative emphasizes in dramatic irony that this offspring comes not through human will or initiative but only through God's supernatural, gracious provision. It is this offspring that is the object of Abraham's faith in 15:6.

4) *The promise of blessing both initiates and concludes the promises of the covenant.* Beyond the general promise of blessing, three things are essentially promised to Abraham in the covenant: offspring, an inheritance of land, and a great name or lasting reputation. Each is given as an eternal or everlasting endowment. The covenant is everlasting—hence Abraham's offspring are eternal and the promise of land is an everlasting possession given to them (13:15; 17:7–8).

The Accounts of Isaac and Jacob

The covenant that God gives to Abraham is subsequently confirmed by God with Isaac and Jacob. The striking similarities in these confirmations speak to a pattern of divine intent within the whole narrative that serves to accentuate the fundamental theological message of the book of Genesis: God intends to bless the patriarchs through the provision of offspring. Sometimes the emphasis is on the multitude of offspring, and other times the emphasis is on a particular divinely provided offspring.

Isaac

There are two recorded occasions where God confirms his covenant with Isaac. The first occurs when Isaac goes to Gerar, apparently because of a famine in the land. Apparently he had also contemplated going to Egypt for further relief. It is on this occasion that the Lord appears to him and says:

> Do not go down to Egypt; dwell in the land of which I shall tell you. Sojourn in this land, and I will be with you and will bless you, for to you and to your *offspring* I will give all these lands, and I will establish the oath that I swore to Abraham your father. I will multiply your *offspring* as the stars of heaven and will give to your *offspring* all these lands. And in your *offspring* all the nations of the earth shall be blessed, because Abraham obeyed my voice and kept my charge, my commandments, my statutes, and my laws. (Gen. 26:2b–5)

On a second occasion in Beersheba the Lord again appeared to him and said:

> I am the God of Abraham your father. Fear not, for I am with you and will bless you and multiply your *offspring* for my servant Abraham's sake. (Gen. 26:24)

The content of the covenantal promises to Isaac echo the same emphases of those God gives to Abraham. On both occasions the promises begin with a *blessing* to Isaac and reaffirm that in Isaac's offspring all the nations of the world will also be blessed. The word *offspring* appears in five different instances, with God's promise to multiply offspring appearing twice. As with Abraham, Isaac is not given the command to "be fruitful and multiply." Rather, God will multiply Isaac's offspring, and he will do it through one appointed twin son and not the other.

Likewise, the promise of land to Isaac's offspring is stated twice. The only notable shift is the change of language from God "cutting a covenant" with Abraham to his "establishing an oath" that "he swore" to Abraham with Isaac. The language confirms our earlier observation that this is a promissory grant covenant in which primary obligation rests with the one who is the *master* in the relationship.

What is surprising in the relatively short narrative of the life of Isaac is his relationship to offspring, the land, and material blessing. After God dramatically intervenes in the life of Sarah to provide Abraham a son, we might expect that Isaac's offspring would come automatically. Instead we find that Rebekah also was barren, Isaac prayed for her, and the Lord responded by providing a fruitful womb (Gen. 25:21). Nor was the land any more hospitable to Isaac than it had been to Abraham. Famine drives Isaac to Gerar, and the implication of the text is that he would have gone down to Egypt had he not been warned by God otherwise (Gen. 26:1–2). Isaac also faced contention with the indigenous population over the use of land resources (26:17–22). While the twin promises of offspring and land required eyes of faith for Isaac, the text is unequivocal regarding God's tangible blessing upon Isaac's livelihood and material well-being. He reaped a hundredfold of what he sowed and became very wealthy, invoking the consternation of the Philistines who lived around him (Gen. 26:12–16).

Jacob

The account of Jacob likewise gives two occasions in which God confirms his covenant. The first occurs while Jacob is fleeing his brother Esau to live with his uncle Laban in Paddan-aram. Jacob falls asleep and sees the angels of God ascending and descending on a ladder up to heaven. Above it stood the Lord, who said to him:

> I am the LORD, the God of Abraham your father and the God of Isaac. The land on which you lie I will give to you and to your *offspring*. Your *offspring* shall be like the dust of the earth, and you shall spread abroad

to the west and to the east and to the north and to the south, and in you and your *offspring* shall all the families of the earth be blessed. Behold, I am with you and will keep you wherever you go, and will bring you back to this land. For I will not leave you until I have done what I have promised you. (Gen. 28:13b–15)

Twenty years later Jacob returns from Paddan-aram to Canaan, and God tells him to return to Bethel and dwell there (Gen. 35:1). There God again appears to Jacob and blesses him, and on this occasion God says to him:

Your name is Jacob; no longer shall your name be called Jacob, but Israel shall be your name. . . . I am God Almighty: be fruitful and multiply. A nation and a company of nations shall come from you, and kings shall come from your own body. The land that I gave to Abraham and Isaac I will give to you, and I will give the land to your *offspring* after you." (Gen. 35:10b–12)

The emphasis on offspring is also prominent in the promises given to Jacob (with the word *offspring* appearing four times in the two passages), although there is also a conspicuous difference. As in the case of Abraham, God not only promises to give Jacob many offspring and land for that offspring, but he also reaffirms the statement given to Abraham that "nations" and "kings" will come from Jacob. But unlike Abraham and Isaac, God also gives to Jacob the Adam/Noah mandate: "Be fruitful and multiply." While for Abraham and Isaac the divinely appointed offspring was only *one* son at the exclusion of other sons, Jacob is the seminal father of the whole nation, and all twelve of his sons conceived via four different women are included within the covenantal blessing. Thus Jacob is commissioned to "be fruitful and multiply" in a parallel physical way to Adam and Noah, in which all his sons become a chosen nation blessed by God through the Abrahamic promises.

Jacob, however, like his father Isaac, though immeasurably blessed materially also faces hardship both in procreation of offspring and with dwelling in the land. Rachel, like Rebekah and Sarah before her, was also barren apart from God's provision. Jacob, like Isaac, also faces trouble with the local inhabitants of the land over the rape of Dinah (Genesis 34), and, of course, it is the famine in the land that ultimately brings Jacob's reunification with his son Joseph at the close of the Genesis story (Gen. 41:57–42:2).

God's confirmation of his covenant with Isaac and Jacob further reinforces the fundamental pattern of his covenant with Abraham. The promise of offspring is the central promise upon which God's blessing and the promise of land also rest. The promise of offspring depends entirely on God's provision, as is made clearly evident in the pattern of barrenness among the patriarchs' wives. In Jacob God is beginning to build a nation; hence he is renamed "Israel" and is commanded to "be fruitful and multiply."

Wrapping Up

By now some readers may be wondering what this discussion in Genesis and the patriarchs has to do with a theology of singleness. After all, from creation through the narrative of the patriarchs the text emphasizes the association of God's blessing with marriage and procreation. Apart from Genesis 2:18, singleness is not appreciably mentioned at all. Thus it is necessary to wrap up a few loose ends and offer a few observations on how the Genesis story relates to the larger picture.

1) Procreation is associated with God's blessing from the very beginning of creation. It is implied in the creation of man as *male* and *female* and with the first mandate to them to "be fruitful and multiply." It is the provision of God within the created order to maintain all life forms in a world subject to physical death (Luke 20:35–36).

2) Marriage, according to the Genesis creation account, has two fundamental purposes. The first is companionship, which has two dimensions: intimacy ("It is not good that the man should be alone," 2:18), and assistance ("a helper fit for him," 2:18). The other purpose for marriage is that it is the means and context for procreation of humankind ("they shall become one flesh," 2:24).

3) The importance of the term *offspring* emerges early and prominently in Genesis. Already in the garden of Eden we have prophetic foreshadowing of the importance of the *offspring* of Eve who will "strike" (RSV) the Serpent's head (Gen. 3:15), and later Eve speaks of God's appointing "another offspring" in Seth (4:25). The importance of offspring also

serves as the central drama within the major storyline of the account of all the patriarchs in Genesis. Not only is it the most prominent of the covenant promises to Abraham, but it is the critical linchpin upon which all covenant promises depend. Moreover, God's blessing comes to the patriarchs through the provision of offspring; and through the provision of offspring, God's blessing comes to the world.

4) The prominence of offspring as a central motif of God's blessing in Genesis might seem to emphasize the importance of human beings marrying and having children as the essential means to realize and effect God's blessing upon the world. Instead, the emphasis is that the *offspring* of the covenant that ultimately mediates God's blessing to the world is ultimately a provision of God himself *rather* than of human initiative. It serves to underscore the theological reality of our full dependence upon God for the provision of all the blessings he wishes to bestow.

2

Living in the Land

Why Every Israelite Man and Woman Married

A number of years ago a little book entitled *The Prayer of Jabez* hit the evangelical best-seller lists.[1] The book considers the obscure biblical figure Jabez, mentioned in 1 Chronicles 4:9–10, who prays to God to bless him and enlarge the borders of his territory—a request that God grants. The premise of the book is that just as Jabez asked God to expand his territory, so then should we, since God has for each of us a storehouse of blessings constrained only by our lack of asking. The book implicitly opened up a pertinent hermeneutical question: To what degree does ancient Israel with its blessings of territorial land and robust family life under the ethical code of the old covenant provide a direct model for those of us living on the other side of the cross in the age of the new covenant?

The Sinai covenant includes blessings of robust fruitfulness in the land to those who keep the stipulations of the covenant. Does this fact mean that Christians who seek to live faithfully in the modern age should also expect to be similarly materially and financially blessed? Many Christians feel uneasy in too quickly presuming such a parallel, recognizing that the blessings afforded to us in the new covenant are of a somewhat different character than those attributed to the old covenant. Jesus himself warns that "one's life does not consist in the abundance of his possessions" (Luke 12:15).

It is with a similar sense of qualification that we turn to the topic of marriage and singleness in ancient Israel, recognizing that while we have a pattern to learn from, we do not necessarily have a pattern to emulate.

We argue in this chapter that the ancient nation of Israel was a society characterized by near universal marriage for those who were able to marry, because marriage and offspring had a fundamental role in the appropriation of the Sinai covenant blessings to the individual Israelite. Not only was the fruitfulness of womb in itself a marker of God's covenant blessing, but having offspring was central to the preservation of two other pillars of importance in Israelite society: the family's inheritance of land, and the postmortem continuance of one's name or legacy. The aim of the present chapter is to show the critical importance of marriage and offspring in relation to these three pillars—covenant, inheritance, and name—and show the interrelationships between them.

Offspring and the Sinai Covenant

The Covenant in Context

After God renews the Abrahamic covenant with Jacob and commissions him to "be fruitful and multiply" (Gen. 35:11), just a few generations later in Israel's history, "the people of Israel were fruitful and increased greatly; they multiplied and grew exceedingly strong" (Ex. 1:7). They became so plentiful that their Egyptian hosts were soon overwhelmed and forced them into servitude and subjugation. The story of the exodus is the story of God's deliverance of the people from their subjugation and his formation of them into a nation with the Lord, Yahweh, as their God.

Though the initial events surrounding God's giving the Sinai covenant to the people are recorded in Exodus 19 and 20, the book of Deuteronomy provides Moses' reiteration of the covenant to the next generation of Israelites as they stood on the plains of Moab ready to take possession of the land (1:5). This renewal of the Sinai covenant was also an occasion to mark God's faithful fulfillment of his promises to the patriarchs. God had formed them into a nation (4:6), multiplied them to be as numerous as the stars of heaven (1:10), and set the land of Canaan before them to possess (1:8).

Whereas the Abrahamic covenant was a "grant" type of covenant similar to those that a lord would employ toward an approved servant, the covenant that God gives to the Israelites at the foot of Mount Sinai finds its closest parallels in the "treaty" type of covenant. This type of covenant placed the greater obligation on the servant and was designed to protect the interests of the lord should the servant fail in fulfilling his or her responsibilities.[2] Meredith Kline and Kenneth Kitchen were pioneers in demonstrating that the book of Deuteronomy itself follows the structural pattern of a mid-second-millennium ancient Near Eastern vassal treaty of this type.[3] The pattern is delineated as follows:[4]

1. *Preamble:* Identifies the author and his right to make the treaty (Deut. 1:1–5)
2. *Historical prologue:* A survey of the past relationship between parties (Deut. 1:6–3:29)
3. *Stipulations:* The list of obligations upon the vassal
   a. *Basic:* (Deuteronomy 4–11).
   b. *Detailed:* (Deuteronomy 12–26)
4. *Deposition and public reading of the text:* Instructions on storage and public reading of texts
   a. *Deposition of the text:* (Deut. 31:9, 24–26)
   b. *Public reading:* (Deut. 31:10–13)
5. *Witnesses:* Normally pagan gods named as witnesses; in Deuteronomy heaven and earth are called upon as witnesses (Deut. 31:16–32:47)
6. *Curses and blessings:* How the author will respond to the treaty in either adherence or violation (in reverse order in Deuteronomy)
   Blessings: (Deut. 28:1–14)
   Curses: (Deut. 28:15–68)

Notable in Deuteronomy is the dominance of the "stipulations" section of the covenant (chaps. 4–26), reinforcing the conditional nature of the Sinai covenant. Unlike the promises given to Abraham, God's blessings in the Sinai covenant were entirely conditioned upon the obedience of the Israelites.

Discussion of marriage and procreation arises in the Sinai covenant both in the covenant stipulations upon the Israelites and in sections delineating God's blessings upon the Israelites for their obedience to the covenant stipulations. Stipulations within the covenant (here including both the formal stipulations in Deuteronomy and also some from Leviticus) are essentially of a restrictive nature. Stipulations on marriage include forbidding a man to marry his wife's sister (Lev. 18:18) or his father's wife (Deut. 22:30); restrictions on the type of woman the high priest can marry (Lev. 21:13–15); restrictions against captives (Deut. 21:11–13); and restrictions on remarrying a wife one has previously divorced (Deut. 24:4). Most significant is the restriction against marrying non-Israelites (Deut. 7:3). The nation was not to assimilate with the surrounding nations but was commanded by God to preserve its racial pedigree by not intermarrying. There is no stipulation, however, *requiring* Israelites to be married or to produce offspring.

Offspring as a Mark of Covenantal Blessing

As in the Abrahamic covenant, marriage and offspring feature prominently among the blessings of the Sinai covenant, but here those blessings come in response to the obedience of the people. The blessings are mentioned in two main places in the Deuteronomic covenant: as part of the *basic stipulations* section in chapter 7 and as part of the *blessings and curses* section in chapter 28. The *basic stipulations* of Deuteronomy 7 give a preview of the covenantal blessings and the importance of marriage and offspring within these blessings:

> You shall therefore be careful to do the commandment and the statutes and the rules that I command you today. And because you listen to these rules and keep and do them, the LORD your God will keep with you the covenant and the steadfast love that he swore to your fathers. He will love you, bless you, and multiply you. He will also bless the fruit of your womb and the fruit of your ground, your grain and your wine and your oil, the increase of your herds and the young of your flock, in the land that he swore to your fathers to give you. You shall be blessed above all peoples. There shall not be male or female barren among you or among your livestock. (Deut. 7:11–14)

We see that God will bless the Israelites if they listen to the "rules" (i.e., stipulations) of the covenant and faithfully keep them. Just as God blessed and multiplied the patriarchs, so too he will bless and multiply them. This blessing is described first and foremost as blessing of the womb but also extends to blessing of the "fruit" of their land—their crops and grain, their wine and olive oil, and their herds and flocks. The primary marker of God's blessing instantiated to the individual Israelite is given here as the "blessing of the womb"; that is, neither they nor their livestock will suffer barrenness of offspring. All of this blessing is built upon a foundation of marriage. The stipulations of Deuteronomy 22:28–29 make clear that if a man violates a virgin not already betrothed, the woman becomes his wife.

In the *blessings and curses* section recorded in Deuteronomy 28, the blessings begin as follows:

> And if you faithfully obey the voice of the LORD your God, being careful to do all his commandments that I command you today, the LORD your God will set you high above all the nations of the earth. And all these blessings shall come upon you and overtake you, if you obey the voice of the LORD your God. Blessed shall you be in the city, and blessed shall you be in the field. Blessed shall be the fruit of your womb and the fruit of your ground and the fruit of your cattle, the increase of your herds and the young of your flock. (Deut. 28:1–4)

As part of the official list of covenantal blessings given for obedience, the blessing of the "fruit of the womb" is again prominently featured with a trifold application that includes the "fruit" of human offspring, the ground (i.e., crops), and livestock. The blessing of the "fruit of the womb" is repeated yet again a few verses later as a description of their promised prosperity:

> And the LORD will make you abound in prosperity, in the fruit of your womb and in the fruit of your livestock and in the fruit of your ground, within the land that the LORD swore to your fathers to give you. (Deut. 28:11)

This restatement of the blessing ties together critical threads that link to the promises of the Abrahamic covenant. The Lord will bless the Israelites *in the land* that he swore to their *fathers* (i.e., the patriarchs) that he would give to them through a combination of prosperity in the land via crops and livestock, but also through providing them their own "fruit of the womb." We see in this blessing not only a fulfillment of God's promises of the Abrahamic covenant but also a range of blessings given to individual Israelites on the condition of their faithful obedience to the stipulations of the Sinai covenant.

The Covenant Curses

Conversely, we find in the more extensive curses section later in the chapter a near reversal of language:

> But if you will not obey the voice of the LORD your God or be careful to do all his commandments and his statutes that I command you today, then all these curses shall come upon you and overtake you. Cursed shall you be in the city, and cursed shall you be in the field. Cursed shall be your basket and your kneading bowl. Cursed shall be the fruit of your womb and the fruit of your ground, the increase of your herds and the young of your flock. (Deut. 28:15–18)

The curse on the "fruit of the womb" as a reference to barrenness is given only once in the formal delineation of covenant curses, again in a trifold formulation that includes crops and livestock. But later in the chapter, as the curses become more grievous and horrific, we find additional curses relating to marriage and offspring. One shall betroth a wife, "but another man shall ravish her" (Deut. 28:30). One's sons and daughters will be given to another people, while eyes "look on and fail with longing for them all day long" (v. 32). Though one fathers sons and daughters, they shall be taken into captivity (v. 41). Under the distress of siege both fathers (vv. 54–55) and mothers (vv. 56–57) will eat the flesh of their own offspring while begrudging even sharing with their spouse.

Near the conclusion of the delineation of curses we find what reads in essence to be a *reversal* of the core promised blessings of the Abrahamic covenant itself:

> Whereas you were as numerous as the stars of heaven, you shall be left few in number, because you did not obey the voice of the LORD your God. And as the LORD took delight in doing you good and multiplying you, so the LORD will take delight in bringing ruin upon you and destroying you. And you shall be plucked off the land that you are entering to take possession of it. (Deut. 28:62–63)

Whereas God promised to multiply the offspring of Abraham to be as the stars of heaven, he will (potentially) reverse this process and make them few in number again. And whereas he had promised to Abraham to give them the land, he will (potentially) remove them from it.

In Deuteronomy 29 we find the clearest example of the particularity of the covenant blessings and curses upon each individual Israelite:

> Beware lest there be among you a man or woman or clan or tribe whose heart is turning away today from the LORD our God to go and serve the gods of those nations. Beware lest there be among you a root bearing poisonous and bitter fruit, one who, when he hears the words of this sworn covenant, blesses himself in his heart, saying, "I shall be safe, though I walk in the stubbornness of my heart." This will lead to the sweeping away of moist and dry alike. The LORD will not be willing to forgive him, but rather the anger of the LORD and his jealousy will smoke against that man, and the curses written in this book will settle upon him, and the LORD will blot out his name from under heaven. And the LORD will single him out from all the tribes of Israel for calamity, in accordance with all the curses of the covenant written in this Book of the Law. (Deut. 29:18–21)

The passage illustrates that even though the covenant was given to the whole nation, every individual was subject to the terms and conditions of the covenant such that if anyone violated the terms of the covenant, he or she *individually* was subject to the full weight of the covenant curses. Such a fate necessarily includes the loss not only of one's own life but also of all one's offspring, as conveyed in the expression of having one's name "*blotted out* [*makhah*] from under heaven."[5] For the average Israelite, the inference of the logic worked both ways. The loss of one's offspring or lack of offspring would serve as a mark of divine disapproval, that one had violated the covenant and therefore was subject to the covenantal curses. Hence for the average Israelite, having surviving offspring was an important marker of divine approval.

The Sinai Covenant: Conclusions

In relating the blessings of the Abrahamic covenant to those given in the Sinai covenant, we observe a link of both fulfillment and qualified continuation. The Sinai covenant testifies of God's fulfillment of his promises to the patriarchs. God has fulfilled his covenant to the patriarchs through giving them innumerable offspring and blessing them with immeasurable fruitfulness in the Promised Land. We see direct continuation between the covenants on the focus of the blessing of offspring. This continuation is qualified in two respects. First, it is broadened to include not just offspring but a trifold "fruitfulness of the womb" and prosperity in the land. The Israelites are to be blessed in their families and material prosperity. Second, it is conditioned upon their individual faithful obedience to the covenantal stipulations. Whereas the innumerable offspring is an unconditional promise to the patriarchs, offspring and prosperity are for the Israelites conditioned upon their adherence to the stipulations of the covenant.

It is thus not difficult to see why it was of utmost importance for each Israelite to marry and beget offspring, for offspring (and thus also marriage) were the *sine qua non* of the individual reception of the covenantal blessings of Sinai. To marry and have offspring was, to an individual, a mark of God's covenantal blessing, and by extension a validation of his obedience to the covenant stipulations. Conversely, to be devoid of children with the result of having one's name "blotted out" of Israel was a mark of his subjection to the covenant curses and by implication a sentence of divine disapproval.

Offspring and the Inheritance of the Land

The Significance of the "Inheritance"

The vocabulary that the Old Testament uses to describe God's apportionment of land to each Israelite family is a window into the theological significance of the land each received. Although a few different terms are used, the most theologically significant term is *inheritance* (*nakhalah*). Strictly speaking, *nakhalah* refers to the portion of a patriarchal estate a joint heir is entitled to receive. Furthermore, it was specific to an inherited portion of a patriarchal estate rather than to property gained or inherited from some other source.[6]

The first detailed description of the allocation of the Promised Land as an inheritance occurs in Numbers 26 after God has Moses and Eleazar take a census of all the people twenty years and older. The tally of individuals totaled 601,730 (Num. 26:51), after which God instructs Moses:

> Among these the land shall be divided for inheritance according to the number of names. To a large tribe you shall give a large inheritance, and to a small tribe you shall give a small inheritance; every tribe shall be given its inheritance in proportion to its list. But the land shall be

divided by lot. According to the names of the tribes of their fathers they shall inherit. Their inheritance shall be divided according to lot between the larger and the smaller. (Num. 26:53–56)[7]

Thus, the land is not simply doled out to each citizen as an entitlement, but rather it is "divided for inheritance" according to each family by lot. As an inheritance, the land is effectively bestowed by God the "patriarch" to the Israelites as "heirs." The designation of the land as an inheritance underscores the importance of offspring, since in the same way that God gives it as a patriarchal bestowment to the first generation of Israelites, so similarly the inheritance as a permanent possession of the household was to be subsequently passed on as a patriarchal bestowment from father to son in successive generations (e.g., Ex. 32:13; 1 Kings 21:3; 1 Chron. 28:8).

The Importance of the Inheritance of Land

It is hard to overestimate the importance of the apportioned inheritance for the individual family unit in ancient Israel.[8] The family's allotment of land represented the portion of God's provision of blessing and sustenance for their livelihood (Num. 32:18; Deut. 19:14). It was the location of the family's homestead and house (Mic. 2:2)—with the Hebrew term for *house* (*bayith*) used to designate both the physical building (Judg. 11:31) and those who dwelled in it (Josh. 24:15).

The inheritance was the place of family security (Lev. 25:18–19) and the location for God's provision of "rest" (Deut. 25:19). It was not to be confiscated by greedy oppressors (note the condemnation of such in Mic. 2:2). It was also the place for burial of one's ancestors (Josh. 24:30). It provided land for growing crops for physical survival and sustenance (Lev. 25:19) and grazing for their flocks and herds (Deut. 7:13; 8:12–13). The inheritance was in every respect the family's tangible wealth engine of the covenantal blessings (Deut. 7:13; 8:12–13; Lev. 25:21).

More broadly, the importance of the land in Israelite society is seen also in its function of preserving economic equality within the nation. The principle behind this legal restriction is articulated in Leviticus 25:23: "The land shall not be sold in perpetuity, for the land is mine. For you are strangers and sojourners with me."

The people did not "own" their inheritance; they merely had the right from God of *usufruct*, to use and live upon the land. Thus they were to regard themselves as "strangers and sojourners" even with respect to their own inheritance of land!

Since the land could not be sold, it also served as a vehicle for maintaining large-scale economic equilibrium, since every fiftieth year (the Year of Jubilee) the individual allotments returned to original families (Lev. 25:13). Thus, only the right to use the land up until the next Year of Jubilee could be bought or sold (Lev. 25:15–16). If one did become poor and was forced to sell the right of usufruct, the law also provided for the right of redemption of the poor man by his nearest kinsman-redeemer (Lev. 25:25). The land as an *inheritance* ensured ongoing economic equality within Israelite society precisely by retaining the individual family allotments within the same family lines.

For the ancient Israelite, one's personal identity was tied to the possession of the family inheritance of land. There were three major concentric levels of identity among the Israelites: the *tribe*, subdivided by *clan*, in turn subdivided by *family* or *house*. Achan is identified in Joshua 7:16–18 as from "the tribe of Judah," "the clan of Zerah," "son of Carmi," "son of Zabdi." Achan himself was a member of the "house of Zabdi," his grandfather. Zabdi's "house" was apparently an extended household including adult grandsons, such as Achan, each with his own children and livestock (Josh. 7:24). With the conquest, the physical geography of the land was allocated to directly correspond to the structure of the nation, with the size of the tribal inheritances being proportionate to the size of the tribe (Num. 26:54). Hence the position of each and every household within Israel was marked in a corresponding position to a plot of land that served as that household's inheritance.

Inheritance and Offspring

The importance of the inheritance of land within Israelite society thus also points to the critical importance in that society of being married and having progeny. For, as important as the inheritance was for a particular Israelite family as a tangible marker of the covenantal blessings of Sinai, the inheritance could be retained within the family line *only* by being passed on to one's progeny—normally one's son. One who had no off-spring or lost his offspring was subject to losing the family's inheritance of land.

The way this was supposed to work is illustrated in the story of Zelophehad's daughters in Numbers 27:1–11. Normally, when the family patriarch passed away, the inheritance was distributed among the sons, while daughters shared in the inheritance of their respective husbands' families. The problem raised by the daughters of Zelophehad in Numbers 27 was that their father had only daughters, at least some of whom were mature but not yet married. As a consequence, Zelophehad's individual inheritance was in danger of being lost and redistributed among his fellow clan members. So the daughters turned to Moses and raised the following complaint:

> Why should the name of our father be taken away from his clan because he had no son? Give to us a possession among our father's brothers. (Num. 27:4)

The daughters of Zelophehad recognized that, in the loss of the possession of the inheritance, their father's name would also disappear from the clan. The presence of one's inheritance was thus a physical manifestation of one's name and existence within the clan. God agreed with their concern and thus responded:

> You shall give them possession of an inheritance among their father's brothers and transfer the inheritance of their father to them. (Num. 27:7)

God's grant to Zelophehad's daughters in this particular incident signified that daughters as well as sons were eligible to retain the family inheritance. A subsequent concern later arises by the clan (Num. 36:1–4): if Zelophehad's daughters marry husbands from other tribes, then his inheritance will be permanently redistributed to those other tribes. The resolution given is that the daughters must marry within their own tribes (Num. 36:6–7).

These texts highlight some important features about the institution of the inheritance within Israel. First, if a man had no offspring, his inheritance was passed to his brothers, or, if no brothers, to his father's brothers, or, if no uncles, to the nearest kinsman within the clan. The inheritance never passed to the widow of the deceased patriarch but only to his male descendants or to his female daughters, if he had no sons (Num. 27:8–11). Second, without offspring the man's inheritance was forfeited to others within the clan. Without an inheritance in the clan, one's name disappeared from remembrance within the clan.

Offspring and One's Name in Ancient Israel

In addition to the importance of covenantal blessings and the continuance of one's family inheritance, we have already seen hints along the way of the importance of one's name in ancient Israel. Among the very worst of the covenant curses was the prospect of having one's name "blotted out" (Deut. 29:20), and Zelophehad's daughters recognize the peril associated with the loss of their father's name in their complaint to Moses over their inheritance (Num. 27:4). The ancient preoccupation with building one's name is seen as early as Genesis 11:4, when Nimrod and the people of Shinar built the tower of Babel to "make a name" for themselves. Among the blessings that God first promises to Abraham in Genesis 12:2–3 is the blessing of making "your name great." Indeed the importance of having one's name remembered in life and preserved after death is pervasive in the Old Testament and is another reason why having offspring was critically important in ancient Israelite society.

The Significance of One's Name

In the Semitic world a person's name signified in a dynamic sense his or her vital (family and heritage), material (property), and spiritual (fame, reputation) aspects.[9] So closely was someone associated with his name that the name could function as a direct substitute for the person (e.g., Solomon is commissioned to build a house for God's *name* in 2 Sam. 7:13; Israel is a people called by God's *name* in 2 Chron. 7:14). The third commandment forbids dishonor to God's name, because to dishonor God's name is tantamount to dishonoring God himself (Ex. 20:7; Lev. 19:12).

In the ancient world naming not only provided an apt description of someone, but also could be determinative of one's coming into existence.[10] This is illustrated, for example, in the opening of the extrabiblical account *Enuma Elish*, which equates naming with existing:

> When on high heaven had not been named,
> firm ground below had not been called by name,
> there was nothing but primordial Apsu their begetter
> *and* Mummu-Tiamat, she who bore them all.[11]

The text of Genesis depicts God creating the heavens and earth and all that is in it through a process of decreeing, forming, and naming their existence. God then shares aspects of his dominion over creation with human beings created in his image by commissioning them to name all the individual animals. Conversely, since one's name and existence were inextricably linked, having one's name destroyed or cut off was a definitive expression of one's ceasing to exist. Thus, one reason that preserving a name was so vitally important to the ancient Hebrews and their contemporaries was that it could survive one's death in a culture with a still shadowy and undeveloped concept of the afterlife.[12] Having one's name continue beyond life was a means of participating in a form of immortality, not through actual postmortem existence but through being incorporated into the existential continuum of the living.[13]

The Importance of Offspring in Preserving a Name

In ancient Israel a name survived postmortem in two ways—through the survival of one's progeny and through the continuance of the inheritance of one's land. Hence, retaining one's name was foremost an effort to keep offspring and land together.[14] But since, as we have seen, the continued possession of one's inheritance also depended on having surviving offspring, the continuance of living offspring was the single most critical factor in preserving one's name.

The name was preserved through offspring in two ways: first, by offspring *carrying* the name of their ancestry (e.g., Israel's name survives in the existence of "Israelites"); and, second, by offspring *remembering* the name of their forefathers. A name lived through the ongoing conversation of offspring recalling and remembering one's life and contributions. Though it was possible in the ancient world that a name could be remembered through other means (e.g., Absalom's pillar), the primary means was through progeny. This linkage can be illustrated in a number of examples:

- When Jacob blesses his grandsons Ephraim and Manasseh, he says, "In them let my name be carried on, and the name of my fathers Abraham and Isaac" (Gen. 48:16).
- Absalom sets a pillar for himself in the King's Valley because, as he reasons, "I have no son to keep my name in remembrance" (2 Sam. 18:18).
- The prophet Nahum condemns Nineveh in saying, "No more shall your name be perpetuated" (Nah. 1:14). Literally it reads, "No more shall your name be sown" (i.e., perpetuated through the lives of your offspring.)

Since the continuance of one's name through a perpetual line of offspring was a means to maintain a sort of immortality, to have one's line of descendants completely terminated at any point was a form of second death. This notion is described frequently in the Old Testament with two rather vivid expressions: having a name "cut off" (*karath*) and having a name "blotted out" (*makhah*). Both expressions convey a graphic sense of finality and represent a termination more pervasive than death, since they imply not only the end of one's physical presence but also any form of one's memory within the society.

The concern to avoid the cutting off or blotting out of one's name is illustrated in numerous examples in the Old Testament. In Psalm 109 David curses his opponent, saying, "May his posterity be cut off; may his name be blotted out in the second generation!" (Ps. 109:13). Since the man has children, David hopes those children will die without offspring so that the man's name will be "blotted" out after one generation.

In an incident when David spares Saul's life and Saul realizes that the kingdom will inevitably pass into David's hands, he pleads with David:

Swear to me therefore by the LORD that you will not cut off my offspring after me, and that you will not destroy my name out of my father's house. (1 Sam. 24:21)

Here, the graphic sense of cutting off one's line of descendants is equated with the destruction of his name.

Since the notion of a name blotted out entailed the extermination of an entire line of offspring, it was applied in the Old Testament on occasion to entire nations, as well as to particular individuals. After the golden calf incident God says regarding Israel, "Let me alone, that I may destroy them and blot out their name from under heaven" (Deut. 9:14).[15] Israel, as part of the conquest of Canaan, was commissioned to "blot out the memory of Amalek from under heaven" (Deut. 25:19). Here again, the nation represents the continuing existence of the individual. Likewise in Isaiah 14:22 the Lord of hosts prophesies against Babylon, "I will rise up against them, and will cut off from Babylon name and remnant, descendants and posterity."[16]

Having one's name "blotted out" (e.g., Deut. 29:20) was the capstone of personal disasters. No surviving children in ancient Israel meant the loss of one's inheritance, name, and covenantal blessings. Conversely, marriage and offspring were fundamentally necessary for the reception of all the covenantal blessings. With them, one was blessed with family, land, and a name that survived beyond death. Without them, all was lost, and one lived under the weight of personally embodying the full gravity of the covenant curses. Given this fact, it is not surprising to find within the Torah codified provisions to mitigate the likelihood of such a disaster occurring. One such provision was levirate marriage.

Levirate Marriage

The term *levirate* comes from the Latin *levir,* which means "brother-in-law." The Old Testament provision of levirate marriage comes from Deuteronomy 25:5–10, although the custom predates the Sinai covenant, as illustrated in the story of Tamar and Judah in Genesis 38.[17] In essence levirate marriage provided a mechanism whereby if a man died without a son, he could have a surrogate son through his brother. The brother was to marry the widow of the deceased and sire a son so that "the first son whom she bears shall succeed to the name [literally "*stand upon the name*"] of his dead brother, that his name may not be blotted out of Israel" (Deut. 25:6). The provision was an exception clause to the incest prohibitions of Leviticus 18:6–18, which in normal circumstances barred a man from having sexual relations with his brother's wife (18:16).

Apart from the deceased brother, it is hard to see how anybody else benefited from the practice of levirate marriage. The provision kept the wife from marrying a new husband outside the clan and beginning a new family. She remained in the household of her deceased husband, bound in a legal sense to her husband's brother, who might already have a wife and family of his own.[18] The brother, in performing his duty as levirate, was in effect acting counter to his own interests, since he would otherwise inherit his brother's estate (Num. 27:9). Additionally, the arrangement apparently did not have the purpose of keeping the deceased man's inheritance within the clan. The widow was not eligible to inherit the land; there was already a legal requirement that it remain within the clan (Num. 27:8–11).

The clear purpose of the provision was to ensure that the name of the deceased was preserved and that his family line did not get blotted out or lose the family inheritance. Levirate marriage, therefore, was a provision to mitigate the difficulties of dying without issue and having one's name forgotten. Implicitly the practice served to reinforce the social gravity of dying without issue—and therefore the value placed upon marriage and procreation within the society as a whole.

Singleness in a Culture of Marriage: The Case of Jeremiah

Given the pervasive importance of marriage and offspring in ancient Israel, it is not surprising that we do not read in the Old Testament of any who remained single voluntarily. One individual called by God to remain single was the prophet Jeremiah. God called Jeremiah not to take a wife as a visible sign of his impending judgment upon the people:

> The word of the LORD came to me: "You shall not take a wife, nor shall you have sons or daughters in this place. For thus says the LORD concerning the sons and daughters who are born in this place, and concerning the mothers who bore them and the fathers who fathered them in this land: They shall die of deadly diseases. They shall not be lamented, nor shall they be buried. They shall be as dung on the surface of the ground. They shall perish by the sword and by famine, and their dead bodies shall be food for the birds of the air and for the beasts of the earth. (Jer. 16:1–4)

Jeremiah was commanded by God to abstain from both marriage and offspring. His life was to be an example of the message that he was to proclaim to the people, namely, that God was judging them because they (and their forefathers) had forsaken the *torah* (the covenant) and they had forsaken the Lord and had served other gods (Jer. 16:11). Consequently, Jeremiah's lack of offspring was to model God's judgment on his people that they too would become bereft of their offspring through pestilence, sword, and famine. Jeremiah's singleness was a visible portent of God's impending judgment upon the nation.

Jeremiah struggled with the implications associated with remaining single in a culture where marriage and offspring were of supreme importance. In an earlier passage we catch a glimpse of Jeremiah's personal angst over threats against his life in his single state, and God's response:

> But I was like a gentle lamb
> > led to the slaughter.
> I did not know it was against me
> > they devised schemes, saying,
> "Let us destroy the tree with its fruit,
> > let us cut him off from the land of the living,
> > that his name be remembered no more."
> But, O LORD of hosts, who judges righteously,
> > who tests the heart and the mind,
> let me see your vengeance upon them,
> > for to you have I committed my cause.
>
> Therefore thus says the LORD concerning the men of Anathoth, who seek your life, and say, "Do not prophesy in the name of the LORD, or you will die by our hand"—therefore thus says the LORD of hosts: "Behold, I will punish them. The young men shall die by the sword, their sons and their daughters shall die by famine, and none of them shall be left. For I will bring disaster upon the men of Anathoth, the year of their punishment." (Jer. 11:19–23)

Jeremiah's lament to God makes clear that both he and his aggressors, the men of Anathoth, were aware of the ramifications of their plot to take his life; namely, that they would destroy "the tree with its fruit" and that in his death, Jeremiah's name would be blotted out and thus "remembered no more." In a form of like-kind retribution (*lex talionis*) God promises to

Jeremiah that the men of Anathoth and their children will die and "none of them shall be left." In other words, God will blot out the name of the men of Anathoth who seek to blot out the name of Jeremiah.

Jeremiah's singleness thus served the prophetic function of reinforcing his message. He in his singleness embodied the impeding judgment of God upon the people, which would entail stripping them of their offspring and exposing them to all the associated consequences of such a fate.

Other Illustrations

Two further Old Testament narratives illustrate well the pervasive importance and interdependence of offspring, inheritance (i.e., land allotment), and name for the ancient Israelites living under the Sinai covenant: the story of Naboth's vineyard and the story of Ruth and Boaz.

Naboth's Vineyard (1 Kings 21:1–29)

In the modern world, most nations recognize the right of *eminent domain*—the right of the state to seize a citizen's private property, with due monetary compensation, but without necessity of the citizen's consent.[19] The story of King Ahab and Naboth is a question of the right of eminent domain in ancient Israel. Ahab comes to Naboth and asks for his vineyard, as it was near the royal palace, in exchange for a better vineyard or monetary compensation (1 Kings 21:2).

From the modern perspective there is nothing apparently exceptional or unethical about Ahab's request. Ahab appears to be willing to compensate Naboth fully—even more than the vineyard itself was worth. But in Israel the land was not a commodity to be freely bought and sold—even by the king (Lev. 25:23). Naboth simply responds, "The LORD forbid that I should give you the inheritance of my fathers" (1 Kings 21:3). Naboth's response makes clear that (1) the land was an inheritance, not merely a possession to be bought or sold; (2) the land had been passed down by his ancestors and therefore *could not* simply be subsumed into the royal estates; and (3) God had explicitly commanded that it not be sold. Ahab is subsequently chastised by his foreign wife Jezebel for not acting king-like in simply taking the land (v. 7). The central drama of the story thus pits the rights of families to their God-given inheritance (a right unique to how God gives them the land) with the right of royal power generally practiced in the ancient Near East.

Because Ahab allows Jezebel to frame and kill Naboth, he receives strident condemnation from God through Elijah the prophet, who confronts Ahab with the question, "Have you killed and also *taken possession?*" (1 Kings 21:19). Ahab is charged with two crimes, murder and forced acquisition. The punishment eked out upon Ahab is in fact the individualized punishment of Deuteronomy 29:20—his name is to be blotted out of Israel. Thus Elijah responds: "Behold, I will bring disaster upon you. I will utterly burn you up, and will cut off from Ahab every male, bond or free, in Israel" (1 Kings 21: 21). Ahab sought to jeopardize the inheritance of Naboth, so God eradicated the offspring and the name of Ahab from the face of Israel.

Ruth and Boaz

The narrative account of Ruth and Boaz is among the richest theological nuggets of the Old Testament and is especially illustrative of the major themes we are considering here. Though Ruth is the heroine, the central drama of the story focuses upon Naomi. Naomi is the one distraught upon whom "the Almighty has brought calamity" at the beginning of the story (Ruth 1:20–21), and she in turn is the one who is blessed and restored in the conclusion of the story (4:14–15). As modern readers we immediately relate to Naomi's tragedy relationally—she has lost both her husband and her two sons. Yet in light of the importance of offspring, inheritance and name for the ancient Israelites in relation to their personal appropriation of the covenantal blessing, Naomi's plight is cloaked with greater gravity than may first appear.

In reconstructing the story as a whole, most probably a famine had devastated Elimelech's family estate in Israel (1:1), forcing him to sell the land to an outsider (Lev. 25:25), and with the money he obtained from the sale, he moved someplace with greater prospects for survival, in this case, Moab.[20] In the course of their ten-year stay as sojourners in Moab, Elimelech died, as did both of his sons, Mahlon and Chilion (Ruth 1:3–5). This has left Naomi in a dire position. She has neither offspring to inherit the land nor land to be inherited (in Moab or Israel) in order. to maintain the family name. Naomi thus experiences the weight of the covenant curses threatened in Deuteronomy 29:20–21 of having her husband's name (and by marriage hers also) blotted out "from under heaven."

Naomi's response also suggests that she interprets her predicament as God's judgment against her. She describes her situation: "The hand of the LORD has gone out *against me*" (Ruth 1:13); "The Almighty has dealt very bitterly *with me*" (1:20); and "The Almighty has brought calamity *upon me*" (1:21). Even if Ruth and Orpah had been Israelite women under the covenant, they would not have faced the same calamitous circumstances, since they were yet young enough to remarry new husbands and start new families. This is assumed in Naomi's statement to them, "The LORD grant that you may find rest, each of you in the house of her [new] husband!" (1:9) as she sends them away.

Naomi returns to Israel on hearing that the Lord has again visited his people with food (Ruth 1:6), along with Ruth, who refuses to return to the home of her parents. The whole town was "stirred" upon seeing them (v. 19), no doubt because of Naomi's dire situation, which is such a contrast to the state in which she had left a decade earlier. The presumption of the story is that upon her return to Bethlehem, Naomi is a bereft widow with no means of support other than to live off the tithes of the townspeople and the remnants of their harvested field, olives, and vineyards (see Deut. 26:12–13; 24:19–21). Naomi's only other thread of hope lies in the redemption of her husband's inheritance by a "kinsman-redeemer" who might in acquiring the land of her husband's inheritance thereafter provide for her sustenance.

The climax of the story occurs in the fourth chapter of the book in the exchange between Boaz and an alternate kinsman-redeemer, who is a closer relative to Elimelech than Boaz and therefore had the right of first option. After Boaz promises Ruth that he will pursue her redemption, he sits down before the city gate with the other redeemer and ten elders of the city and begins the exchange:

> "Naomi, who has come back from the country of Moab, is selling [*makhar*] the parcel of land that belonged to our relative Elimelech. So I thought I would tell you of it and say, 'Buy it in the presence of

those sitting here and in the presence of the elders of my people.' If you will redeem it, redeem it. But if you will not, tell me, that I may know, for there is no one besides you to redeem it, and I come after you." And he said, "I will redeem it." Then Boaz said, "The day you buy the field from the hand of Naomi, you also acquire Ruth the Moabite, the widow of the dead, in order to perpetuate the name of the dead in his inheritance." Then the redeemer said, "I cannot redeem it for myself, lest I impair my own inheritance. Take my right of redemption yourself, for I cannot redeem it." (Ruth 4:3b–6)

Part of the complication of this little dialog is the fact that two different transaction customs, described in the Pentateuch, are both alluded to here: the kinsman-redeemer custom of property redemption (Lev. 25:23–34) and the custom of levirate marriage (Deut. 25:5–10). In addition, though the verb *makhar* most commonly means "to sell," it seems most unlikely here that she is "selling" Elimelech's land.[21] Most likely, the verb here means "to transfer or surrender the rights to."[22] In other words, Naomi, as the representative of what is left of Elimelech's estate, carries the right to redeem to the land from its present owners but, being destitute, she transfers this right to the next of kin, who is also the designated kinsman-redeemer.

The apparent presumption of the other kinsman-redeemer is that, by accepting the right to purchase the land, he would purchase the land from the resources of his own estate and assume responsibility for the maintenance of Naomi and presumably Ruth. But since Naomi is bereft of offspring, the land, upon her death, would be added to his estate because he is the nearest kin (see Num. 27:11).[23] He would be under no obligation to exercise levirate duties with respect to Naomi or Ruth, since this responsibility fell only upon the deceased man's brothers.

But Boaz then ups the ante when he adds further expectations of the transaction: the kinsman-redeemer must not only purchase the land but also perform levirate duties with Ruth to restore to Elimelech a legitimate heir. In this case he would be forced to spend resources from his own estate to purchase the inheritance of Elimelech, only to eventually surrender the land again to Elimelech's heir.[24] Thus, the alternate kinsman-redeemer suddenly reverses course and cedes the option to Boaz.

Boaz, in being willing to serve both as kinsman-redeemer to restore the land and as *levir* to restore Elimelech's heir, thereby "perpetuates the name of the dead in his inheritance" (Ruth 4:5). The sense of the Hebrew verb *perpetuates* (*qum*) here connotes the sense of "revive."[25] In other words, the *name* of the dead that had been effectively blotted out was now, through the act of Boaz, revived again with the inheritance intact.

The story concludes with a further surprising twist in the words of the women of the town who celebrate the Lord in providing for Naomi a kinsman-redeemer:

> Blessed be the LORD, who has not left you this day without a redeemer, and may his name be renowned in Israel! He shall be to you a restorer of life and a nourisher of your old age, for your daughter-in-law who loves you, who is more to you than seven sons, has given birth to him. (Ruth 4:14b–15)

In the women's praise to the Lord, the referent for the kinsman-redeemer suddenly shifts from Boaz to the child of Ruth and Boaz, Obed. There is some inherent logic in the shift, for the name and the inheritance are ultimately saved (hence, redeemed and restored) not through the presence of Boaz but through the presence of the offspring. And indeed, as the author of the narrative appears eager to point out, this is not just *any* offspring, but Obed the grandfather of King David (4:18–22). The dramatic point that concludes the story cannot be missed: God, who provides in the line of David the redemptive offspring who is the restorer of life.

The Nature of the Israelite Nation

The importance of tribal pedigree within ancient Israel points to a critical difference in the character of God's chosen people in the Old Testament, the nation of Israel, and God's chosen people in the New Testament, the church. In one sense the difference is readily apparent: the Israelites were an ethnically homogeneous people, while the church is ethnically heterogeneous. The implication of this distinction is this: *in the Old Testament God was primarily building and forming his covenant people through the mechanism of physical procreation.* This means that apart from special exceptions, those who were not the physical offspring of Jacob were not included in God's covenant people. One might object to this conclusion, noting the Pentateuch's high commitment to ethically just treatment of the sojourner, who was not an ethnic Israelite. Rahab and Ruth, for example, were both foreigners who not only were welcomed into the covenant community but were even part of the royal ancestral line of King David and Christ.

As Figure 2.1 illustrates, with regard to claim to the covenant there were three distinct classes of individuals. The first was the native citizens, called in Hebrew the *'ezrakh*, which simply designates those "born in the land." The second class was the "sojourner" or *ger*, those of alien birth who had come to live in the land and abide by its customs—resident aliens. The two classes are often paired in legal texts to emphasize that in God's eyes there is no difference in how they should be treated; the Israelites after all were once sojourners in the land of Egypt.[26]

Figure 2.1: God's Covenant People in the Old Testament:
Citizens and Foreigners

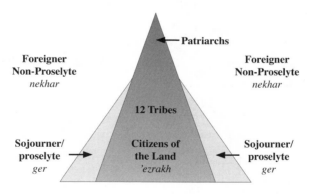

The third class of foreigner, designated with the Hebrew term *nekhar*, is generally referred to less favorably than the *ger*. The term *nekhar* simply means "foreign" and designates a foreign person, a foreign land, or a foreign god. Sometimes an individual was referred to as a *ben-nekhar* or "son of foreign land," designating one born outside the land who nevertheless retained his native customs and identity (e.g., Gen. 17:12; Lev. 22:25; 2 Sam. 22:45–46; Neh. 9:2; Isa. 56:3, 6). The law regarded the status of the *nekhar* very differently from the *ger*. The *ger* was included in the Passover (Num. 9:14), whereas the *nekhar* was strictly banned from participation (Ex. 12:43). The *ger* participated with the native *'ezrakh* in burnt offerings (Lev. 22:18), but no animals obtained from the hand of a foreigner (*nekhar*) were acceptable for an offering to the Lord (Lev. 22:25). It is the *nekhar* that routinely tempts Israel to the worship of foreign gods (e.g., Deut. 7:1–4; 31:16; 1 Kings 11:8).

What is important in the two types of foreigners is that while occasional foreigners were drawn to the nation and covenant of Israel—and those who did so were welcomed into the covenant of Israel—most remained outside the covenant and were potential sources of sin and temptation for Israel into the worship of other gods. Though Israel was to be a holy nation through whom all the nations of the world would be blessed (Ex. 19:6; Gen. 22:18), they were not commissioned to proselytize the foreign *nekhar* to become Jews. Rather, Israel itself was to be God's "treasured possession" among all the nations (Ex. 19:5). Israel was intended to retain its ethnic identity as the offspring of Abraham while also welcoming the occasional foreign sojourner, the *ger*, who sought to live under the covenant of the Lord God of Israel. But the full proclamation of good news for the nations would have to wait until the "fullness of time" (Gal. 4:4), when God would send forth his Son and when his reconciling grace would be proclaimed through the gospel message of the New Testament.

The Davidic Covenant

The other covenant that arises during the preexilic period of Israel involves a set of promises that God gives to David in 2 Samuel 7. Though the word *covenant* occurs nowhere in the account, it is referred to numerous places elsewhere in the Old Testament (2 Chron. 13:5; 21:7; Ps. 89:3; Jer. 33:21). The Davidic covenant is of the unilateral grant type similar to the covenant God made with Abraham.[27] The essential portion reads as follows:

> And I will make for you a great name, like the name of the great ones of the earth. And I will appoint a place for my people Israel and will plant them, so that they may dwell in their own place and be disturbed no more. And violent men shall afflict them no more, as formerly, from the time that I appointed judges over my people Israel. And I will give you rest from all your enemies. Moreover, the LORD declares to you that the LORD will make you a house. When your days are fulfilled

and you lie down with your fathers, I will raise up your offspring after you, who shall come from your body, and I will establish his kingdom. He shall build a house for my name, and I will establish the throne of his kingdom forever. I will be to him a father, and he shall be to me a son. When he commits iniquity, I will discipline him with the rod of men, with the stripes of the sons of men, but my steadfast love will not depart from him, as I took it from Saul, whom I put away from before you. And your house and your kingdom shall be made sure forever before me. Your throne shall be established forever. (2 Sam. 7:9b–16)

As Table 2.1 illustrates, there are a number of distinct parallels between what is promised in the Abrahamic and Davidic covenants. Like Abraham, David is also promised a great name and physical offspring. What is promised to David's offspring, who is referred to with the singular pronoun—is not land, but an eternal kingdom, the opportunity to build "a house for my name," and the endowment of God's faithful love. The promises are partially realized in Solomon, who builds the temple and represents the continuance of the Davidic dynasty. But they are not fully realized in Solomon with the capitulation of the house of Judah to the Babylonians in 586–587 BC.

Table 2.1: Key Points of Similarity between the Abrahamic and Davidic Covenants

Abrahamic Covenant (Genesis 12–22)	Davidic Covenant (2 Samuel 7)
I will . . . make your **name great,** so that you will be a blessing (12:2). In you all the families of the earth shall be blessed (12:3).	I will make for you a **great name,** like the name of the great ones of the earth (v. 9).
I will make of you a great **nation** (12:2). You will be father of a multitude of **nations** (17:4).	The LORD will make you a **house** (v. 11). Your **house** . . . shall be made sure forever before me (v. 16).
I will make your **offspring** as the dust of the earth (13:16). . . . The stars (15:5). . . . The sand on the sea-shore (22:17).	I will raise up your **offspring** after you, who shall come from your body (v. 12).
For all the **land** you see I will give to you and your off-spring forever (13:15). I will give to you and to your offspring after you the **land** of your sojournings, all the **land** of Canaan, for an ever-lasting possession (17:8).	I will establish his **kingdom** (v. 12) I will establish the throne of his **kingdom** forever (v. 13). Your throne **[kingdom]** shall be established forever (v. 16).

Thus, once again we detect messianic expectation in the promise of

David's coming offspring. The offspring will be given an eternal kingdom. God himself "will be to him a father" and he shall be to God "a son," and God's love will not depart from him. Though Solomon sinned and committed iniquity and was disciplined by God (1 Kings 11), it is the suffering servant rather than Solomon who bears the "stripes" or "afflictions" of men mentioned in Isaiah 53:5.

Though clear parallels emerge between the promises that God gives in the Davidic covenant and those he gives in the Abrahamic covenant, there is a visible narrowing in the scope of those promises. Abraham is to be father of many nations, while God promises David a *house* within a single nation—a particular eternal dynasty. God promises Abraham a vast *multitude of offspring*, whereas the promise to David speaks of a *particular offspring* that God will "raise up." To Abraham and his multitudinous offspring God promises the broad expanse of the *land* of Canaan, whereas to David's particular offspring God promises a future eternal *kingdom*. Where Abraham's many offspring each inherit a *portion of the land*, David's single offspring is to inherit the *whole kingdom*.

As in the case of the promise given to Abraham, all the promises given to David also depend on the promise of physical offspring. But the attention in the Davidic covenant narrows from the promise of generic offspring and descendants to focus upon the promise of a very specific individual and his particular kingdom. Whereas in the Abrahamic covenant the promises related to offspring are wide and diffuse, in the Davidic covenant they are narrowed and focused with increasing messianic overtones. A new and dramatic work of God is in the wind.

Wrapping Up

What we have attempted to demonstrate in this chapter is the fundamental role marriage and procreation played in Israelite society under the Sinai covenant. Core to the covenant blessings was fruitfulness of one's womb, livestock, and land. The distinguishing mark of God's blessing upon the nation in comparison to the surrounding peoples was encapsulated in the statement: "There shall not be male or female barren among you or among your livestock" (Deut. 7:14). Whereas the patriarchs were given an unconditional promise of offspring, the Israelites under Sinai were conditionally promised fruitfulness of the womb and the land. Marriage, children, and material prosperity in the land were markers of covenantal obedience. Thus, for an individual in Israel to be devoid of spouse, children, and land, such as Naomi on her return to Israel, was to feel the weight of divine judgment (Ruth 1:20–21).

Beyond being fundamental markers of God's covenantal blessing, marriage and offspring were vital in Israelite society in two other respects. First, marriage and offspring were necessary for retaining one's inheritance of allocated land within the family. Second, offspring and the land were necessary for preserving one's name after death. To have no offspring resulted in losing one's land and consequently having one's name blotted from remembrance within the clan and the nation—a fate worse than physical death itself.

Consequently, we have no known examples of those within Israel who voluntarily chose to remain single. To have done so would have been to voluntarily embrace God's judgment. One visibly single person in the Old Testament was Jeremiah, who was commanded by God to remain single as a direct portent of God's judgment upon the nation, that they will lose their offspring born in the land (Jer. 16:1–4). In short, marriage was the universal practice in ancient Israel because to be married and have offspring was evidence of God's blessing *and* by implication evidence of faithfulness to the covenant.

Finally, a few thoughts are appropriate regarding the place of the Sinai covenant within the larger framework of the developing biblical storyline of God's redemptive work of reconciling a people to himself. The nature of God's relationship with the people in the Sinai covenant was largely on temporal-physical terms. Marriage and procreation were the primary means by which God was building his covenant nation Israel. If the nation obeyed the terms of the covenant, God would bless them with physical offspring, an allocated inheritance of land, and material prosperity in the land. But because Israel largely failed to live according to stipulations of the covenant, the corresponding material blessings of the covenant were to be lost, as Jeremiah prophesied through his message and corresponding singleness.

The thread of hope of God's ongoing redemptive work in human history thus would pass ultimately from the Abrahamic covenant, not through the failed Sinai covenant but through the unilateral Davidic covenant in which the hope of humankind was to be found in the promise of a future royal offspring and his accompanying kingdom. It is the prophets who speak more of the unilateral hope of God's ongoing redemptive plan.

3

Prophetic Paradox

How Failure of a Nation Brings Blessing to the World

Among my favorite optical illusions is a famous sketch of an old woman with a headscarf (see Figure 3.1), which simultaneously depicts a younger woman looking to the rear of the picture. What is most enjoyable about the picture is that it presents us with two different pictures of two different women. Though both pictures exist simultaneously, the one

we begin to see first is governed by the way our brain assembles all the data present on the page.

Reading the Old Testament prophets can be a bit like a picture of this sort. Though we may at first understand the text to convey one picture, a second look reveals that the prophet is conveying a second and greater picture.

We find this in Isaiah. The fundamental paradox of Isaiah's message is that amidst a message of utter condemnation of Israel for its failure to

Figure 3.1: Illustration of a Woman live according to the covenant, we find God's ultimate message of hope for humankind. What is especially surprising about Isaiah's thread of hope is that it comes not through the reformation of the nation but despite its recalcitrance; it comes not through the merits of human endeavor but exclusively through the provision of God himself. The story of Isaiah is simultaneously a story of two types of offspring—the physical offspring of the Israelite nation and a new off-spring that emerges from the power and provision of God.

The story begins where we left off—with the physical offspring of Abraham in the nation of Israel. From there we shall examine a few of the major themes within Isaiah's message, a message that moves from the outright condemnation of Abraham's physical seed, to Isaiah's mission and the prophecy of a coming new offspring, to his depiction of the suf-fering servant and results of the servant's sacrificial death, to a portrait of the culmination of his spiritual seed in a picture of the new creation. We will look briefly at the new covenant of Jeremiah and the portrait of Daniel as an exemplar of the Old Testament prophet who lived singly and faithfully before his Lord. We will conclude with how these themes contribute to the larger picture of a coherent biblical theological under-standing of singleness.

The "Offspring of Evildoers"

Judgment on the Nation

The heart of the message of the preexilic prophets to both Israel and Judah is a message of God's judgment upon both kingdoms for their failure to adhere to the stipulations of the Sinai covenant. As a result of their disobedience, the people were liable to the curses of the covenant, and God would hold them to account. Not surprisingly the prophets also appeal to themes related to marriage and offspring in their condemna-tion, both literally and metaphorically. Hosea, a prophet of the eighth century, was commanded by God to marry an adulterous wife as an object sign of Israel's adultery in forsaking the Lord (Hos. 1:2). Amos condemns the priest of Bethel (of the cult of Jeroboam) to death "in an unclean land" with his children falling by the sword, a fate equivalent to his name being "blotted out" (Amos 7:17). Upon the whole of the nation Amos proph-esies a famine that will result in the "lovely virgins and the young men" fainting from thirst rather than marrying (Amos 8:13).

Isaiah is among the most graphic of the early prophets in using offspring language and imagery in his condemnation of the southern kingdom of Judah. The book opens with the Lord speaking of the people as "children I have reared and brought up" (Isa. 1:2). Though they are his children, they have rebelled against him and are thus "offspring of evildoers, children who deal corruptly" (Isa. 1:4). Later, in 57:3–4, he again refers to them as "offspring of the adulterer and the loose woman" and "children of transgression, the offspring of deceit."[1]

In chapter 48 God again speaks through the prophet: "For my name's sake I defer my anger, for the sake of my praise I restrain it for you, that I may not cut you off" (v. 9). In the same chapter the Lord laments:

> Oh that you had paid attention to my commandments! Then your peace would have been like a river, and your righteousness like the waves of the sea; your offspring would have been like the sand, and your descendants like its grains; their name would never be cut off or destroyed from before me. (vv. 18–19)

In this section he links their corruption, adultery, and deceit to their failure to obey the commandments of the law. Had the people not ignored the stipulations of the covenant, their offspring would have continued to flourish and their name would not have been subject to being cut off. Only for the sake of God's name was God's anger restrained, such that the entire *house of Jacob* was not cut off (Isa. 48:1–11).

In 3:25–4:1 Isaiah offers a glimpse of the reproach of barrenness from a female perspective. After the men fall by the sword and die in battle (3:25), the women left in the land face the prospect of not having enough men for them to marry and have children:

> And seven women shall take hold of one man in that day, saying, "We will eat our own bread and wear our own clothes, only let us be called by your name; take away our reproach." (Isa. 4:1)

For a woman in ancient Israel not to marry was not only to be denied the covenant blessings but also to be a reproach. As the antithesis of honor (Prov. 14:31), reproach was associated with shame, scorn, and disgrace (Ps. 71:13). The picture presents the ripple effect of war. After the young men die in battle and have their names cut off, the remaining women are likewise devoid of mates and the opportunity to bear offspring and ultimately also have their names cut off.

Judgment on the Royal Line

While Isaiah explicitly condemns the people as a whole for violating the terms of the covenant and puts forth the potential consequences of losing their offspring and having their names and family lines cut off, the prophets also levy similar pronouncements of judgment upon the Davidic royal line of kings who successively reigned over the southern kingdom. Whereas the northern kingdom had cycled through a series of distinct dynasties,[2] the southern kingdom maintained the single Davidic dynasty in fulfillment of God's promise to David (2 Sam. 7:16). Nevertheless, the royal line of Judah was eventually also blotted out because of the egregious sin of Manasseh (2 Kings 21:9).

This blotting out of the dynastic line of Judah occurs over a series of prophecies and incidents. The first inkling of this occurs when Hezekiah receives envoys from the king of Babylon, and Isaiah prophesies to Hezekiah on that occasion:

> Behold, the days are coming, when all that is in your house . . . shall be carried to Babylon. . . . And some of your own sons, who shall be born to you . . . shall be eunuchs in the palace of the king of Babylon." (2 Kings 20:17–18)

The implications of this prophecy were ominous. The offspring of the king, among whom should have been the very ones to continue Hezekiah's dynasty, would be instead eunuchs, men *without* any hope for offspring or dynasty of their own, serving in the court of a foreign king.

It is with the sin of Manasseh, Hezekiah's son, that the judgment upon the Davidic dynasty becomes absolute. Because Manasseh's sin exceeded even that of the Amorites who were blotted out in the Israelite conquest of Canaan, and because his sin had likewise led Israel into sin, God was going to stretch over Jerusalem the "plumb line of the house of Ahab" and "wipe Jerusalem as one wipes a dish" (2 Kings 21:11–13). The Hebrew word for *wipe* in this pronouncement is *makhah*, the same word that means "to blot out." The parallel with the house of Ahab made the judgment incontrovertible; because of the sin of Manasseh, God was going to blot out the royal house of Judah, just as he had done to the house of Ahab. Even the subsequent exemplary reforms of Josiah do not reverse God's judgment upon the house of Judah and the impending disaster to come upon the nation in the form of "all the curses that are written in the book" (2 Chron. 34:24).

The actual pronouncement of judgment falls upon Josiah's sons Jehoiakim and Zedekiah. Jeremiah first condemns Jehoiakim:

> He shall have none to sit on the throne of David, and his dead body shall be cast out to the heat by day and the frost by night. And I will punish him and his offspring and his servants for their iniquity. (Jer. 36:30b–31a)

Similarly he condemns Jehoiakim's son Coniah (Jehoiachin),[3] with a pronouncement of childlessness:

> Thus says the LORD: "Write this man down as childless, a man who shall not succeed in his days, for none of his offspring shall succeed in sitting on the throne of David and ruling again in Judah." (Jer. 22:30)

Jehoiachin is cut off from the royal line of Judah, as there is no future kingship for either him or his offspring, for he, in regard to the dynasty, shall be regarded as childless. God's judgment is not complete annihilation of Jehoiachin's physical line but only of the Judean dynasty of kings, as confirmed by Jehoiachin's favorable treatment in Babylon (2 Kings 25:27–30) and the genealogies that list his descendants (e.g., 1 Chron. 3:17; Matt. 1:11).

The fate of Zedekiah's line was less fortunate. Nebuchadnezzar replaces Jehoiachin as king of Judah with his uncle Zedekiah (2 Kings 24:17). But Zedekiah rebels, and consequently Nebuchadnezzar returns and captures the city, slaughters the sons of Zedekiah before his eyes, and takes him prisoner to Babylon (25:7–11). Zedekiah's house and name were completely blotted out.

The Prophetic Tension

The preexilic prophets condemn both kingdoms of Israel for their failure to abide by the stipulations of the Sinaitic covenant. The covenants God gave to Abraham and David were unconditional, but the Sinai covenant was conditioned on the people's obedience. However, though both the people and their rulers failed, the hope embodied in God's eternal covenant promises remained. On account of their disobedience, the Israelites were subject to the loss of their land, their offspring, and, for some, their name. Yet God would bless the nations through the offspring of Abraham. Likewise, on account of moral failure, the royal house of Judah was to cease with Jehoiakim and Zedekiah. But God would raise up David's offspring and establish the throne of his kingdom forever. Thus, the prophets' message at its core is a message of both condemnation and hope: though the people had failed, the work of God had not. It is this paradoxical element that emerges in a dramatic fashion in God's calling of Isaiah.

The Hope of a New Offspring

Isaiah's Prophetic Call: Isaiah 6

The call of Isaiah to his prophetic mission, recorded in Isaiah 6, is as surprising as it is dramatic. The chapter opens with Isaiah's encounter with the Lord in his holiness sitting upon his throne in heaven surrounded by the seraphim. Immediately aware of his own sin, Isaiah cries, "Woe is me! . . . For my eyes have seen the King, the LORD of hosts!" (v. 5). One of the seraphim then touches Isaiah's lips with a burning coal to symbolize the atonement of his sin and the removal of his guilt. The dramatic encounter prepares the prophet for his commissioning. He had to be completely cleansed of his impurities in order to be fully prepared for a most perplexing assignment.

Isaiah's call is surprising in its appearance of utter futility. He is commissioned:

> Make the heart of this people dull, and their ears heavy, and blind their eyes; lest they see with their eyes, and hear with their ears, and understand with their hearts, and turn and be healed. (Isa. 6:10)

The Hebrew of this text says that the effect of Isaiah's preaching will be to "make fat" the heart, to "make heavy" the ears, and to "shut" the eyes of the people.[4] Through a relentless call to repentance, Isaiah's mission was to harden the people from the very repentance that was the essence of his message.[5]

Isaiah's reaction in 6:11 is evidence of the difficulty he had with such a personally unrewarding sort of assignment.[6] "How long, O Lord?" he asks, with the inference, "How long, O Lord, *must I carry on in such a fruitless endeavor?*" God's response is startling once again in its severity. Isaiah must carry on his mission until "cities lie waste without inhabitant" (6:11b); "houses [are] without people" (6:11c); "the land is a desolate waste" (6:11d); "the LORD removes people far away" (6:12a); and "the forsaken places are many in the midst of the land" (6:12b).

Isaiah's stark assignment will be complete when the land is stripped of its people and, conversely, the people are stripped of their land. The two fundamental blessings of the Sinai covenant—the fruitfulness of the womb in abundant offspring and the fruitfulness of the land via a prosperous inheritance—are to be fully rescinded.

The final verse of the chapter contains the lone ray of hope in the whole depiction of Isaiah's tragic mission:

> "And though a tenth remain in it, it will be burned again, like a terebinth or an oak, whose stump remains when it is felled." The holy seed is its stump. (Isa. 6:13)

Though a tenth remain, it too will be burned, that is, completely destroyed as trees that were cut down, leaving only a stump. The holy seed is the stump. The Hebrew word translated here as "seed" is *zera'*, the same word for "offspring" that is central to the promises and blessings of the covenants. The verse is especially difficult textually and exegetically; nevertheless, as the capstone of God's commission to Isaiah, it is a theological linchpin for understanding the thrust of Isaiah's entire prophecy.[7]

Isaiah 6:13 begins with a statement reinforcing the degree of destruction described in the previous verses. Even if some should appear to be spared God's judgment, they *too* will be judged—they will be as trees cut down, leaving only a "stump." The conclusion reads as an interpretive note: the stump that remains *is* the holy seed. The final sentence appears to offer a ray of hope and raises two questions: (1) Who is designated by the term *holy seed*? and (2) What is the stump?

Three major views have been proposed for what is meant by the term *stump* (*matstseveth*) in Isaiah 6:13. The dominant view takes *matstseveth* as the stump of a tree, which is likely just a contextual guess without additional semantic support.[8] Others have argued for *cultic pillar*, resulting in an interpretation of the clause as condemnatory of the holy seed rather than as offering hope.[9] But Isaiah never describes the people in their disobedient state with the divinely associated term *holy*. A third view sees *matstseveth* as referring to "new planting," based on the Aramaic and Syriac translations.[10] This translation is not far from the idea of "root stock"—the part of the dead tree that enables new life—and this idea is popular among some interpreters.[11] That view makes sense when we consider that the stump of a tree contains its potential for new growth. Thinking of *matstseveth* as "potential for new growth" means that the holy seed is its stump, its potential for new growth.

If the holy seed is designated as the potential for new growth in a dead tree, who or what is the holy seed? Of the seventy occurrences of the word *holy* (*qodhesh*), in the book of Isaiah, it is most commonly seen in the phrase "the Holy One of Israel," which occurs twenty-five times. Shorter or indirect references to Yahweh as "holy" account for an additional eleven occurrences. Only three times is it used as an adjective for Israel, and when it is, either the eschatological redeemed Israel or an idyllic prototypical Israel appears to be in view; never is it used to describe the sinful nation.[12]

Even before chapter 6 we can observe a distinction in Isaiah between the "offspring of evildoers" who "have despised the Holy One of Israel" (1:4), and a picture of the future survivors of Israel who will "be called holy" (4:3), having had their filth washed away by a spirit of judgment and burning. Isaiah himself encounters the thrice-holy God in 6:1–7 and must have his sin atoned for through his lips' being seared by a burning coal. Thus, the term "holy seed" in 6:13 likely signifies someone intensely associated with Yahweh himself, the Holy One of Israel. Furthermore, other uses of the term *holy* throughout the book of Isaiah suggest that the "holy seed" of 6:13b is a *qualitatively* different type of "seed" from the people "laden with iniquity, offspring of evildoers" of 1:4, who were hardened to Isaiah's message in 6:9–10 and merit the destruction of 6:11–13a.

The qualitative distinction to be drawn between the holy seed and a physical remnant of the nation is also underscored by the juxtaposition of "a tenth" in 13a with "the holy seed" in 13b. Though a tenth still remains, it too will be subject to burning. Gerhard Hasel has observed that while it is obvious that the remnant motif is evident in the expression of the remaining tenth, here it contains no positive aspect.[13] Isaiah appears to be correcting a misconception regarding the nature of the remnant. It is not to be regarded as a certain portion of the existing populous that was mercifully spared the divine judgment. Rather, the point to be realized in 13a is that *these too* will be subject to destruction. Brevard Childs writes:

> Indeed, Isaiah does not speak here of a remnant of a pious group who escaped judgment. All of Israel must perish: "houses without people." The radical quality of this imagery resonates with the intensity of 587. There is no continuity from the old to the new.[14]

Instead, the hope is to be exclusively found in 13b, that out of the *complete* judgment of the existing nation something new will arise, something qualitatively different from what had existed before. This is the *holy seed.*

The potential ambiguity of the singular "seed" again raises the question of whether the referent is to be understood as singular and messianic (as in the case of Gen. 3:15; 4:25; and most likely 2 Sam. 7:12) or if a holy race of people is in view. In favor of the former possibility is the observation that, given the opening reference to the death of King Uzziah in 6:1, it would offer tidy symmetry to conclude the passage with a reference to the emergence of a *new* king.

John's Gospel also appears to reinforce the messianic link. In explaining why the Jews were unbelieving of Jesus' message, John cites Isaiah 6:9–10 and adds, "Isaiah said these things because he saw his glory and spoke of *him*" (John 12:39–41). On the other hand, if the condemnation expressed in Isaiah's message is of a corporate nature, there remains an implicit expectation that the hope expressed is also corporate in nature. If God commissions Isaiah to preach to effect the destruction of one people, it is only because this is essential in order to bring about the emergence of a new people. But given the possibility that the singular messianic "seed" also serves as the progenitor of a new race of plural "seed," ultimately the distinction itself becomes moot; both are simultaneously in view.[15]

Portraits of the Anticipated Offspring

It is likely no coincidence that, immediately after Isaiah is given his commission to preach to the people in order to harden them for destruction and thereby prepare the ground for an anticipated "holy seed," in the subsequent five chapters Isaiah provides a series of portraits of a *child* as the emblem of his hope.[16] Each portrait serves to reinforce the picture that the hope of the emerging holy seed will take the form of a coming child.

The Virgin Shall Conceive: Isaiah 7

The first portrait follows immediately on the heels of the promised holy seed of Isaiah 6:13. In chapter 7 Isaiah gives the account of King Ahaz, who is under the threat of war from the combined alliance of the kings of Syria and Israel. God sends Isaiah *with his son* Shear-jashub, meaning "A remnant shall return," with a message of hope for the king. Together they inform Ahaz that he does not need to fear the threat of these "two smoldering stumps of firebrands" (v. 4), and they invite Ahaz to ask the Lord for a sign as verification (v. 11). Ahaz's unwillingness to ask for a sign (v. 12) epitomizes the complete dull-heartedness of the people—he is unable to respond even to a message of deliverance. The king's complete lack of faith results in God's providing the sign in 7:14—"The virgin shall conceive and bear a son, and shall call his name Immanuel" (meaning "God with us").

Ahaz's contempt in the face of God's deliverance effectively nullifies for him any positive benefits of the deliverance, for the cure, in the form of the king of Assyria, will prove for Ahaz worse than the dangers associated with the previous kings that threatened him. Thus while Ahaz, through his flagrant disbelief, exemplifies the national response that results in God's judgment, God simultaneously remains faithful to his promises to Abraham and David in his provision of the divine-human messiah, Immanuel.

The portrait of Immanuel presented by Isaiah is a child, yet he is no ordinary child. His name, "God is with us," implies that he himself represents the very presence of God among the people. As a helpless child, Immanuel represents deliverance to the nation, for before he "knows how to refuse the evil and choose the good," the two threatening aggressor nations will be deserted (v. 16). After the initial announcement of his birth in 7:14, Immanuel is mentioned two more times, in 8:8 and 8:10.

In Isaiah 8:8 Isaiah prophesies the sweeping down of Assyria upon the nation of Judah. It will overflow the nation, "reaching even to the neck, and its outspread wings will fill the breadth of your land, O Immanuel." Though occasionally the land of Israel was linked as a political unit to the king (e.g., to David in 2 Sam. 24:13), usually the land of the whole nation is associated with the Lord himself (e.g., Lev. 25:23; 1 Kings 8:36; Ezek. 36:5). Immanuel is the owner of the whole land, against whom Assyria's threats are ultimately lodged. This Immanuel cannot be an ordinary son of Isaiah or Ahaz; it can only be the Messiah in whom all hope resides.[17]

Not only is Immanuel the ultimate possessor of all the land, but Isaiah makes clear in a pun that Immanuel is the sole ultimate source of hope. He says to any and all the aggressor nations, "Take counsel together, but it will come to nothing; speak a word, but it will not stand, for God is with us" (i.e., "Immanuel") (8:10). Immanuel is simultaneously the promised child deliverer, the presence of God himself, the owner of all the land, and the only ultimate refuge against the onslaught of the nations.

The Hope of Isaiah's Offspring: Isaiah 8

A second portrait of children that Isaiah presents in chapters 6 through 12 is the "sign" represented by his own children. The Lord sends Isaiah initially to Ahaz with his son Shear-jashub, which means "A remnant shall return," offering a promise of deliverance. Then Isaiah is instructed to have another son and call his name Maher-shalal-hashbaz, meaning "the spoil speeds, the prey hastens" (8:1–4). While the first child is a portent of hope, the second seems to represent both hope and judgment, as his name signifies the inevitable arrival of the king of Assyria who not only will destroy Judah's enemies but will also sweep quickly into Immanuel's land, to plunder the land of its spoils.

In 8:18 Isaiah refers to both himself and his children as "signs" and "portents" from the Lord:

> Behold, I and the children whom the LORD has given me are signs and portents in Israel from the LORD of hosts, who dwells on Mount Zion.

The language of signs and wonders (or portents) recalls the dramatic signs that God gave in Egypt to show his power over the Egyptians and their gods (Ex. 7:3; Deut. 6:22; Jer. 32:20). But Deuteronomy 28:46 describes the fulfillment of the covenant curses as signs and wonders against the Israelites and their offspring, as reminders of their disobedience. Jeremiah's calling by God not to marry and have children (Jer. 16:1–4) was a prophetic demonstration to the Israelites of the fulfillment of such signs and wonders of God's judgment of complete barrenness upon the people for their disobedience. Conversely, Isaiah here is told to *have* children, and this too is a sign and wonder, but one of hope, both for Ahaz in the near term and for the coming ultimate deliverance of God in the anticipated holy seed.

Unto You a Child Is Born: Isaiah 9

Isaiah's third portrait of hope is the familiar "for to us a child is born" prophecy found in Isaiah 9:6. The setting for this third image is linked to the preceding context through the initial reference to "gloom" and "anguish" (9:1) that echo 8:22. Isaiah with his two children are simultaneous portents of both judgment and hope. But the people, following the course of Ahaz, look not to the hope of the Lord but inquire instead of their mediums and necromancers (9:19). And because they look to the earth and to the dead for their guidance, they have no dawn and will be thrust into the darkness—a darkness inevitably brought on by the blindness of their hardened hearts in response to Isaiah's ministry (6:10).

It is amidst the darkness of the blinded people that Isaiah's third portrait of hope appears. This emblematic child comes not to Jerusalem but to Zebulun and Naphtali, areas that were among the first to fall to Assyria and become Assyrian provinces. He comes to Galilee of the Gentiles.

Whereas in chapter 8 Isaiah's children were signs and portents of what was to come, in Ahaz's time attention shifts from the gloom and anguish of the "former" time to the "latter time" (9:1). This third image depicts a future child separate and distinct from anything of Isaiah's own day.

The dominant depiction of the child is one with royal authority to govern. He has the government "upon his shoulder" (9:6) of which "there will be no end" (v. 7) and is the "Prince of Peace" (v. 6). But this child is not just any ruler; rather, he is the heir to the "throne of David" who will uphold it "forevermore" (v. 7). His identity with the throne of David not only makes him the fulfillment of God's promise in the Davidic covenant to establish David's throne forever (2 Sam. 7:16) but necessarily also means he is the *offspring* of Abraham and the ultimate fulfillment of the prophecy God gives to Abraham that kings shall arise from him (Gen. 17:6).

Though he is heir to the dynasty of David, there is no suggestion that his kingdom is confined to the geopolitical structure of the former nation of Israel, for this king arises to reign from Galilee of the Gentiles. This government will be a continuation of the throne of David, the permanent reign of Abraham's seed, eternally established in justice and righteousness, over not just the remnant of Israel but over all the nations.

As in the case of Isaiah's depiction of the Immanuel child, this child also possesses divine identity. All four titles given to the child in 9:6 underscore the deity of the coming child.[18] In contrast to the folly of human wisdom characteristic of those spiritually dead, the coming child will be called "Wonderful Counselor" (literally "Wonder-Counselor"), one who embodies *supernaturally wondrous* counsel. The term *wonder* in the Old Testament most frequently refers to a mighty and glorious deed of God (Ex. 15:11; Pss. 77:11, 14; 78:12; 89:5; Isa. 25:1; 29:14).[19] "Mighty God" is the most direct divine appellation—wherever the term appears elsewhere in the Old Testament, it undeniably refers to God (Deut. 10:17; Isa. 10:21; Jer. 32:18).[20] While kings often claimed the title of "Father" of the country (e.g., Caesar Augustus assumed the title *pater patriae*, "Father of the Fatherland") only God assumes the designation "everlasting" (Gen. 21:33; Isa. 40:28) and can assume the appellation "Everlasting Father" of the nation. Similarly, it is God alone and his representative who usher in true and lasting peace (e.g., Isa. 52:7; 53:5; 54:10; 66:12) worthy of the designation "Prince of Peace."

The Shoot and Root of Jesse: Isaiah 11

It is perhaps quite fitting that Isaiah's concluding portrait of new life in 11:1–9 returns to imagery reminiscent of that in 6:13. While the image of new life arising from the trunk of a tree reminds us of the seed offspring that emerges from the burned stump of the desolated nation (6:13), the word *stump* in 11:1 denotes more simply the source of the shoot devoid of any associations of judgment:

> There shall come forth a shoot [*khomer*] from the stump [*geza'*] of Jesse, and a branch [*netser*] from his roots [*shoresh*] shall bear fruit.

The parallelism in imagery but not vocabulary between "shoot" and "stump" in the first clause of the verse and the "branch" and "root" in the second clause suggests that the image of new life emerging from the stock of the old is more important here than particular vocabulary—vocabulary also different from the seed-offspring emerging from the burned stump of 6:13. Whereas Isaiah's point in 6:13 is to disassociate the holy seed-offspring from the sinful people, the point of the image in 11:1 is to reinforce the messianic identity of the seed-offspring as the physical offspring promised to David in 2 Samuel 7:12–13 who will establish his kingdom eternally.

Isaiah gives a surprising twist to the image of the messianic shoot *from* Jesse later:

> In that day the root of Jesse, who shall stand as a signal for the peoples—of him shall the nations inquire, and his resting place shall be glorious. (Isa. 11:10)

Here the messianic figure is described as the "root" (shoresh) of Jesse, one of the words used in 11:1 to depict the source from which he as a "branch" emerges. While this may appear to be just a result of Isaiah's fluid use of vocabulary, it seems to point out aspects of the messianic figure worth differentiating. On the one hand, the coming messianic seed-offspring is the physical offspring of Jesse and serves to fulfill the prophecy given to David that God will raise up an offspring from his own body (2 Sam. 7:12). As offspring of David, it is also ultimately the physical offspring of the everlasting covenant promised to Abraham in

Genesis 17:19 through whom the nations shall be blessed (Gen. 22:18) and hinted at also to Eve in Genesis 3:15 and 4:25.

But the use of "Jesse" rather than "David" may also suggest that this king is not just another king within David's line but that he himself is a new David, another *son of Jesse* to whom all others are to be compared. All other kings were compared to David, the son of Jesse (e.g., 1 Kings 14:8), but no other king is ever also referred to *as* a son of Jesse.[21] Furthermore, he is not merely the *shoot* from Jesse, one amidst many within God's existing people, but he is the *root* of the eternal world-encompassing nation of God's own people, the source out of which the true eschatological people of God ultimately emerge.

Isaiah's dual image looks both back and forward. The messiah is both the uniquely born fulfillment of the promised offspring to Abraham and David—the *shoot* of Jesse—but also he is the seed of something genuinely new, the *root* of Jesse, the new King David who will establish a people unto his own qualitatively different from what was earlier. Glimpses of the qualitative differences in his rule and kingdom are evident in the description that Isaiah gives in 11:1–10. The "Spirit of the LORD shall rest upon him" guiding him in wisdom, counsel, and knowledge (v. 2). His rule will be characterized by complete righteousness (vv. 3–5). His kingdom will be characterized by the eschatological peace in which the wolf dwells with the lamb and the lion eats straw like the ox (vv. 6–8). The earth will be full of the knowledge of the Lord (v. 9), and all the Gentile nations will inquire of him and his glorious resting place (v. 10).

Conclusions

Like a seasoned artist, Isaiah weaves together a tapestry of images to make his point. Isaiah's prophetic message is one of simultaneous condemnation and of hope. It is a message of condemnation for one kind of seed, the offspring of evildoers, but it is also a message of hope of a coming future messianic holy seed. This coming messianic seed will come in the form of a child, a shoot of the physical line of Jesse and of Abraham but who is also divine as "Immanuel" and "God Almighty." He will rule and have a kingdom, but both his rule and his people will be qualitatively different from the returning exilic remnant of Israel. He is the root of a new kind of holy offspring, a people marked by righteousness who are to usher in God's eschatological kingdom.[22]

The Servant and His Offspring

Who Is the Servant of Isaiah?

The theme of "the servant" is a recurring motif in latter portions of Isaiah (chaps. 40–66). In a number of different passages, Isaiah refers to the Israelite nation as a servant (41:8, 9; 42:19; 44:1, 2, 21; 45:4). Amidst these passages, he also interweaves a series of four portraits of an individual servant, portraits which are known collectively as Isaiah's Servant Songs (42:1–9; 49:1–7; 50:4–9; 52:13–53:12). After the series of Servant Songs, the term *servant* appears eleven additional times in Isaiah 54–66,[23] but only in the plural, whereas the singular uniformly appears in twenty instances in chapters 40–53.[24]

Despite the differences, Isaiah's three classes of servants may be linked together. The sinful shortcomings of the Israelite nation as God's chosen servant (who in 42:19–20 is blind and deaf, in the pattern of 6:9–10), is ultimately vindicated in the faithfulness of the single suffering servant of Yahweh, who, as part of Isaiah's eschatological vision in chapters 54 through 66, produces other "servants" in his pattern.

This pattern of Isaiah's successive servants may find some parallel with varying types of offspring that Isaiah describes throughout his book. Whereas in his opening chapter the prophet describes the nation as "offspring of evildoers" (1:4), the climax of his vision is the announcement of an anticipated coming "holy seed" (6:13), a term that, as we suggested already, seems to embody notions of both a single holy individual and the nucleus of a forthcoming holy race. In the fourth servant song in the aftermath of the servant's suffering, we find such a holy race of offspring reemerging.

The Servant Songs and the Suffering Servant of Isaiah 52:13–53:12

As we have observed, the beginning of the book of Isaiah offers a series of portraits of hope in the form of a young child and new growth, and the latter portion of the book offers a series of portraits of a mature man—the faithful servant of the Lord—the servant who ultimately suffers and dies on behalf of the people. The presumption that both series of portraits represent the same individual cannot be taken for granted, but there is at least one reference that strongly suggests that the child portrayed early in the book is the same individual as the suffering servant of Isaiah 53. This reference is found in 53:2, where the upbringing of the servant is described:

> For he grew up before him like a young plant, and like a root out of dry ground; he had no form or majesty that we should look at him, and no beauty that we should desire him.

While here again Isaiah varies the vocabulary slightly, the recurrent imagery is an undeniable reference to the shoot/root imagery of 11:1–10.[25] The word for "young plant" is a synonym for "shoot," which is used in 11:1, while "root" is the same word as appears in 11:10. In this context both shoot and root emphasize new growth—the shoot or young plant grows upward toward the sun, while the root grows downward toward better water and nutrients in the soil. Nevertheless, the reappearance of the distinct shoot and root imagery in reference to the servant provides a point of continuity with the shoot and root child described in Isaiah 11.

The climax of the fourth servant song occurs in 53:10, and here we find a reference to the servant's seed/offspring:

> Yet it was the will of the LORD to crush him; he has put him to grief; when his soul makes an offering for guilt, he shall see his offspring; he shall prolong his days; the will of the LORD shall prosper in his hand.

It is within the midst of this verse that the mood of the song takes a decisive turn. Prior to this verse the mood is somber with language anticipatory of death and divine judgment. The servant was "smitten by God, and afflicted" (53:4), "crushed for our iniquities" (v. 5), "oppressed . . . afflicted . . . like a lamb that is led to the slaughter" (v. 7), "cut off out of the land of the living" (v. 8), to make "his grave with the wicked" (v. 9).

The climax appears in the clause "when his soul makes an offering for guilt," after which the tone turns decidedly restorative and hopeful.

It is from this point that the servant "shall see his offspring; he shall prolong his days" (v. 10); "he shall see and be satisfied," making "many to be accounted righteous" (v. 11), so that "he shall divide the spoil with the strong" (v. 12). The change in tone speaks of the benefits that follow the death of the servant. Though the Hebrew verb for *atone* is not used here, the context clearly has in view the positive effect of the servant's victorious self-sacrifice.[26]

When the servant's soul makes an offering for sin, the result will be that "he shall see his offspring" (v. 10). But what sort of offspring does the servant *see* through his death? As most scholars have concluded, the most plausible understanding of the text is that the servant's offspring are spiritual offspring rather than physical offspring.[27] One indication of this is that elsewhere in the Old Testament where blessing is associated with seeing one's offspring[28] (Gen. 50:23; Job 42:16; Ps. 128:6), it is grandchildren rather than direct children that are primarily in view. One is blessed through having children, but seeing grandchildren is a marker of a long and fruitful life. But the suffering servant is blessed with prolonged days in seeing only his offspring, not his grandchildren.

Another indication that the offspring the servant sees are his spiritual rather than physical children is the language used to describe the servant's suffering:

> By oppression and judgment he was taken away; and as for his generation, who considered that he was cut off out of the land of the living, stricken for the transgression of my people? (Isa. 53:8)

Here we read, regarding the servant, that "he was cut off out of the land of the living." The Hebrew verb used here for *cut off*, *gazar*, bears a meaning nearly identical to the somewhat more common term *karath*, which, as we have seen, often incorporates not only the notion of one's death but also the elimination of one's posterity or the potential for posterity. In 2 Kings 9:8 both Ahab and his posterity were to be "cut off," while in Jeremiah 11:19 Jeremiah's enemies plot to "cut him off from the land of the living" and thereby "destroy the tree with the fruit."

The choice of language in Isaiah 53:8 suggests that something similar is in view. The servant is to be "cut off" out of the land of the living. This conclusion becomes even more apparent given a proposal by John Oswalt, that the syntax and structure in this verse favor understanding "generation" as the direct object of the verb "consider" and should be understood as a direct reference to the hypothetical progeny of the servant. This would render the sense of 53:8 similar to the NIV translation: "And who can speak of his descendants? For he was cut off from the land of the living." Oswalt concludes that what is described in 53:10 after the servant's acceptable sacrifice is in direct antithesis to what is described in 53:8–9:

> What the Servant will experience is in direct contrast to what was said about him in vv. 8–9. These verses describe a completely futile life. The Servant dies without children and is not even permitted to be buried among honorable people. But here the very opposite is said about him.[29]

Whereas the servant dies as a cursed man without family or progeny, in his death he becomes exalted of God (Isa. 52:13) and blessed with an abundance of spiritual offspring who visibly emerge through the results of the obedience of his sacrificial death. It is the new vision of these offspring that Isaiah further develops in the ensuing chapters of his book in vocabulary of "offspring" and "servants" of *the Servant*.

The Song of the Barren Woman: Isaiah 54

A vivid picture of the suffering servant's spiritual offspring appears in the song of the barren woman, which immediately follows in chapter 54.[30] The song begins with the following depiction:

> "Sing, O barren one, who did not bear;
>   break forth into singing and cry aloud,
>   you who have not been in labor!
> For the children of the desolate one will be more
>   than the children of her who is married," says the LORD.
> "Enlarge the place of your tent,
>   and let the curtains of your habitations be stretched out;
> do not hold back; lengthen your cords
>   and strengthen your stakes.
> For you will spread abroad to the right and to the left,
>   and your offspring will possess the nations

and will people the desolate cities.
Fear not, for you will not be ashamed;
    be not confounded, for you will not be disgraced;
for you will forget the shame of your youth,
    and the reproach of your widowhood you will remember
        no more.
For your Maker is your husband,
    the LORD of hosts is his name;
and the Holy One of Israel is your Redeemer,
    the God of the whole earth he is called." (vv. 1–5)

Although some commentators see little direct connection between the fourth servant song and what follows in Isaiah 54–55, a thematic connection arises between the depiction of the "offspring" of the suffering servant, who dies childless (53:10), and the description of the multitude of "offspring" of the barren woman (54:3).[31] Indeed, just as the suffering servant was faced with the social stigma of dying childless and being "cut off" from his people, so too the barren woman faced the social reproach of being childless. Four separate designations are given for the public humiliation she faced for being unable to bear children. She faced the continual prospect of being "shamed" and "disgraced," having already endured the "shame" of youth, and the "reproach" of widowhood (54:4).

In chapter 54 we find a picture of a woman shamed in her youth on account of her barrenness but who now sings for joy. Her "song" symbolizes entering into a blessing provided by another's efforts.[32] As in the case of the servant, some sort of miraculous or nonphysical birth appears to be in view. The text is emphatic that these children are not her physical offspring; her physical incapacity is described with four different designations. She is: "barren"; one who "did not bear"; one who has "not been in labor"; and "the desolate one" (v. 1). She is without a human husband, as the Lord himself will be her husband (v. 5).

The only specific information provided about the woman to whom the barren one is compared is that she is married with sons, presumably having had children through conventional childbirth (v. 1). Further reinforcing the nonphysical nature of the barren woman's "offspring" is that they will "possess" the nations. The language here recalls God's covenantal land promise to Abraham (Gen. 15:7) and echoes victorious plunder given to the servant in the aftermath of his death in Isaiah 53:12.[33] The nonphysical nature of her offspring is underscored both in the implied extent of them (so many as to possess the nations) and in the international language (her offspring will incorporate all the races of the nations).

What emerges from the overall picture is that Isaiah 54:1–5 describes a reconstituted people in the aftermath of the servant's death. Alec Motyer offers the following helpful summary:

> So here, the *barren woman* sings, not because she has ceased to be barren but because the Lord has acted in his Servant with the effect that his 'seed' become her *children/*'sons.' . . . The contrast here is between one who has no chance of having children (being deprived of a husband's care and support . . .) and one naturally placed to be fruitful (who *has a husband*). Thus, the gathering family cannot be explained naturally as a fact (she is *barren*, she *never bore* a child, was *never in labour* and *is desolate*) and is more than can be explained naturally in extent (her children are *more than of her who has a husband*). The church, the Lord's people are created by supernatural birth.[34]

The offspring the servant sees as a result of his death (Isa. 53:10) now emerge in the form of a reconstituted people of God (54:1–5). They are no longer physically related to each other or ethnically defined as they possess the nations. Rather, they are the spiritual offspring of the servant and the true recipients of the promises of Abraham.

The Eunuch and the Foreigner

Only two chapters later we find another portrayal of restoration and hope. This time the portrait is that of the castigated male in the figure of the eunuch. Isaiah 56:3–7 presents an astounding picture of hope to two different classes of people excluded from the assembly of the Lord and cut off from the covenant blessings—the foreigner and the eunuch:

> Let not the foreigner who has joined himself to the LORD say,
>   "The LORD will surely separate me from his people";

and let not the eunuch say,
    "Behold, I am a dry tree."
For thus says the LORD:
"To the eunuchs who keep my Sabbaths,
    who choose the things that please me
    and hold fast my covenant,
I will give in my house and within my walls
    a monument and a name
    better than sons and daughters;
I will give them an everlasting name
    that shall not be cut off."
And the foreigners who join themselves to the LORD,
    to minister to him, to love the name of the LORD,
    and to be his servants,
everyone who keeps the Sabbath and does not profane it,
    and holds fast my covenant—
these I will bring to my holy mountain,
    and make them joyful in my house of prayer;
their burnt offerings and their sacrifices
    will be accepted on my altar;
for my house shall be called a house of prayer
    for all peoples."

As we discussed briefly in the previous chapter, the "foreigner" (*nekhar*) was separated from the covenant and its blessings by reason of birth. Foreigners were not offspring of Abraham and therefore not heirs of the promises given in the Abrahamic covenant. While the occasional "sojourner" (*ger*) or resident alien of foreign birth was assimilated into people of Israel, foreigners who lived outside the nation remained separated from the covenant. With the loss of territorial boundaries in the exile, the nation would face ever-increasing pressure to assimilate with its foreign neighbors through intermarriage. Thus, with the return and resettlement of the exiles we find both Ezra and Nehemiah emphasizing endogamous marriage. Ezra binds all the returning exiles with an oath to put away all their foreign wives and children (Ezra 10:1–5). Nehemiah reacts even more passionately, cursing those who had intermarried and beating them and pulling out their hair (Neh. 13:23–25).

Although commentators have often argued for a postexilic historical setting for Isaiah 56–66, Isaiah's use of these two figures, the foreigner and the eunuch, as model recipients of God's salvation and deliverance would be very surprising, given what we know of the returning community of Jewish exiles.[35] As castration was never an Israelite practice, any returning Jewish exiles who had been made eunuchs would have been subjugated in the service of foreign (e.g., Assyrian or Persian) kings. Thus, both figures represent a foreign presence within the community. But as the Ezra and Nehemiah texts demonstrate, the emphasis of the postexilic community was upon endogamous marriage and maintaining ethnic purity. In addition, both eunuchs and foreigners were excluded from access to the assembly in Deuteronomy 23:1–8, and Ezekiel 44:9 reiterates the exclusion of foreigners from the temple.

However, in light of the expanding horizon of those who comprise the servant's spiritual offspring, Isaiah's choice of these figures makes appropriate sense. The foreigner had been excluded from participation in the covenant of God's people by virtue of his birth and ethnicity. The eunuch, as one devoid of offspring, was subject to the covenantal curses and being blotted out from any future within the community.[36] But being the servant's offspring requires neither physical ancestors nor physical descendants—and so both the eunuch and foreigner are now eligible to be joined to the Lord and his people.

The imagery of the dry tree used in Isaiah 56:3 to describe the childless eunuch is reminiscent of the threat against Jeremiah to "destroy the tree with its fruit" (Jer. 11:19) and presents a reverse image of the flourishing shoot and root of the servant. The eunuch is now *no longer* to consider himself a dry tree, perhaps in part because he, in the pattern of the barren woman, may also bring forth a new form of offspring. But even more important for the eunuch is the promise of a new and everlasting relationship with the Lord himself. God will reverse the prohibition of Deuteronomy 23:1 that denied him access to the assembly and the temple.

Three conditions are placed upon the eunuch: he is to "keep my Sabbaths," "choose the things that please me," and "hold fast my covenant." The reference to keeping the Sabbath here is probably a metonym for keeping the legal requirements of the covenant, so the repetition may be here to reinforce the picture of one who upholds both the letter and spirit of the law.[37] What the eunuch is given here speaks to the three things denied him as a single man: offspring in the form of sons and daughters, an inheritance in the land, and a name to be remembered after his death.

He is given a permanent place, a memorial within God's house and within God's city. The expression "a monument and a name" (v. 5) is unique within the Old Testament and is probably a hendiadys, in which the two terms are taken together to represent a single concept. The Hebrew word for *monument* (*yad*) recalls Absalom setting up a monument to his name in 2 Samuel 18:18. The Greek Septuagint translates the expression as "named place," again reinforcing the idea of a *permanent place* within the house of God identified with the eunuch. The concept is reminiscent of the inheritance given to the individual Israelite that was also to serve as an everlasting *place* identified with that individual.[38] Likewise, it appears to anticipate Jesus' own reference to preparing a "place" for his disciples within his Father's house (John 14:2). Having this sort of permanent inheritance within the house of God is better than sons and daughters, for such an inheritance is one that cannot be cut off; it is not dependent on the existence and continued presence of one's progeny but is truly everlasting.

The idea of a permanent name also seems to anticipate New Testament references to having one's name written in the book of life (Phil. 4:3; Rev. 3:5; 13:8; 17:8; 20:15; 21:27), a place from which it can never be blotted out, as described in the letter to the church of Sardis:

> The one who conquers will be clothed thus in white garments, and I will never blot his name out of the book of life. I will confess his name before my Father and before his angels. (Rev. 3:5)

Beyond the blessings of a permanent name and place within the house of God that is better than sons and daughters, the prohibition that barred the eunuch from access to the temple and the priesthood (Deut. 23:1; Lev. 21:20) has also been reversed. Now the eunuch not only has restored access to the house of God but has a permanent place within it; i.e., he is given a priestly position.

It seems more than coincidental that among the very first accounts of Gentiles coming to Christian faith we have an account of the Ethiopian eunuch, a man who fits the description of *both* the foreigner and the eunuch described in Isaiah 56. Acts 8:26–40 records the story of a court eunuch of Candace, queen of the Ethiopians, who had come to Jerusalem to worship, presumably having visited the temple, and was now returning in his chariot to his home country. The Spirit sends Philip to intercept the man and meet him as he was traveling on the desert road to Gaza. The eunuch, moreover, is found by Philip to be reading from Isaiah 53:7–8, depicting the humiliation and childlessness of the suffering servant, and asks him for assistance in understanding what he is reading. Philip, under the inspiration of the Spirit, proceeds to speak to him about the good news of Jesus, "beginning with this Scripture" (Acts 8:35).

It is difficult to imagine a clearer and more specific fulfillment of Isaiah's depiction of the restoration and inclusion of the single and childless eunuch within the people of God than what is described in Acts 8. He is a single and childless court eunuch, a foreigner worshiping in Jerusalem and grappling to understand the fulfillment of the prophecy of the suffering servant in Isaiah 53. One can only wonder the further amazement that would have been in his eyes if he had continued reading on to the account of the eunuch and the foreigner in Isaiah 56.

Offspring in Isaiah 57–66

The two types of offspring with which Isaiah begins his prophecy also reappear in the closing portions of his book. In 57:1–13 we are again presented with a portrait of the sin and waywardness of the nation, which, devoid of the Spirit, had followed the sin and idolatry of the surrounding nations, a picture reminiscent of the "offspring of evildoers" seen in 1:4. In 57:3–4 God's people are described as "offspring of the adulterer and the loose woman," "children of transgression," and "offspring of deceit."

Elsewhere in Isaiah, those redeemed of the Lord are spoken of positively. They are referred to as his "Holy People" (62:12). Isaiah 59:20 speaks of a "Redeemer" who will come to Zion to those who turn from transgression and then, in verse 21, comes a description of God's covenant:

> "This is my covenant with them," says the LORD: "My Spirit that is upon you, and my words that I have put in your mouth, shall not depart out of your mouth, or out of the mouth of your offspring, or

out of the mouth of your children's offspring," says the LORD, "from this time forth and forevermore."

Several important features of the people of the Redeemer are given in this dense verse. They are characterized by God's Spirit upon them, and the presence of his Spirit is intrinsic to the covenant (presumably a *new* covenant) that God makes with them. God's words are put in their *mouths*. What defines this people is verbal dissemination of God's words, and not only in their mouths but, literally, also "out of the mouth of your offspring, or out of the mouth of your offspring's offspring" (AT).

The ESV translates "your *children's* offspring" for variation, but there is no presumption here that these must be *physical* offspring.[39] Indeed, what binds them all together is the word of God in their mouths, the proclamation of God's word rather than physical bloodlines. This is the covenant that the Lord now establishes with the coming of a redeemer from Zion from "this time forth and forevermore."

In Isaiah 61:8–9, we find another reference to the covenant that God will make with this new people: all who see them will acknowledge that "they are an offspring the LORD has blessed." In addition, their offspring shall be known "among the nations"; that is, they will constitute an ethnically diverse rather than homogeneous identity. They are not a people blessed by the Lord in *having* offspring but in *being* his offspring. Just before this comes the passage that Jesus later cites as having been fulfilled in him:

The scroll of the prophet Isaiah was given to him.
　　He unrolled the scroll and found the place where it was written,
"The Spirit of the Lord is upon me,
　　because he has anointed me
　　to proclaim good news to the poor.

He has sent me to proclaim liberty to the captives
　　and recovering of sight to the blind,
　　to set at liberty those who are oppressed,
　　to proclaim the year of the Lord's favor." (Luke 4:17–19)

Isaiah also incorporates the offspring theme within his eschatological vision of the new heavens and new earth that closes out the final two chapters of his book. He describes the eschatological people of God as those who "shall *not* labor in vain or bear children for calamity" (65:23). Rather, they shall be in themselves "offspring blessed of the LORD" and "their descendants with them."[40] Just as in 61:9, the fundamental blessing in 65:23 is not found in having or bearing children but in *being* offspring. The word "descendants" (*tse'etsa'*) is one that Isaiah routinely uses as a parallel for "offspring" (*zera'*).[41] Thus, in keeping with Jesus' pronouncement that in the resurrection there will be neither marrying nor giving in marriage (Luke 20:35) and Isaiah's own picture of offspring who generate offspring through the word (Isa. 59:21), the reference to descendants here is likely best understood as referring to *spiritual* rather than *physical* progeny.

Isaiah concludes his book with a fitting rejoinder to his condemnation in 48:18–19 of the sinful nation. There he laments to the nation: "That you had paid attention to my commandments . . . your offspring would have been like the sand, and . . . their name would never be cut off." In his final eschatological vision Isaiah again uses language of "offspring" and "name," but he presents his vision of the gathering, beginning in 66:18, not just with Israel but with all nations and tongues where all the nations see and declare his glory:

> For as the new heavens and the new earth that I make shall remain before me, says the LORD, so shall your offspring and your name remain. From new moon to new moon, and from Sabbath to Sabbath, all flesh shall come to worship before me, declares the LORD. (Isa. 66:22–23)

The reference here to "your offspring" and "your name" applies to the new redeemed humanity gathered from all the nations and also designated "your brothers" (66:20).[42] They are gathered from all the nations, brought together as brothers, and now share together in the designation of "your offspring" and the possession of an eternal name. The condemnation of the offspring of evildoers has been permanently superseded in the eternal blessing given to the offspring of the servant.

Nehemiah and Daniel

The prophetic restoration of the eunuch that Isaiah presents raises the possibility that a couple of Old Testament figures in their positions of service to foreign kings may have been eunuchs. The tradition of employing castrated men for court service dates back at least to the ninth-century BC Assyrian queen Semiramis[43] and became commonplace throughout the Persian Empire under the Achaemenean kings (559–330 BC).[44] Nehemiah was cupbearer for King Artaxerxes (465–424 BC) of Persia (Neh. 1:11), a position that demanded absolute loyalty to the king.

Beyond his position and the time and place in which he served, there is further evidence to suggest that Nehemiah was a eunuch. After Shemaiah advises Nehemiah to flee to the temple for the safety of his life, Nehemiah responds, "What man such as I could go into the temple and live? I will not go in" (Neh. 6:11). Nehemiah's reluctance to enter the temple for safety is logically explained by the prohibitions barring eunuchs from the temple or priestly service (Deut. 23:1; Lev. 21:20). Although we do not have definite proof that Nehemiah was a eunuch, there is good circumstantial evidence to suggest he was.[45]

There is more evidence to suggest that Daniel was a eunuch, but here, too, the case is probabilistic rather than definitive. Like Nehemiah, Daniel and his three friends were in positions of high confidence, serving as royal advisors to Babylonian and Medo-Persian kings. Isaiah had prophesied to Hezekiah that some of his own sons would become "eunuchs in the palace of the king of Babylon" (Isa. 39:7). Nebuchadnezzar, the king of Babylon, commands Ashpenaz, his chief eunuch, to bring some from the royal family, literally "the offspring of the kingdom," from Israel to stand in the king's service (Dan. 1:3–4). Daniel and his friends are then placed under the tutelage of the chief of the eunuchs who gives the men new names befitting their new positions of service within the Babylonian court (v. 7). Jewish interpretive tradition also favored the view that Daniel was indeed a castrated eunuch, and the rabbis regarded Daniel as a fulfillment of Isaiah's restored eunuch.[46] Some considered the preservation of the book of Daniel itself as a fulfillment of the promise in Isaiah 56:5 of an everlasting name that will never be cut off.[47]

The narrative drama within the first six chapters of Daniel may also subtly corroborate the likelihood that Daniel served as a eunuch. His impeccable moral faithfulness was exceptional among Old Testament figures generally, perhaps reflecting the high standard of Sabbath keeping described in Isaiah 56:4. The narrative backdrop for the book has Daniel standing in service before human kings. In the king's service, the faithful eunuch was the exemplar of loyalty and faithfulness to the throne. Since he could not have a dynasty of his own, he was not a threat to the ruling monarch and his dynasty. Conversely, since the eunuch had no children to care for him in old age, he was completely dependent on the auspices of the throne for his future welfare. Thus, since the eunuch depended fully on the king's power and provision for his future survival, further-ing the interests of the king and his kingdom was the eunuch's constant and primary concern. Though Daniel is a model of faithful eunuch-like service, the central drama of the book concerns the question of *which* king Daniel was really serving: the human king who employed him or the Lord God king of the universe. In a repeating pattern of narrative episodes (the defiled food, the fiery furnace, the lions' den), Daniel must choose between faithfully serving the Lord God and obedience to the human monarch. Daniel's continued faithfulness results in God's miracu-lous pattern of continued provision and care for him, even in the midst of the life-threatening consequences of his choices. Daniel thus serves as the exemplar Old Testament eunuch of the Lord, completely loyal and faithful to his Lord's commandments while trusting and depending upon him fully for the provision of his welfare.

The New Covenant of Jeremiah

We have already seen repeated reference within Isaiah to a covenant between God and the new kind of holy offspring that emerges in the aftermath of the servant's atoning sacrifice (e.g., Isa. 59:21; 61:8–9). Jeremiah's well-known "new covenant" prophesy is perhaps the most explicit reference and description of this new covenant found among the prophetic authors of the Old Testament:

> Behold, the days are coming, declares the LORD, when I will make a new covenant with the house of Israel and the house of Judah, not like the covenant that I made with their fathers on the day when I took them by the hand to bring them out of the land of Egypt, my covenant that they broke, though I was their husband, declares the LORD. But this is the covenant that I will make with the house of Israel after those days, declares the LORD: I will put my law within them, and I will write it on their hearts. And I will be their God, and they shall be my people.

And no longer shall each one teach his neighbor and each his brother, saying, "Know the LORD," for they shall all know me, from the least of them to the greatest, declares the LORD. For I will forgive their iniquity, and I will remember their sin no more." (Jer. 31:31–34)

Jeremiah succinctly frames the essential distinctions between the Sinai covenant God made with the nation of Israel and the new covenant that God establishes with the new offspring that emerge from his servant. The old covenant was formed in the context of God's deliverance of the people through the exodus, but it was a covenant that they broke.

The marriage imagery here is striking in anticipation of the same metaphor applied by Paul in Ephesians 5:32 to the people of the new covenant. The old marriage, however, is broken and thus God now offers a new covenant—a *new* marriage with his new people. This marriage covenant is characterized by a qualitatively different character that defines his new people. They have the law of God within them, they know the Lord, and they have their sins forgiven.

Ezekiel and Isaiah also characterize this new people of God as those who possess God's Spirit (Isa. 44:3; 59:21; Ezek. 11:19; 36:26). Indeed, this new people of God, who are in a new covenant with God, are also born of a new birth, one that is spiritual, that comes by the Spirit, and identifies them as servants in the form of the suffering servant.

Wrapping Up

Like the two-faced Roman god Janus who looked back while also looking forward, the prophets both look back upon the previous covenant God gave the nation at Sinai and look forward to the new covenant that God will make with his people in the future. Their message is a paradox of condemnation and hope, for the very condemnation of judgment upon the people for their failure to live as God's faithful covenant people becomes the soil for God's raising up of a new holy seed to grow and flourish. This new *seed* or *offspring* is both singular and plural. It is first the promise of an individual coming child who possesses the power and presence of God himself. He is both the "shoot" that grows from the lineage of Abraham and David, and also the "root" of qualitatively *new* people of God. He is the suffering servant who, through his sacrificial death, sees his offspring, who become servants in his image and are the heirs of the new creation.

With the prophetic transition between the old and the new comes a dramatic reversal of fortune for a single person in the dual images Isaiah presents of the barren woman and the eunuch. The figures are complementary—the barren woman represents the female unable to bear children, while the eunuch is the male unable to beget. Both were figures of reproach for the Israelites living in the land under the Sinai covenant. Fundamental to the blessings of the Sinai covenant was fruitfulness of the womb, and, as we have seen, all the blessings of the covenant depended in one way or another on having physical offspring. But in the aftermath of the work of the suffering servant, both the barren woman and the eunuch are *blessed*.

The barren woman, who was unfruitful in producing physical offspring, is now able to bring forth something profoundly greater— spiritual sons and daughters in the pattern of the servant. Her legacy of offspring is even greater than the fertile woman, since the Lord himself is her husband. The eunuch, conversely, who had been denied access to temple service, is now given an eternal and permanent place within God's house. Instead of being a figure of reproach, he becomes the model of uncompromisingly loyal and devoted service to the Lord in the pattern of Daniel the prophet. In his inheritance within the walls and house of the Lord, he shall inherit a legacy and name even better than sons and daughters. Though the barren woman and the eunuch are gendered portraits, as we shall see, the blessings they represent are not gender specific. Both are begetters of spiritual offspring and can serve as models of devoted service to the Lord. It is in the life and ministry of the church that Isaiah's vision takes hold.

4

Good News for the Gentiles

How Abraham's Offspring Come from Jesus Alone

Imagine a young boy who has his heart set on owning a stuffed dog he sees in the window of a local toy shop. It is the only dog of its kind, and each time the boy sees the dog in the window, he grows in his longing to take the dog home to be his play companion and loyal friend. As Christmas approaches, the boy shares his desire for the stuffed dog with his parents. Confident that his parents have heard his request, the boy scampers down the stairs Christmas morning with every expectation that the stuffed dog will be there waiting under the Christmas tree. To his surprise, he finds out that his parents had something much greater in mind. Waiting for him on Christmas morning is not the stuffed dog from the window of the toy store but a real dog. The boy is overjoyed, for the fulfillment of his desire for a play companion far exceeded his expectations. The nature of his parents' provision far surpassed the boy's comparatively modest expectation.

The difference between the expectation of the boy and the fulfillment that came is a reminder to us that God too sometimes fulfills his promises in ways that far exceed our expectations, and so much so that it shifts our whole paradigm of expectation. A simple example appears in the Abrahamic narrative. God promised Abraham that one coming from his own body would be his heir (Gen. 15:4). Abraham, presuming it was not physically possible to produce a child with his wife, yielded to her proposal to beget a child with her servant Hagar as a surrogate. But God, not bound by natural limitations, had something greater in mind and gave Abraham a son directly through supernatural provision to aged Sarah (Gen. 17:16).

On a much larger scale we have seen a paradigm shift of expectation occurring in the prophetic storyline of Isaiah. The fulfillment of a multitude of promised offspring to Abraham will ultimately be accomplished not simply in the procreation of the physical offspring that formed the Israelite nation but through a particular divinely appointed *holy seed* (6:13) and the offspring that he produces by means of his sacrificial death (53:10).

In the three remaining chapters of this book we will wrestle with the distinctive and surprising treatment of the subject of singleness in the New Testament—how it differs from the Old Testament and what accounts for those differences. At the root of these differences is the paradigm shift between an expectation of how God would fulfill his promises to Abraham and the reality of how he did so. This shift is fundamental to the differences between the Testaments on singleness and marriage because of the very central role that *offspring* plays in these promises and the inherent link between the procreation of offspring and the marriage relationship.

The paradigm shift in how God would provide the promised offspring that Isaiah saw and depicted in prophecy, the New Testament writers see and explain even more clearly from a post-crucifixion perspective. Hence, a theological exploration of how and why the New Testament writers speak about singleness and marriage must start with an examination of how the New Testament develops and understands the paradigm shift that Isaiah so vividly portrayed. So we begin by exploring how the New Testament explains and develops Isaiah's paradigm shift in light of the life, death, and resurrection of Christ and reflecting on some of the implications that this theological paradigm shift has upon the nature of singleness, marriage, and procreation in the new covenant.

The Expected Paradigm: The Plural Seed of Abraham

Let us recall the prevailing expectation of how God would fulfill the promises of the covenant with Abraham, the covenant at Sinai, and the covenant with David.[1] First, God gave a direct promise to Abraham that he would multiply his offspring to be as numerous as the stars of the sky (Gen. 15:5; 22:17), the dust of the earth (Gen. 13:16), and the sand of the seashore (Gen. 22:17). Although Abraham was to be the father of kings and a multitude of nations (Gen. 17:4, 6), God was going to make of him a particular "great nation" (Gen. 12:2). To Abraham's offspring God would give an inheritance of land as an everlasting possession (Gen. 13:15–17; 15:18–21; 17:8). God was going to bless Abraham and make his name great, and through him bless all the "families of the earth" (Gen. 12:2–3).

The expectation, therefore, was that through Abraham's physical offspring, God would create a great nation (Israel) that would receive an everlasting inheritance of land and, as a nation, would be a blessing to all other nations of the earth. As a people chosen by the Lord to be his treasured possession among all the nations of the earth (Ex. 19:5; Deut. 7:6) they were to be a kingdom of priests, a holy nation (Ex. 19:6), worshiping the Lord and functioning as his representative among the nations. It was to be a nation led by the house of David and his offspring whose kingdom and throne would be eternal (2 Sam. 7:12–13). This offspring was to build a house for God's name (2 Sam. 7:13) on the mountain of the Lord to which all the nations would stream (Isa. 2:2–3).

The distinguishing mark of the Lord's chosen nation was the righteous law that God himself had set before it (Deut. 4:8) and the people's faithful adherence to it. They were to lay up the words of the law in their hearts, bind them on their hands and foreheads, teach them to their children, and write them on the doorposts of their houses (Deut. 11:18–20). In response, God would bless the fruit of their womb, the fruit of their livestock, and the fruit of their land (Deut. 7:13). They would be marked out as "blessed above all peoples" in this: there would not be "male or female barren" among them or their livestock (Deut. 7:14).

Marriage and offspring were fundamental to the vision of the expected fulfillment of God's covenantal promises in three respects. First, God's blessing to the nations was to come through the physical seed of Abraham. Marriage and procreation were the means by which God was building his holy nation of priests that would be a vehicle of blessing to the world. Second, marriage and children were a mark and confirmation of God's covenantal blessing for every individual Israelite. Third, marriage and procreation were a means of retaining identity after death. Through children, one's name was carried and remembered, and one's allocated inheritance of land was passed to the next generation. Not to marry and have children was to have one's name and identity permanently blotted out after death.

But Israel did not fulfill its mission, and Isaiah and the prophets began to speak of a new and different way that God would fulfill his promises—a coming seed. From a post-resurrection perspective, Paul sees and explains this paradigm shift in his letter to the Galatians.

Jesus, the Single Seed

The most common Greek translation of the Hebrew term for *offspring* or *seed* (*zera'*) is *sperma*, and this term is no less important among New Testament authors, who were aware of its theological importance in the Old Testament. The most striking theological claim of the New Testament regarding offspring occurs in a verse where the word appears three times:

> Now the promises were made to Abraham and to his *offspring*. It does not say, "And to *offsprings*," referring to many, but referring to one, "And to your *offspring*," who is Christ. (Gal. 3:16)

Just as in English and Hebrew, so too in Greek the singular term *seed* can refer to either an individual seed or a collective seed (e.g., "the man sowed seed in his field"). Here Paul argues that when God gave promises to Abraham and his offspring (or seed), those promises were not granted to Abraham's collective descendants but only to a particular descendant. Commentators have struggled to explain *why* Paul would make such a seemingly unprecedented claim that the collective sense of the term should be rejected in favor of interpreting the term in the particular sense.[2] But Paul's interpretive move here is neither naïve nor manipulative.[3] Paul's claim serves as a succinct consolidation of what the Old Testament had already anticipated—that Jesus Christ is *both* the unique anticipated fulfillment of the promised seed of Abraham *and* the ultimate heir of the Abrahamic promises. What the prophet Isaiah had vividly depicted as the anticipated coming *shoot* and the *root* of Jesse, Paul now makes explicit. He has come in the person of Jesus Christ.

Jesus as the Promised Seed

Paul's claim comes within the context of a letter he is writing to the Galatians. The premise for writing the letter appears to be that a group of Judaizers had arisen within the church, and the group was insisting that Gentile Galatians within the church must be circumcised and compelled to adhere to the law of Moses (1:6–7; 3:1; 4:21; 5:2–12; 6:12–13). The potential confusion among early Greco-Roman converts between the Christian gospel that was being proclaimed by Jews and the full tenets of Judaism would have created a natural setting for traditional Jews to attempt to blur the distinctions and draw new Gentile Christians into the full orbit of Judaism. From the topic and content of Paul's argument, it is likely that such Judaizers appealed to various Old Testament Scriptures to make their case (e.g., Deut. 27:26, which Paul references in Gal. 3:10), and Paul found himself needing to correct their misguided interpretations.[4]

The Jewish proponents could also find some basis for their claims by appealing to the Abrahamic covenantal promises in which *all* the families of the earth (i.e., Gentiles) were to be blessed through Abraham and his offspring (Gen. 12:3; 18:18; 22:18). These promises, they might have claimed, were finding fulfillment in the inclusion of Gentiles via the proclamation of the gospel. But the promises that God gave to Abraham did not go to all his descendants (e.g., the Ishmaelites) but only to his offspring in Isaac. Thus, the Gentiles were to have no share in promises of Abraham apart from being adopted into the Abrahamic seed by circumcision and legal observance.[5] Paul thus likely found himself needing to correct a fundamental misunderstanding of the Old Testament in which adherence to the legal stipulations of the Sinai covenant was linked to the unconditional promissory tenets of the Abrahamic covenant.

Paul's radical claim in Galatians 3:16 implies that the Abrahamic promises were not ultimately to be fulfilled through the physical Jewish nation but through Christ. The promise given to Abraham—that through him all the families of the earth would be blessed—was not to be mediated through the Jewish nation's commitment to Sinaitic law but solely through Christ's atoning death. Thus, in Galatians 3:13–14 Paul asserts that *Christ* became "a curse for us—so that in Christ Jesus the blessing of Abraham might come to the Gentiles."

The implications of this exegetical move are profound. God's blessing to the world was indeed to be mediated by means of the vehicle of offspring, and specifically Abraham's offspring—but not all of Abraham's offspring or even a select subset of his offspring, but a single offspring—who in his atoning death was the means of righteous standing before God. The offspring that represents and brings the true blessing of God is not many, but one—Jesus Christ. With one bold swipe Paul neutralizes two arguments of the Jewish legalists. Adherence to the law was not necessary for maintaining righteous standing before God, nor was it a vital link in the fulfillment of God's promises to Abraham to mediate blessing to the world.

Paul's exegetical move was not an arbitrary sleight of hand. The concept of a special divinely provided offspring was a recurring Old Testament theme. Beginning with Eve (Gen. 3:15; 4:25), it appears again in the account of Abraham (Gen. 17:16), in the story of Ruth and Boaz (Ruth 4:12–15), in God's covenant with David (2 Sam. 7:12–13),[6] and in four consecutive images of the prophet Isaiah (Isaiah 7–11). Also, the identification of the key word *offspring* as a messianic referent was not a Pauline innovation. Jewish thought and exegesis had already made this move.[7] A clear reference to a messianic interpretation of the offspring of David in 2 Samuel 7:12 occurs in the Dead Sea Scrolls,[8] and John 7:42 indicates it was well ingrained in Jesus' own day that the Christ was to be from the offspring of David.[9]

A standard Jewish exegetical device known as *gezerah shavah* was commonly used to transfer the interpretation of one instance of a particular term or expression to another where the same term or expression is also used. Hence the expression "your *offspring* after you," which occurs in reference to David's offspring in 2 Samuel 7:12 and to Abraham's offspring in Genesis 17:7, would have provided Paul sufficient exegetical warrant for also seeing a messianic reference in Abraham's offspring in Genesis 17:7.[10] Paul chose to appeal to a messianic singular interpretation of *sperma* to make his fundamental point: the true seed of Abraham were those who identified with the unique messianic seed, who is Christ.

Paul's claim, identifying Christ as the offspring of Abraham, has profound implications. God was blessing the world not through a multitude of offspring but through a particular offspring, and that offspring was being announced through the proclamation of the gospel. At the same time, Paul's claim also implies another bold conclusion—the fulfillment of the Abrahamic and Davidic promises was being accomplished through Christ alone, independently of God's covenant with Israel at Sinai. The law and covenant at Sinai were not necessary for the fulfillment of God's covenant promises to Abraham. Any claim by the Judaizers that Gentile Christians needed to adhere to the Mosaic law was moot.

Jesus as the Heir of the Promises

Jesus is not only the promised offspring that fulfills the Abrahamic covenant, but he is also the heir of the Abrahamic covenant promises. This is expressed in Paul's statement in Galatians 3:16 that "the promises were made to Abraham and to his offspring." Paul goes on to clarify that the law, by contrast, was added "because of transgressions, until the offspring should come to whom the promise had been made" (Gal. 3:19). Let us examine the context that bridges these verses more closely:

> Now the promises were made to Abraham and to his offspring. It does not say, "And to offsprings," referring to many, but referring to one, "And to your offspring," who is Christ. This is what I mean: the law, which came 430 years afterward, does not annul a covenant previously ratified by God, so as to make the promise void. For if the inheritance comes by the law, it no longer comes by promise; but God gave it to Abraham by a promise. Why then the law? It was added because of transgressions, until the offspring should come to whom the promise had been made. (Gal. 3:16–19a)

A peculiar aspect of Paul's language here is his tendency, when speaking of the Abrahamic covenant, to refer to both "promises," plural, and "promise," singular. In 3:16 the reference is plural (also in 3:21), while in the four instances in 3:17–19 the singular is used. Verse 18 may provide the clue behind Paul's thinking—the "inheritance" is the substance for Paul of the covenant promises under discussion. This raises two questions: (1) What were the promises given both to Abraham and his offspring in Genesis? and (2) What does Paul mean by the term *inheritance*?

The Nature of the "Promises"

F. F. Bruce once observed that wherever in the Genesis narrative the promises are given "to" Abraham's offspring[11] as Paul says in Galatians, the reference is invariably to land (e.g., Gen. 12:7; 13:15; 15:18; 17:8; 24:7). Bruce adds, "The reference to the land, however, plays no part in the argument of Galatians."[12] While the observation may be technically correct, it fails to fully appreciate Paul's use of "inheritance" language in this context.

In addition to the land promise, both Abraham and his offspring are given similar promises that they will be agents of blessing to the world, although these do not occur together in the same verse. In Genesis 12:3 a promise is given to Abraham that "in you all the families of the earth shall be blessed."[13] Later, in Genesis 22:18, a promise is given that "in your offspring shall all the nations of the earth be blessed."[14] Paul appears to combine these two expressions when he identifies this blessing with the preaching of the gospel:

> And the Scripture, foreseeing that God would justify the Gentiles by faith, preached the gospel beforehand to Abraham, saying, "In you shall all the nations be blessed." (Gal. 3:8)

Paul attributes the promise as given to Abraham with the "nations" language promised to Abraham's offspring. Thus Paul attributes to Abraham and his offspring the promise of being a blessing to all the nations (i.e., the Gentiles) and that this would occur by means of the preaching of the gospel for justification of the Gentiles. While the wording of the promise in both cases is that "in" Abraham and his offspring the nations would be blessed, the preposition is part of the wording of the promise itself—it is understood from context that it is to both Abraham and his offspring that these promises are given.

Bruce's corollary observation that the land promise plays no part in Paul's present argument fails to appreciate the direct connection between the promise of land in Genesis and Paul's immediate reference to the "inheritance" in Galatians 3:18.[15] It is probably no coincidence that the central drama of the Abraham narrative concerns Abraham's lack of an heir (Gen. 15:3) and God's provision of not only an heir (Gen. 15:4) but also an inheritance (Gen. 15:7). Paul's reference to "inheritance" in Galatians 3:18 is a clear allusion to the "land" promise of Genesis.

That Paul speaks both of "promises" and "the promise" in the same context is possibly explained in that the promise of Abraham and his offspring being a blessing to the world was directly tied to the nature of the inheritance they brought to the world. It is to the nature of this inheritance that we next turn.

The Nature of the Inheritance

Paul's use of the term *inheritance* (*klēronomia*) in Galatians 3:18 is surely not accidental in light of the fact that land features prominently in Genesis as the promise given to *both* Abraham and his offspring, and that *inheritance* was a theologically significant designation for God's provision of the land to the people. Nevertheless, it is not immediately clear from the context what Paul intends by the term here in Galatians. There are no previous occurrences of the term *inheritance* or its cognates (i.e., *heir* or *inherit*) in Galatians, and this is the only appearance of *inheritance* in the letter. But from the usage of the term elsewhere in the New Testament, it is possible to construct a relatively good picture of the significance of the term here.[16] Like the Hebrew term for *inheritance, nakhalah,* the Greek term *klēronomia* reflects a similar aspect of outside provision involved— something that is decided or provided by another party.

Whereas the dominant theological association of *nakhalah* in the Old Testament is with the divinely provided land of Canaan, *klēronomia* in the New Testament consistently designates an inheritance of a spiritual nature, but no less divinely provided. This shift in focus from the geographical land of Canaan to more intangible spiritual realities was not exclusive to the New Testament writers. With the loss of the land in the exile, writers in Second Temple Judaism were already applying the concept of "inheritance" in more eschatological directions.[17] Some expanded the promises of an inheritance to Abraham to include the whole earth[18] or reapplied these to the elect.[19] Elsewhere we find the concept of "inheriting" being extended to expectations for the afterlife.[20]

One direct parallel to Galatians 3:18 occurs in Romans 4:13, where Paul again is discussing the promises to Abraham and his offspring:

> For the promise to Abraham and his offspring that he would be heir
> of the world did not come through the law but through the righteous-
> ness of faith.

Paul's reference here to being "heir of the world" is probably not to a temporal repossession of the world but is rather an eschatological reference, since for Paul the present form of the *kosmos* was already passing away in anticipation of the next (1 Cor. 7:31). Elsewhere Paul's use of *inheritance* is also exclusively reserved for the eschatological inheritance in heaven, or in reference to the kingdom of God. This inheritance comes through the word of grace (Acts 20:32), as the eschatological hope to which God has called those in Christ (Eph. 1:18), with the Spirit given as the guarantee until the saints acquire full possession of it (Eph. 1:14). This inheritance is ultimately the "inheritance in the kingdom of Christ and God" (Eph. 5:5; see also 1 Cor. 6:9; 15:50), a reward of the servants of the Lord Christ (Col. 3:24) and not for the immoral or impure (1 Cor. 6:9–10; Gal. 5:21).

Paul was not alone in viewing the inheritance in the new covenant as a spiritual entity, the kingdom of God that broke into history in the coming of Christ but which will be fully consummated in the new creation of the age to come. The Synoptic Gospels speak on repeated occasions of what is required to inherit eternal life (Matt. 19:29; Mark 10:17; Luke 10:25; 18:18), and in Matthew's eschatological judgment, the "blessed" are called to "inherit the kingdom prepared . . . from the foundation of the world" (Matt. 25:34).

The author of Hebrews almost echoes Paul when he describes Christ as the "heir of all things" (1:2) and the "mediator of a *new* covenant, so that those who are called may receive the promised *eternal* inheritance" (9:15). The author even regards Abraham and the patriarchs as anticipating this eschatological inheritance. Abraham "was looking forward to the city . . . whose designer and builder is God" (11:10). All the patriarchs desired "a *better* country, that is, a *heavenly* one," a city that God has prepared (11:16). Peter picks up a similar theme when he refers to his readers as "sojourners and exiles" (1 Pet. 2:11), who have been "born again to a living hope" through Christ "to an inheritance that is imperishable, undefiled, and unfading, kept in heaven for you" (1:3–4).

The contrast between the anticipated inheritance of land described in the Old Testament and the eventual inheritance of the kingdom of God described in the New Testament reveals a dramatic shift between expectation and ultimate fulfillment. Both were to be eternal bestowments, the land through marriage and procreation to the next generation, the kingdom through eternal life of its recipients. Yet, as the author of Hebrews reveals, even the patriarchs themselves were looking toward a better and more permanent inheritance—the city whose designer and builder is God.

The One Heir and the Many

What then does Paul mean by designating Christ as the *heir* of the Abrahamic promises? It means, first, that he is the vehicle of God's consummate blessing to the nations. How he does this is not through power and force but through his atoning and sacrificial death by which he reconciles humankind to God. It means, second, that Christ is the entitled recipient of *the* promised inheritance—not the original land of Canaan but the eschatological inheritance of the kingdom of God, inaugurated in the present age through the proclamation of the gospel and the establishment of the church, and consummated in the new heavens and earth of the age to come. These aspects are also directly related, since those whom Christ reconciles with God also become co-heirs of his promised inheritance.

This Paul goes on to clarify in the remainder of Galatians 3. The law was given as our "tutor," *paidagōgos*, for the sake of our sins only until the offspring of the promise should come (vv. 19, 24). Everything was thus imprisoned under sin so that the promise might be given by faith in Jesus Christ to those who believe (v. 22) and are "of Christ" and are now also Abraham's offspring—*heirs* according to the promise, as he makes explicit in 3:29:

> And if you are Christ's [lit. "of Christ"], then you are Abraham's offspring, heirs according to [the] promise.

This verse succinctly encapsulates a theological earthquake! Paul now links all those "of Christ" with Christ. When Paul grammatically constricts the meaning of offspring in Galatians 3:16 to the singular reference to Christ, it is only in anticipation of redefining a new aggregate offspring of Abraham. These offspring are not defined physically but are those who share union with the particular "offspring," Jesus Christ. All these who share a spiritual union with the unique physical offspring of Abraham are now also reckoned to be Abraham's offspring. These offspring, because of their union with Christ, are also reckoned to be "heirs according to the promise," that is, heirs of the eschatological inheritance mentioned in 3:18. The designation of Christians as heirs or co-heirs is one that appears a number of places in the New Testament (Rom. 8:17; Gal. 4:7; Eph. 3:6; Titus 3:7; James 2:5; 1 Pet. 3:7) but the weight of its significance is never so greatly seen as when we reflect on the theological paradigm shift that it represents.

In a single theological stroke Paul articulates the paradigm shift in God's fulfillment of his promises to Abraham. The true offspring of Abraham are no longer defined physically through their ethnic identity but spiritually through their union with Christ through faith. Moreover, as Abraham's offspring and heirs, they can anticipate receiving an inheritance—again, not a physical piece of real estate but a spiritual inheritance, one that is imperishable, undefiled, and unfading and kept in heaven (1 Pet. 1:4).

The essence of this paradigm shift represented by the very core of the Christian gospel has profound implications for all areas of life, including how we as Christians understand marriage and procreation. For whereas marriage and physical procreation were the necessary means of building the physical nation of Israel, the spiritual people of God are built through the process of spiritual regeneration. Moreover, whereas marriage and physical procreation were necessary for maintaining one's physical inheritance for the next generation, they are not necessary for preserving one's spiritual inheritance within the eternal kingdom of God.

Christ is thus *the* promised offspring and also the heir of *the* promised inheritance, bringing God's blessing to nations. It is this offspring of God, whom Isaiah so vividly depicts—the shoot and the root of Jesse—who brings this blessing to the world not by means of power and positing but through his sacrificial death as the Suffering Servant of the Lord.

Abraham and Allegory: Two Covenants and Two Births

Paul's allegorical interpretation of the account of Hagar and Sarah (Genesis 16–21) and their offspring in Galatians 4:22–31 provides the theological capstone for his argument against the Galatian Judaizers and in an important way also provides a capstone illustration of the essential difference between the old and the new covenants and the nature of participation in each. Though the passage is interpretively difficult, not only does it become easier to understand in light of our present exploration of the covenantal importance of begetting, offspring, and marriage, but it also serves to marvelously illustrate the essential paradigm shift that arises between the old and the new covenants and confirms afresh Paul's theological coherence with the prophet Isaiah. In that sense it also provides an illustrative capstone to our present exploration of the place of marriage, procreation, and offspring through the developing storyline of Scripture.

> For it is written that Abraham had two sons, one by a slave woman and one by a free woman. But the son of the slave was born according to the flesh, while the son of the free woman was born through promise. Now this may be interpreted allegorically: these women are two covenants. One is from Mount Sinai, bearing children for slavery; she is Hagar. Now Hagar is Mount Sinai in Arabia; she corresponds to the present Jerusalem, for she is in slavery with her children. But the Jerusalem above is free, and she is our mother. For it is written, "Rejoice, O barren one who does not bear; break forth and cry aloud, you who are not in labor! For the children of the desolate one will be more than those of the one who has a husband." Now you, brothers, like Isaac, are children of promise. But just as at that time he who was born according to the flesh persecuted him who was born according to the Spirit, so also it is now. But what does the Scripture say? "Cast out the slave woman and her son, for the son of the slave woman shall not inherit with the son of the free woman." So, brothers, we are not children of the slave but of the free woman. (Gal. 4:22–31)

C. K. Barrett suggests that the passage may have been a response to the climax of the scriptural evidence put forth by the Judaizers in making their case.[21] Even if Paul could claim Christ to be Abraham's true offspring, how could he then also include Gentiles as his offspring?

He could not deny the Genesis account, that Abraham had *two* sons: Isaac, who was father of the Jewish nation—those who were blessed in being given the law and the prophets—and Ishmael, who was father of Gentile descendants who had neither the law nor the prophets. But Paul not only turns the conventional Jewish interpretation on its head but also concludes his exegesis with an appeal to Genesis 21:10 as scriptural warrant for the Galatians to "cast out" the Judaizers from their midst.

The Crux of the Comparison

It is understandable that at a surface level Paul's argument would have been shocking to most Torah-observant Jews. Paul argues in essence that in *contrast* to the traditional understanding of the account of Ishmael and Isaac, Ishmael represents not Gentiles devoid of the law but the Jewish descendants of Abraham, who maintain adherence to the law. Isaac does not represent the Jews, who maintain the law, but the Galatian Gentiles, free from law. This is the case he proceeds to argue *from* the law in Galatians 4:21 when he challenges his opponents, "Tell me, you who desire to be under the law, do you not listen to the law?" To the faithful Jew, the claim that the Torah, rightly read, warrants rejection of law keeping would be outrageous.[22]

Paul proceeds with his conclusions through an allegorical interpretation of the text (v. 24); that is, the figures and events of the narrative are to be understood symbolically as representing a deeper meaning or truth. But Paul's use of allegory was not an arbitrary means to force the text to produce his desired conclusion. Paul surely was well aware of the significance of offspring in the Old Testament covenants. Likewise he would have known the Old Testament theme of two different types of offspring evident from the creation account of the birth of Eve's two children in Genesis 4, the two sons of Abraham in Genesis 16–21, and the contrast between the two types of offspring that Isaiah describes in 54:1–5 (to which he appeals in v. 27). In addition, Paul had the benefit of living on the other side of the cross and resurrection and having seen the outpouring of the Spirit upon the Galatians. In short, Paul's allegorical interpretation was far from arbitrary. Rather, it rested on the depth of his Spirit-illuminated understanding of the whole biblical storyline.

Paul introduces the text in Galatians 4:22 as being about Abraham's two sons, one by a slave woman, and one by a free woman. But the precise objects of his comparison appear to shift as he proceeds. Verses 22 and 23 compare the two sons of Abraham, Ishmael and Isaac. In verse 24 the categories shift attention from the sons to their respective mothers. In verse 27 he appeals to the comparison of two women in Isaiah 54:1, and he concludes in verses 28 through 31 with attention upon the application of the allegory to the present context of the Galatians. Though the contrasts he draws involve elements pertaining to both the sons and their respective mothers, the essential parallels are provided in Table 4.1.

Table 4.1 Paul's Allegorical Comparison of Galatians 4:22–31[23]

Verse	Ishmael/Hagar	Isaac/Sarah
22	[born] of the slave woman	[born] of the free woman
23	**begotten according to flesh**	**[begotten] through promise**
24	[covenant] from Mount Sinai	[covenant from Mount Zion]
24	**begetting into slavery**	**[begetting into freedom]**
24	Hagar	[Sarah]
25	Mount Sinai in Arabia	[Mount Zion in Judea]
25–26	Present Jerusalem	Jerusalem above
25–26	[is] in slavery with her children	is free
26	[she is not our mother]	she is our mother
27	*[fertile]*	*barren*
27	*[one who bears]*	*who does not bear*
27	*[one who is in labor]*	*one who is not in labor*
27	*has a husband*	*desolate*
27	*[fewer children]*	*more children*
28	[The Judaizers, like Ishmael are not children of the promise]	You, like Isaac, are children of the promise
29	**begotten according to the flesh**	**[begotten] according to the Spirit**
29	persecutes	[is persecuted]
30	The son of the slave woman will not inherit	The son of the free woman [will inherit]
31	We are not children of the slave woman	[We are children] of the free woman

It is important to observe in the table that although over the course of the argument the objects of comparison change along the way (e.g., women, sons, mountains, etc.), the fundamental distinction that appears to critically link the objects together and remains parallel throughout the comparison is that of *begetting*.

The Two Types of Begetting

Paul's point in the allegory is that Hagar and Sarah, in the way they give birth to their respective sons, represent the cosmic drama between the two different elected peoples of God. One is defined through physical birth and progeny, with a covenant of law, and a temporal inheritance marked by the present Jerusalem. The other is characterized by a non-physical birth by the Spirit, with a covenant consisting of grace and freedom from the law and an eschatological inheritance symbolized by the heavenly Jerusalem. Paul uses the verb *beget* to highlight three distinctions (bolded in Table 4.1) between Abraham's two types of progeny.[24]

The first distinction occurs immediately upon introduction of Abraham's two sons (Gal. 4:22–23). The son of the slave woman was born "according to the flesh," while the son of the free woman was born "through [the] promise." This distinction harkens back to the central drama of the Abrahamic narrative, that God would give Abraham his own son as an heir (Gen. 15:4), even though Sarah was barren. Ishmael was born through the human initiative of Sarah and Abraham, while Isaac was born through the supernatural provision of God, through the word of God's own promise (Gen. 17:16), and via a process that was impossible in human terms, as evidenced in Abraham and Sarah's laughter (Gen. 17:17; 18:12).

In Galatians 4:24 Paul moves to a second distinction of birth, one that parallels two covenants. Here Hagar represents the covenant of Sinai, begetting into (or for) slavery. No explicit parallel is offered on the part of Sarah, but the contrast between slavery and freedom that runs throughout the letter (e.g., Gal. 2:4; 4:22, 23, 25–26, 30; 5:1) suggests that it is between those bound to a sense of legal obligation to the Torah and those without such obligations. Those born into such legal obligations are ethnic Jews.

Earlier in the chapter Paul provides an example of the direct connection between birth as a Jew and one's presumed legal obligation to the Torah. In Galatians 4:4–6 he describes Jesus as sent by God "born of woman, born under the law" (i.e., born physically as a Jew) in order to "redeem those who were under the law" that they might become adopted sons and heirs. Paul's logic with this designation is that one who claims the necessity of keeping the law is under the slavery of law and therefore cannot be a true son and heir of Abraham but is instead a son of Hagar, Abraham's slave.

The third distinction occurs in Galatians 4:29, where Paul again contrasts the one born "according to [the] flesh" with the one born "according to [the] Spirit." This dichotomy of birth he immediately applies to his readers' context to contrast those insisting on the primacy of Jewish pedigree and law with his predominantly Gentile Galatian converts. Whereas the "flesh/promise" dichotomy in Galatians 4:23 focuses on the empowering agency of birth, comparing the one who bears via the human process and one who bears through the supernatural word of God's promise, the dichotomy here focuses on the fundamental nature of the birth. One is a physical birth "according to the flesh," while the other is a nonphysical but spiritual birth "according to the Spirit." Whereas the Judaizers could claim to be Abraham's physical offspring, through faith in Christ, the Galatian Gentile converts could claim to be Abraham's spiritual offspring.

The three distinctions taken together provide a more robust contrast between the two types of births that Paul is describing. On the one hand are those born physically of Abraham who are under a form of slavery in their obligation and bondage to the law—these in their slavery are not true sons of Abraham or heirs of his eschatological inheritance. On the other hand are those born supernaturally as a result of God's promise to Abraham, that through him all the nations would be blessed, born through the Spirit apart from the law and who are the true sons of Abraham and his eschatological heirs.

The Covenants and the Quotation of Isaiah 54:1

Commentators have disagreed over precise identification of the two covenants represented by the two women in Galatians 4, whether they represent the Sinaitic covenant and the new covenant,[25] the Sinaitic covenant and the Abrahamic covenant,[26] or other covenants not biblically identified.[27] Perhaps the best solution is to suggest that what Paul has in view is the paradigm shift between the presumed linkage of the Abrahamic covenant with the Sinaitic covenant and the proposed linkage of the Abrahamic covenant directly with the new covenant. In linking the Abrahamic covenant with the Sinaitic covenant, the Abrahamic promises are realized in the physical birthright of Israel and its unique commitment to the Sinaitic law, whereas in linking the Abrahamic covenant with the new covenant, the promises are realized through new birth and faith in the atoning work of Christ. Here again, the fundamental contrast between the old paradigm and the new is the nature of one's entrance or "birth" into the covenant.

Interpreters of this allegory have typically found it difficult to explain why Paul cites Isaiah 54:1 to bolster his allegorical interpretation. Barrett went so far as to suggest that Paul's use of the text was "arbitrary,"[28] while Richard Hayes admits that "the aptness of the quotation is not immediately evident."[29] J. Louis Martyn suggests that Paul appeals to the text because "it provides him with pairs of opposites with which he can supplement those he has already found in the Genesis stories."[30]

There is one obvious verbal link, found in the word *barren*, between the barren woman in Isaiah 54:1 and Sarah, who is described by that word in Genesis 11:30. It is tempting to use this link as a basis for aligning the remaining correspondences between the two sets of women; i.e., Sarah corresponds to Isaiah's barren and desolate woman who has no husband and has never been in labor, while Hagar corresponds to the woman married who bears physical children conventionally.[31] The difficulty is that the correspondences do not fit very well. Sarah was the one with a husband, and she presumably had labor pains. Hagar was the one without a husband who eventually was made desolate in the wilderness—but was not barren. Thus, Paul's purpose in using the citation cannot be because of obvious correspondences between the two sets of women.

Hayes has turned to a more involved explanation, suggesting that in an otherwise "blunt letter," here "Paul employs Scripture in an allusive, echo-laden manner." Hayes's solution proposes that Paul's use of Isaiah 54:1 makes his point—that Sarah is linked to an eschatologically restored

Jerusalem—by presupposing another text, Isaiah 51:2, where this link is more apparent.[32] But if Paul's primary purpose is to link Sarah to eschatological Jerusalem, this raises a question as to why Paul did not choose to use Isaiah 51:2 to make his point in the first place.[33] Moreover, how does this link in itself serve to strengthen Paul's argument?

But in light of our previous walk through Isaiah's multifaceted treatment of offspring in relationship to singleness and barrenness, perhaps a simpler explanation might help reduce some of the interpretive difficulties. To this end a few observations are necessary. First, the thrust of Paul's purpose in offering his allegorical interpretation of Sarah and Hagar is to demonstrate scripturally how it is that Gentile Galatian Christians can claim to be the legitimate offspring, sons and heirs, of Abraham, *over against* Judaizers, who otherwise make exclusive claim to their identity as sons and heirs of Abraham by means of their ethnic pedigree and social conformance to the Mosaic law. As part of his argument Paul appeals to Isaiah 54:1 as a proof-text, so we expect that some essential aspect of the text somehow supports that argument.

Second, the quotation of Isaiah 54:1 is linked to Paul's argument with the conjunction *for*. Thus it serves to support Paul's immediately preceding proposition that "Jerusalem above" (Gal. 4:26) is *our* mother. Contemporary Jewish sources suggest that "Jerusalem above" is a depiction of God's eschatological city, which can be designated either by the name "Jerusalem" or "Zion."[34] This Paul contrasts with the "present Jerusalem," the geographical epicenter of first-century Judaism. Hence Paul's appeal to Isaiah 54:1 somehow demonstrates that the Gentile Galatians, rather than ethnic Jews, have a greater claim to being the true children of eschatological Jerusalem.

Third, though Isaiah in numerous places describes a restored eschatological Zion as a woman fruitful in land and children (e.g., 49:21–23; 51:2–3; 62:4–5; 66:7–14), only here does he highlight her status as *barren*. Contrary to Sarah, who was previously barren but later was in labor and bore Isaac, the woman described in the Greek rendering of Isaiah 54:1 is still barren: "Rejoice, O barren one who *does not bear*; break forth and cry aloud, you who *are not in labor*!"[35] The point is that one who does not physically bear or even have a husband has more children than the one who does bear. Thus, neither Sarah nor Hagar can be in view. The fundamental contrast to be drawn is between the barren woman who bears children spiritually and the married woman who bears children physically.

Fourth, the contrast between Sarah's bearing Isaac by means of supernatural divine provision and Hagar's bearing Ishmael through mere conventional means provides a typological picture of the contrast between physical and spiritual offspring. But this is the precise difference exemplified in the contrast between the women in Isaiah 54:1, and thus Paul draws upon it to make his point. The text suggests that the children of eschatological Jerusalem are born spiritually rather than physically, and Paul can thus bolster his argument that it is the Gentile Galatians, born spiritually rather than physically, who are the true heirs of Abraham.

While the point of Paul's allegorical interpretation of Sarah and Hagar is to demonstrate scripturally how Gentile Galatian Christians are the true offspring of Abraham and heirs of the promises, it is not a theme unique to this letter or to Paul's other New Testament epistles. In Romans 4:13 Paul argues that "the promise to Abraham and his offspring that Abraham would be heir of the world did not come through the law but through the righteousness of faith." Paul's emphasis in Romans 4 is that Abraham was justified by faith, and it must be so "in order that the promise may rest on grace and be guaranteed to all his offspring—not only to the adherent of the law but also to the one who shares the faith of Abraham, who is the father of us all" (v. 16).

Not that Paul was arguing for inclusivism of both types of offspring, as he later clarifies:

> For not all who are descended from Israel belong to Israel, and not all are children of Abraham because they are his offspring, but "Through Isaac shall your offspring be named." This means that it is not the children of the flesh who are the children of God, but the children of the promise are counted as offspring. (Rom. 9:6b–8)

Here again the same radical redefinition of the exclusivity of "Isaac's off-spring" is in view. Only some of Abraham's offspring belong to eschato-logical Israel—those who come through Isaac. But the true sons of Isaac are not his children of the flesh but his children of the promise, not those born to him physically, but those born spiritually by grace through faith.

Paul's allegorical appeal to the Hagar and Sarah episode vividly illustrates that the fundamental difference between God's elect under the old Sinai covenant and his elect under the new covenant is the respective nature of their birth into the covenant. The former were God's people through procreation by means of their physical birth as descendants of Abraham. The latter are God's people through regeneration by means of their spiritual new birth through union with the single seed of Abraham, Jesus Christ. As our previous exploration confirms, Paul's observation of this distinction was not an innovation on his part, but it was an appeal to a theme already underscored within the Old Testament storyline from Genesis to Isaiah. And, as we shall see, this distinction is not unique to Paul in the New Testament but appears among numerous other authors and books.[36] Moreover, it is this fundamental distinction that also shapes differing covenantal perspectives regarding the purpose of marriage, singleness, and procreation within the people of God as a whole.

Jesus and the Blessings of the New Covenant

From the beginning of our journey through the storyline of the biblical text we have seen the strong link between the provision of offspring and divine blessing. In the creation account God blessed the man and the woman and said, "Be fruitful and multiply" (Gen. 1:28). As we have seen, God not only promised to Abraham in a covenant that he would be blessed and have offspring (Gen. 12:2; Isa. 51:2) but also that the world would be blessed through him and his offspring (Gen. 12:3; 22:18). God likewise promised to the Israelites in the Sinai covenant that if they kept the stipulations of the covenant, they would be "blessed above all peoples," and, "There shall not be male or female barren among you" (Deut. 7:12, 14). Offspring through marriage was thus a fundamental marker of God's covenant blessing to the individual Israelite (Deut. 28:11). In the book of Ruth, the women of Bethlehem blessed the Lord for his provision to Naomi of a grandson (Ruth 4:14), and Psalm 127:5 declares a man blessed who fills his quiver with children. Isaiah describes God's blessing upon Zebulun and Naphtali in the advent of the coming messianic child (Isa. 9:1–5), and concludes his prophecy with a vision of the eschatological people of God as "offspring blessed of the LORD" (Isa. 61:9; 65:23, AT).

Not surprisingly the connection between divine blessing and off-spring also features prominently in the new covenant, but not in the way we might expect. Paul again speaks to the subject in the Galatians passage we have been examining:

> Christ redeemed us from the curse of the law by becoming a curse for us—for it is written, "Cursed is everyone who is hanged on a tree"—so that in Christ Jesus the blessing of Abraham might come to the Gentiles, so that we might receive the promised Spirit through faith. (Gal. 3:13–14)

In the new covenant Jesus Christ, the begotten offspring of God, reversed the curse of the law by becoming a curse for us in being hanged on a tree so that the divine blessing of Abraham might be realized in us through faith in his atoning sacrifice for our sin. In short, Jesus Christ—the offspring of God—is himself, in his atoning and reconciling work, the vehicle of God's blessing to the world. This comes apart from the law and covenant of Sinai but through faith, so that "those who are of faith are *blessed* along with Abraham, the man of faith" (Gal. 3:9).

This nexus between God's blessing and Christ's atoning sacrifice as a fundamental feature of the new covenant arises prominently in the description of the cup of Communion. At the Last Supper Jesus takes the cup, saying, "This cup that is poured out for you is the new covenant in my blood" (Luke 22:20), a statement Paul cites in 1 Corinthians 11:25. Elsewhere Paul refers to the Communion cup as the cup of *blessing*: "The cup of blessing that we bless, is it not a participation in the blood of Christ?" (1 Cor. 10:16). Thus our participation in the blood of Christ poured out on our behalf in the cup of Communion is also our participation in the very blessing of God bestowed to us in the new covenant.

Paul recognized that the magnitude of the covenantal blessing that comes through Christ in the new covenant dwarfs by comparison all other "material" blessings of God that feature prominently in the Sinai covenant. In the new covenant we find no mention of the familial blessings of offspring and marriage or of a fruitful and prosperous land so prominent as markers of God's blessing in the Sinai covenant. Rather, the fullness of God's blessing comes to us through Christ and his sacrificial death on the cross whereby he has fully reconciled us to God and made us co-heirs in the inheritance of his kingdom. Thus Paul, a single man, devoid of wife, children, house, home, land, possessions, and financial prosperity, nevertheless recognized that he, even as a simple itinerant missionary on this earth, possessed "the *fullness* of the blessing of Christ" (Rom. 15:29).

Ephesians 1 provides one of the most vivid descriptions of the new covenant blessing that we have anywhere in the New Testament. Paul begins his account in classic style by blessing God for blessing us:

> Blessed be the God and Father of our Lord Jesus Christ, who has blessed us in Christ with every spiritual blessing in the heavenly places, even as he chose us in him before the foundation of the world, that we should be holy and blameless before him. In love he predestined us for adoption as sons through Jesus Christ, according to the purpose of his will, to the praise of his glorious grace, with which he has blessed us in the Beloved. (Eph. 1:3–6)

Paul describes the nature of God's blessing to us in Christ here in three ways. First, it is complete in that it envelops "every" blessing he has to give. Second, these blessings are fundamentally of a "spiritual" rather than material nature. Third, these blessings are "in the heavenly places" and are therefore directed heavenward rather than being fully consummated on earth. What is the essence of these blessings to us? First, he "chose us" before the creation of the world that we should be "holy" and "blameless" before him (v. 4). He also "predestined *us*" to be his adopted sons in Christ (v. 5)—in other words, he counted us as his own *adopted* offspring through the sacrificial atoning work of his *begotten* offspring. This he has done for the praise of his grace, with which he has graced us. God does this act of adopting and graciously giving us status as "sons" as a single act "in love" (v. 4) through his own "beloved" begotten Son (v. 6).

In verses 7 through 10 he gives additional aspects of God's blessing that comes according to this grace he has lavished upon us *in Christ*. "In him," God has given us "redemption" through his blood, which equates to the "forgiveness" of our trespasses (v. 7). And through this grace he has "[made] known to *us*" the mystery of his will to "unite" all things in heaven and earth under the headship of Christ (vv. 9–10).

The picture concludes in verses 11 through 14 with a view of the promised inheritance that comes to us *in Christ*. "In him" we have "obtained an inheritance" as a result of the principle blessing of being predestined by him (v. 11). Moreover, "in him" we were sealed with the Holy Spirit, who "is the guarantee of our inheritance until we acquire possession of it" (vv. 13–14).

The picture here is of a single unified fount of divine blessing. *All* God's blessings come by his grace through the sole material blessing—the provision of his Son, the begotten offspring of God himself. These blessings consist of, first, our complete reconciliation with God through our redemption and the forgiveness of sin, and, second, an eternal inheritance within his kingdom to be consummated at the end of the age. This is by God's design to bring all things in heaven and earth under his headship for the praise of his glory (vv. 6, 14). Indeed, offspring is the centerpiece of God's covenant blessing in the new covenant as well as in the old.

Wrapping up
The Shape of God's Fulfillment
In Galatians 3–4 we have a condensed articulation of the paradigm shift that occurred in how God fulfilled his covenant promises to Abraham. The true offspring of Abraham are not defined by their natural birth but by their spiritual birth in union with Christ. In Christ they have received all the blessings of the new covenant so that they are completely blessed and have an imperishable eternal inheritance irrespective of the circumstances of their lives.

Thus whereas marriage and procreation play a critical role in the expected fulfillment of God's covenantal promises to and through Abraham, they do not do so in the actual fulfillment that comes through the new covenant in Christ. God's blessing to the nations has come through the unique offspring of Abraham and his atoning sacrifice. Spiritual regeneration rather than procreation is the means by which God is now building his holy nation (1 Pet. 2:9). Neither marriage nor children is a fundamental marker of being blessed of God in the new covenant, as all spiritual blessings come through Christ (Eph. 1:3). Nor are marriage and procreation necessary to maintain one's covenantal inheritance, for those in Christ have an imperishable inheritance in heaven.

This reality does not diminish the inherent joy and fulfillment that come in marriage and children, nor does it diminish the profound gospel witness potential that a Christian marriage can exhibit to the unsaved world. But it does mean that marriage itself is *not* fundamental to our life in the new covenant in the way it was under the old Sinai covenant of the Old Testament. This is a freeing truth that has exciting theological implications.

The Sufficiency of Christ for the Covenant Blessings

In the Sinai covenant, being married and having offspring played a fundamental role in fulfilling the blessings of the covenant. Moreover, as the narrative of Ruth aptly illustrates, the messianic seed itself was to come through the physical procreation of individual Israelites. Physical procreation was the divinely ordained means by which God in his appointed time was going to ultimately bless the world through the provision of his Son. In the new covenant the picture is different. All the blessings of the new covenant come to us through Christ. He is the sufficient source. All other material blessings of creation—whether the blessings of food, clothing, shelter, monetary provision, healthy bodies, marriage, family, and even life itself—all these utterly *pale* in comparison to *the* blessings that God has given to us in Christ. These blessings include our full and complete reconciliation to God himself and our glorious inheritance as members of his eternal kingdom. Nothing, and I mean *nothing*, can remotely compare with the glory and weight of these new covenant blessings. To suggest that to be a fulfilled or complete Christian in the new covenant requires anything *more* than Christ is to deny the fundamental sufficiency of Christ as the sole vehicle of covenantal blessing.

Some explanation is needed regarding what we *don't* mean. We are not saying that all else in creation save our relationship with Christ is to be disparaged as worthless, of no value. Nor are we suggesting that health, marriage, children, family, wealth, career, and so on are not also blessings of God. Every good gift comes to us from God alone (James 1:17). What we are saying is that if, heaven forbid, we should lose our health, marriage, wealth, or whatever, we are no less fully blessed in Christ as children of the new covenant and fully anticipating an imperishable inheritance awaiting us in his kingdom. And if we should never find a spouse, or find ourselves unable to produce a child or stricken prematurely with a terminal illness, we are no less blessed of God *in Christ*. Unlike the Sinai covenant, in the new covenant barrenness is not a sign of reproach or disobedience. Single persons, whether "eunuchs" by birth, social convention, or personal choice, are no less blessed as participants in the new covenant than those with the sweetest marriage and a "quiverful" of children and grandchildren.

Looked at positively as a celebration of the complete sufficiency of Christ, singleness can be a powerful witness for the gospel. Whereas in Judaism, Islam, and Mormonism being married and having children are expected norms, in Christianity they are not. In choosing a life of singleness for the sake of kingdom service, one can freely demonstrate the complete sufficiency of Christ for being a fully blessed member of the new covenant, despite being without the fulfillment of a spouse and children. This is not to say that every Christian single person consciously sees his or her singleness in this way. Christian marriages can similarly be a powerful tool for proclaiming the gospel when the husband and wife respectively seek to model their marriage in the pattern of Christ and the church described in Ephesians 5. But not every Christian spouse consciously does so. Likewise, one's singleness can be a powerful testimony to the sufficiency of Christ for all things when one realizes and lives out this covenantal truth. Not every single person consciously does so, but the opportunity remains.

The Opportunity for Spiritual Offspring

An intriguing question then arises: did Paul see himself, ostensibly unmarried and without issue, in the pattern of the barren woman bearing spiritual children on behalf of the suffering servant? Our first clue occurs immediately in the context of the Galatians passage we just examined. Only two verses prior to that passage, Galatians 4:19, Paul speaks of the Galatians as "my little children, for whom I am again in the anguish of childbirth until Christ is formed in you."

Such language is not unique in Paul's epistles. Paul uses similar begetting language in 1 Corinthians to distinguish his authority over other teachers within the church: "For though you have countless guides in Christ, you do not have many fathers. For I *begat* you in Christ Jesus through the gospel" (4:15, AT). He writes to admonish them as children (v. 14), as the Corinthians were yet "infants" and not ready for the solid food that he would give them (3:1–2). In his second letter he exhorts them as "children" to open their affections for him (6:12–13) and acknowledges his financial relationship with them as that of parents to children (12:14).

Both male and female imagery is used in the case of the Thessalonians to whom he speaks: "We were gentle among you, like a nursing mother taking care of her own children" (1 Thess. 2:7). Subsequently he describes his exhortation and encouragement to them as "a father with his children" (v. 11). Paul felt orphaned from them in his great desire to see them (v. 17), for they were his "crown of boasting," his spiritual legacy before the Lord in his coming, and, as his spiritual progeny, they were his "glory and joy" (vv. 19–20).

Paul speaks of spiritually begetting and parenting individuals as well as churches. To Philemon Paul appeals, "For my child, Onesimus, whom I begat in my imprisonment" (Philem. 10). Timothy is addressed similarly as "my legitimate or lawfully begotten child in the faith" (1 Tim. 1:2), "my beloved child" (2 Tim. 1:2), "my beloved and faithful child in the Lord" (1 Cor. 4:17), and "you then, my child" (2 Tim. 2:1).[37] Likewise, Titus is referred to as "my lawfully begotten child in a common faith" (Titus 1:4).

Did Paul have children of his own? Lots of them: Timothy, Titus, and Onesimus, to name a few, and whole churches of followers of Jesus Christ. We too, like Paul, are called to be spiritual parents. Not only in begetting children through the gospel but in raising them in the nurture and admonition of the Lord until they too are mature disciples. Paul's letters to his churches are examples of his parenting of his young churches. And, like Isaiah's barren woman, Paul's legacy was greater than that of any physical parents, for Paul's progeny were those begotten in Christ through the limitless power of the gospel for an eternal inheritance in heaven.

5

The King and the Kingdom

Jesus' Surprising Statements on Singleness and Family

I have always been amazed by Jesus' apt use of images, illustrations, and stories to make his points. Yet, having heard many of Jesus' stories and illustrations so many times, I have come to think that we often become desensitized to the original shock value of what Jesus actually *says*. Think of Jesus' parable of the good Samaritan in Luke 10:25–37. We call it that because the Samaritan in the parable is selfless and generous. We may in turn use the label, "a good Samaritan," for anybody in our world who responds kindly and generously to others.

But we often neglect to recall the extreme antipathy Jews and Samaritans had for each other. Nor do we observe that in the chapter before the parable in Luke's Gospel, Jesus and his disciples were rejected by a Samaritan village, and James and John asked Jesus for permission to call down fire from heaven to utterly consume the Samaritans (Luke 9:21–56). When Jesus asked the inquiring lawyer which of the three men who had passed by the stricken man proved to be a neighbor, the lawyer did not name the Samaritan outright but only referred to him as "the one who showed him mercy" (Luke 10:37). Much of the shock value of the story involves the degree of antipathy the original hearers had for Samaritans. If even the utterly despised Samaritan treated a Jew in distress as his neighbor, could anyone in need not also be their neighbor?

In this chapter we will see that much of what the Gospel writers recorded for us of Jesus' teaching fully resonates with the new-covenant paradigm shift that we considered in the previous two chapters. Here, we will focus especially on Jesus' discussion of birth and new birth in the kingdom. We will also examine Jesus' direct teaching on the topic of singleness in two key texts: Matthew 19:10–12 and Luke 20:34–36. We shall then proceed to a brief look at a number of Jesus' surprising statements on family and new family and contemplate whether Jesus was a "family man." In this chapter we want to listen afresh to some of Jesus' teachings on the topic of singleness, marriage, and family and to appreciate anew some of the surprising statements he made and how these may have been heard originally. In the process we will begin to see how Jesus' teaching on these various topics fits together in a logical way. The chapter will conclude with some reflection on the patterns evidenced in the whole.

Jesus on Birth and Procreation
The New Birth

The language of birth used to describe one's entrance into the new covenant is not unique in the New Testament to Paul's letter to the Galatians. Titus 3:5 refers to the "washing of rebirth" (*palingenesia*), while James 1:18 concurs that God "of his own choice gave birth to us through the word of truth."[1] Peter uses the Greek word meaning "to beget again" (*anagennaō*) two different places in his first epistle (1:3, 23). The short book of 1 John makes no less than eight references to being "born of God" (see 1 John 2:29; 3:9; 4:7; 5:1, 4, 18), as a metaphor for genuine Christian conversion. The frequent appeal to this distinctive metaphor by various New Testament writers suggests all the more strongly that it recalls language that Jesus himself used in his encounter with Nicodemus (John 3).[2] It is no doubt this encounter with Nicodemus that provides the defining text on the concept.

Nicodemus was a Jew of eminent credentials. He was not only a teacher and a Pharisee but also a "ruler of the Jews" (John 3:1, 10)—a member of the ruling class of Jewish elders known as the Sanhedrin. He was part of the ruling elite, the pinnacle of authority and stature in the Jewish community of first-century Palestine. From the standpoint of the Jewish Sinai covenant, he had every reason for being confident that he was a member of God's covenant people and could anticipate being part of the eventual vindication of God's people in the eschatological age. There was apparently some interest on Nicodemus's part in Jesus' teaching or "signs," which caused him to come to Jesus at night to question him further. Was this man Jesus a mere pious rabbi, a prophet, or the coming Messiah expected to usher in the vindication of God's people? Nicodemus approached him with deference and caution, addressing him not as a peer rabbi but as a teacher who had "come from God."[3] Jesus responded, in turn, with a surprising declaration to launch the discussion:

> "Truly, truly, I say to you, unless one is born again he cannot see the kingdom of God." Nicodemus said to him, "How can a man be born when he is old? Can he enter a second time into his mother's womb and be born?" Jesus answered, "Truly, truly, I say to you, unless one is born of water and the Spirit, he cannot enter the kingdom of God. That which is born of the flesh is flesh, and that which is born of the Spirit is spirit. Do not marvel that I said to you, 'You must be born again.' The wind blows where it wishes, and you hear its sound, but you do not know where it comes from or where it goes. So it is with everyone who is born of the Spirit." (John 3:3–8)

Nicodemus probably lacked a cognitive category for Jesus' assertion that he needed to be born *again* in order to see the kingdom of God. For a first-century Jew with the convictions of Nicodemus, to "see the kingdom of God" meant not only seeing the consummation of God's kingly rule but participating in the world to come and experiencing the resurrection life.[4] Moreover, all Jews had a part in the world to come unless they were explicitly excluded.[5] The Jewish Mishnah makes this explicit:

> All Israelites have a share in the world to come, for it is written, "Thy people also shall be all righteous, they shall inherit the land for ever; the branch of my planting, the work of my hands that I may be glorified."[6]

Jewish tradition thus presumed that all Israelites were to share in the world to come and were to "inherit the land forever."

Jesus' statement would have been completely unanticipated and indeed shocking to Nicodemus, for he was calling into question a fundamental Jewish presumption: apart from a few dishonorable exceptions, participation in the world to come was an entitlement of Jewish birth. For postexilic Jews having lost the original land of Israel, to share in the world to come was another way that God's material land promise to Abraham could yet be fulfilled. They were to be vindicated as righteous and were to "inherit the land forever." But Jesus redirects this entitlement to those of a different birth—those born *again*. The Greek word used here, *anōthen*, is an adverb that can mean either "again" or "from above." Elsewhere in his Gospel John seems to use it exclusively to mean "from above," but here both meanings could be in view: one needed to be born a second time, by being born "from above."[7] Jesus' surprising statement to such a high-ranking Jew is that the promise to Abraham and his offspring of inheriting the land was not an entitlement of Abraham's physical offspring but to those who were born *anōthen*.

Nicodemus's response (John 3:4) indicates that he had no working category for Jesus' statement.[8] He interpreted *anōthen* to mean literally being born again and responded that it is physically impossible for a grown man to reenter his mother's womb. His painstakingly literalistic interpretation of Jesus' words reveals at very least his confusion (v. 10) and disbelief at Jesus' statement (v. 12) but perhaps even a degree of scorn.[9]

Jesus then repeats the pronouncement (v. 5), but this time he rephrases "born *anōthen*" with "born of water and spirit,"[10] and "see the kingdom of God" with "enter the kingdom of God." The substitutions both emphasize his point and remove potential ambiguities. One must be born *differently*, that is "of water and spirit," in order to enter into the kingdom of God. The reference to "water and spirit" vividly recalls Ezekiel's eschatological vision of God's people:

> I will sprinkle clean water on you, and you shall be clean from all your uncleannesses, and from all your idols I will cleanse you. And I will give you a new heart, and a new spirit I will put within you. And I will remove the heart of stone from your flesh and give you a heart of flesh. And I will put my Spirit within you, and cause you to walk in my statutes and be careful to obey my rules. (Ezek. 36:25–27)

The imagery of the sprinkling of water also recalls baptism and John the Baptist's statement, "I have baptized you with water, but *he* will baptize you with the Holy Spirit" (Mark 1:8).[11] As both Ezekiel and John the Baptist recognized, full conversion required not only the repentance of one's sin symbolized by the cleansing water but also a changed heart through the agency of God's Spirit.

In John 3:6 Jesus clarifies that he is making a fundamental distinction between two different kinds of birth, and here the dichotomy parallels Paul's dichotomy of flesh and spirit in Galatians 4:29. Jesus' statement is blunt: "That which is born of the flesh is flesh, and that which is born of the Spirit is spirit," but two distinctions are apparent. First, the *nature* of the new life—one is physical and the other spiritual. Second, the *bearer* of the new life is different. While human flesh gives birth to human flesh, it is the Spirit, namely, God's Holy Spirit, that gives birth to spirit. This birth occurs only by divine provision and agency.

In John 3:8 Jesus offers a further illustration. Here he makes use of a wordplay in Greek. *Pneuma* can mean either "spirit" or "wind." Just as we see evidence of the wind (*pneuma*) that blows (*pneō*) without knowing either where it comes from or where it goes, so too we see evidence of those *born* of the spirit (*pneuma*) without being able to explain how it came to be so.

Jesus makes clear Nicodemus's lack of understanding at this point: "Are you the teacher of Israel and yet you do not understand these things?" (John 3:10). This bit of situational irony reinforces Jesus' stated point—the new birth is neither an entitlement of human birth or credentials nor an act of human will. It is the work of God's Spirit and God's will alone. Human beings can see the effects of the Spirit, but they cannot control its movement. Nicodemus's Jewish pedigree and outstanding credentials did not entitle him to the inheritance of the kingdom of God. He had to be born "from above," regenerated by the Spirit of God.

As with Paul, the new birth for John comes through one's identification with God's physical son, Jesus, through faith in him. As John clarifies, God has provided the world with his unique, only begotten Son, such that whoever exercises faith, or believes,[12] in him shall have eternal life (John 3:16). As John describes it, Jesus is the uniquely begotten, physical offspring of God, but to all who receive him and believe in his name, God also gives the right to become "children of God" who are "born of God" (John 1:12–13). Thus, through believing in the name of *the begotten* offspring of God, we too become born into God's family as his children. Paul uses language of adoption to distinguish the Christian's relationship to God as *son* from Jesus' unique relationship to God as *Son*.[13] John refers to Christians as *children* of God and to Jesus as the *only begotten* Son of God. The language is different but the concept is the same.

What our brief foray into the Gospel of John shows is that Paul's paradigm shift resonates with the language and teaching of Jesus himself. For Jesus, like Paul, the fundamental contrast is one of *birth*. Though physical birth could assure one's Jewish status as a physical descendant of Abraham, this was not sufficient for entering into the ultimate inheritance of the kingdom of God. Rather, it was necessary for one to be born from above into spiritual new life through the agency of God's Spirit. This was offered to those who believe in Jesus and abide in him and his Word, bearing fruit and thereby authenticating their status as Jesus' true disciples. While Jesus does not use explicit "offspring" language to describe his disciples' relationship with him, all the fundamental conceptual ingredients are present. The disciple is modeled after his teacher and seeks to be like him in thought, word, and deed. As Jesus' followers seek to emulate him and be fully his disciples, they are his children indeed.

The New Mandate

Although the New Testament never explicitly reiterates the Genesis creation mandate to "be fruitful and multiply," it does recognize that it is the pattern of the present created age to marry and have children (Matt. 19:4–5; 24:37–78; Luke 20:34). But unlike what appears in later rabbinic sources,[14] the New Testament does not interpret the mandate given to Adam, Noah, and Jacob as a divine imperative impingent upon all. Nor are traditional marriage, procreation, and material prosperity explicitly associated with covenantal blessing in the new covenant. Instead, the central message of the New Testament is in proclaiming the good news of the coming kingdom of God (Mark 1:15).

Jesus' primary concern in his ministry is not to provide a prescription for living well in the land but to bestow spiritual life—a new life in the Spirit that is eternal life. Such new spiritual formation is the process of becoming Jesus' disciple. Hence, though in the New Testament we are not given any explicit mandate to marry and procreate physical human beings, we are given a new mandate to create more spiritual human beings, disciples in the form of Jesus as we find in the words of Matthew's Great Commission:

> Go therefore and make disciples of all nations, baptizing them in the name of the Father and of the Son and of the Holy Spirit, teaching them to observe all that I have commanded you. And behold, I am with you always, to the end of the age. (Matt. 28:19–20)

The gospel mandate is not distinctive to Matthew but reverberates through the New Testament (Luke 10:1–2; John 20:31; Acts 1:8; 15:7; Col. 1:23; 2 Tim. 4:5; Rev. 14:6). Likewise, it is not Jesus' task alone but one which he commissions to his disciples. Disciples are to make disciples. Paul exhorts his converts to imitate him as he, in turn, imitates Christ (1 Cor. 4:16; 11:1; 1 Thess. 1:6; 2 Thess. 3:7–9). Like the barren woman of Isaiah, they too are to produce spiritual offspring in the pattern of the Offspring, servants in the pattern of the Servant. It is with this in mind that we turn to Jesus' surprising statements on singleness and marriage.

Jesus on Singleness

One of the challenges of theological inquiry is that what the Bible chooses to discuss does not necessarily correspond to the questions that we bring to it to answer. Scripture is concerned with its own purpose and questions, questions that may not be the same ones vexing us at the particular moment we look to it for answers. Should we desire to reflect theologically on the subject of singleness, marriage, or anything else, we face the immediate constraint of working with limited and occasional sources. Where we look for Paul's general principles on marriage and singleness, we find only his response to a particular Corinthian situation. How and what we generalize from first-century Corinth to our own context becomes our challenge.

Jesus' teaching on the topic of singleness is no different. What he says is limited and occurs in the context of other discussions about other questions. Two occasions where the topic arises are found in Matthew 19:10–12 in the context of a discussion on the topic of marriage and

divorce, and in Luke 20:34–36 in the context of a discussion on the resurrection. While neither is a systematic treatment, both provide windows
into Jesus' thinking on the subject.

Eunuchs for the Kingdom

The eunuch *logion* recorded in Matthew 19:10–12 includes the most
direct instruction of Jesus' in the New Testament on the topic of singleness. However, it is a text often sidelined by Protestant interpreters.[15]
Although only Matthew records it, the eunuch reference serves as the
concluding point of a larger pericope on marriage and divorce that occurs
in both Matthew 19:3–12 and Mark 10:2–12. Three aspects of this text
are important for drawing out its theological implications: (1) the discussion that precedes the *logion*; (2) the figure of the eunuch that Jesus uses
to make his point; and (3) the inherent logic within Jesus' response.

The Discussion

The setting for the discussion occurs in the context of a question on
divorce, presented to Jesus by the Pharisees, intended to lure him into a
running legal debate between two sects of Pharisees, the Shammaites and
the Hillelites, regarding the legal grounds for divorce given by Moses.[16]
"Is it," the Pharisees ask, "lawful to divorce one's wife for *any* cause?"[17]
Jesus does not take the bait but instead redirects the focus to the creation
account. His response, "Have you not read . . . ?" may imply a slight
chastisement that they were centering their discussion on Moses' exceptional allowances rather than on God's intended design for marriage in
creation. Jesus instead appeals to the authority of God's original design
by juxtaposing the creation of gender in Genesis 1 with the "one flesh"
pronouncement in Genesis 2:

> Have you not read that he who created them from the beginning made
> them male and female, and said, "Therefore a man shall leave his father
> and his mother and hold fast to his wife, and the two shall become
> one flesh"? So they are no longer two but one flesh. (Matt. 19:4b–6a)

Since God created them *male* and *female* (Gen. 1:27), *therefore* a man
shall join his wife, and they shall become "one flesh" (Gen. 2:24). Jesus

follows the citation of the Genesis account with his pronouncement on the matter: "What therefore God has joined together, let not man separate" (Matt. 19:6b). Jesus' response sets up an antithesis between God, the one who unites, and the married man, who all too frequently in Jesus' day was the one who separated the marriage God had joined together.[18]

In a bit of situational irony, the Pharisees seek to turn the discussion back to divorce: "Why then did Moses command one to give a certificate of divorce and to send her away?" (Matt. 19:7). Jesus' response reinforces his chastising antithesis: "Because of your hardness of heart Moses allowed you to divorce your wives, but from the beginning it was not so." Jesus then gives a second pronouncement:

> And I say to you: whoever divorces his wife, except for sexual immorality, and marries another, commits adultery. (Matt. 19:9)

Divorce and remarriage for any reason except "sexual immorality" equates to adultery.[19] Jesus opts for a much higher standard of marriage than any of his listeners had expected. The design of creation testifies to the truth that marriage is a union established by God himself, and man is not to "separate" it.

After Jesus' second pronouncement on marriage and divorce, Matthew recounts a secondary mini-discussion between Jesus and his disciples about marriage, a discussion found only in his Gospel:

> The disciples said to him, "If such is the case of a man with his wife, it is better not to marry." But he said to them, "Not everyone can receive this saying, but only those to whom it is given. For there are eunuchs who have been so from birth, and there are eunuchs who have been made eunuchs by men, and there are eunuchs who have made themselves eunuchs for the sake of the kingdom of heaven. Let the one who is able to receive this receive it." (Matt. 19:10–12)

This stark pronouncement caused the disciples to recoil and respond with an immediate objection that if "such is the case" with marriage, it is better not to marry at all.[20] In other words, such a high view of the permanency of marriage with virtually no legitimate ground given for a man to terminate the relationship (not many Jewish wives were prone to sins of sexual immorality) raises the question of whether it is beneficial or advantageous for a man to commit to marriage in the first place.

Although some commentators have read this as a genuine proposition on the part of the disciples,[21] there is reason to believe that their response was intended to force Jesus to either back down on his extreme view on the indissolvability of marriage or conclude with them the untenable alternative that it *is* better not to marry. The disciples' statement corresponds to language commonly recognizable in the first-century Greco-Roman world as originating from the classic marriage debate among philosophers and rhetoricians. That debate concerned whether it was more advantageous for the wise man to marry or to remain single.[22]

But the context here is a debate *among Jews* over Jewish law, and there was *no* debate among Jewish legal experts about whether it was fitting or beneficial to marry, as rabbinic sources later confirm. Rabbi Eleazar is quoted as saying, "Any man who has no wife is no proper man; for it is said, Male and female created He them."[23] Rabbi Joshua confirms, "Do not say, 'I shall not get married,' but get married and produce sons and daughters and so increase procreation in the world."[24] Marriage was necessary in order to fulfill the command of the law to "be fruitful and multiply," one of the 613 recognized commandments of the Torah, and one required of every Jewish male.[25] Moreover, as we have seen, marriage and procreation were necessary for the reception of God's covenantal blessings. Deliberate avoidance of marriage was not only against God's law for the traditional law-observant Jew, but it was an outright rejection of God's covenantal blessings.

But such a strict view on divorce as Jesus was proposing in forbidding a man from divorcing his wife even for "pious" reasons, such as her infertility[26] or wickedness,[27] might force even a law-observant Jew into the Greco-Roman camp of thinking twice about marriage at all! That is why, if the disciples here were appealing to the Greco-Roman marriage debate, it was probably meant to compel Jesus to a more moderate and practical view.

This is not the only example where the disciples were so astonished by Jesus' words that they drew an extreme conclusion. They were also astonished at Jesus' pronouncement on how hard it is for a rich man to enter the kingdom of heaven (Matt. 19:24; Mark 10:25) and responded,

"Who then can be saved?" In other words, "If it is impossible for the elite, it is surely impossible for all!"

Jesus' response to the disciples in Matthew 19:11 is equally shocking. If the disciples ventured to think they had Jesus between a rock and a hard place, he was to surprise them once again. For rather than softening his prohibitive view of divorce, he responded by *commending* their statement on not marrying. The shock of his response may get missed by us now, being on the other side of hundreds of years of monastic tradition, but to Jewish ears it was shocking indeed![28] And if his tacit agreement with their proposal was not shocking enough, Jesus was going to add one more. He turned to the despicable figure of a eunuch to make his point.

The Figure of the Eunuch

Jesus' use of the eunuch figure in Matthew 19:12 to illustrate the point that it might be beneficial not to marry may have been an even greater shock to Jewish ears than the point itself. But the use of this figure could also have been a deliberate way to distance himself from a Greco-Roman-styled approach to the marriage question, as the image had no better reception in the Hellenistic world than it did in traditional Jewish circles.

We have already touched on the figure of the eunuch in chapter 3, but let us quickly recap the general disposition of Judaism toward eunuchs and emasculation. The Old Testament gives three explicit references to emasculation. Leviticus 21:20 bars any with physical defects, including "crushed testicles," from the priestly responsibilities of making offerings to God. Likewise, Leviticus 22:24 bars offering up any animal that has "its testicles bruised or crushed or torn or cut." Deuteronomy 23:1 prohibits any whose "testicles are crushed or whose male organ is cut off" from entering the worshiping "assembly."

Although the Old Testament does not explicitly forbid the practice of emasculation, Jewish interpretive tradition understood it to be forbidden. Some rabbis regarded the practice of emasculation to be a violation of the mandate in Genesis 1:28 to "be fruitful and multiply";[29] others spoke of it as prohibited in light of Deuteronomy 23:1;[30] and others regarded it among the precepts that God forbade to Noah in Genesis 9:1–7 (note the recurrence of "be fruitful and multiply" in 9:1, 7).[31] Josephus refers to castration as a Persian institution that "with us" is a capital crime, and other references in Jewish literature also refer to the prohibition.[32]

Of course, not all who were deemed eunuchs were so because of physical castration. The early rabbinic sources distinguished between those who were born eunuchs "by nature," that is, those who lacked the power to reproduce by nature, and those who had been emasculated as "man-made" eunuchs.[33]

Beyond the legal prohibition on physical castration, eunuchs, from whatever cause, were opportune subjects for ridicule within Judaism. Characteristic is the jeer Rabbi Joshua made to a eunuch who mocked him for his baldness:

> O eunuch, O eunuch, you have enumerated three things to me, [and now] you will hear three things: the glory of a face is its beard; the rejoicing of one's heart is a wife; the heritage of the Lord is children.[34]

From the Jewish perspective, the eunuch was devoid of the essential blessings that led to rejoicing in life: having a wife and children.

Beyond this, the eunuch forfeited his inheritance, and his name was to be "blotted out" of remembrance.[35] Since the eunuch had no family, he (and any man without children) was ineligible to serve on the Sanhedrin.[36] Eunuchs were associated with affliction from the Lord, since, like one afflicted, a eunuch who embraces a maiden can only groan.[37] Likewise, the threat of castration and being made into a eunuch by the Gentiles was regarded as potential punishment by the Lord for the sin of becoming involved in "revolting gentile affairs" of licentiousness and idolatry.[38]

Josephus also derides eunuchs in a comment upon Deuteronomy 23:1:

> Shun eunuchs [*gallos*] and flee all dealings with those who have deprived themselves of their virility and of those fruits of generation, which God has given to men for their increase of our race; expel them even as infanticides who withal have destroyed the means of procreation. For plainly it is by reason of the effeminacy of their soul that they have changed the sex of their body also. And so with all that would be deemed a monstrosity by the beholders. You shall castrate neither man nor beast."[39]

The word Josephus used for *eunuch* here is not the word typically used, *eunouchos*, but the more specific term, *gallos*, which was commonly used for eunuch priests of Cybele,[40] an oriental cult from Asia Minor that practiced celibacy. Josephus's language surely has in view those who practiced self-emasculation for the sake of cultic purposes.[41]

What we can detect in this quotation is that part of the reason eunuchs were held in disdain is the perception that they represented sexual ambiguity. They had manipulated the sex of their bodies and had become human monstrosities. Philo of Alexandria also comments on exclusion of eunuchs from the worshiping assembly in Deuteronomy 23:1, describing them as "men who belie their sex and are affected with effemination, who debase the currency of nature and violate it by assuming the passions and the outward form of licentious women."[42] Like Josephus, Philo also associates eunuchs with effeminacy and violation of nature. To the average Jew, the image of a eunuch was a reprehensible figure.

The perception of eunuchs among the Greeks and Romans was no better. To the Greeks the castration of living creatures was fundamentally alien.[43] Classicist David Hunt sums up the secular Hellenistic perspective: "To the classical world eunuchs were despised figures who haunted the courts of oriental monarchs."[44] Herodotus refers to castration as a "wicked practice" and gives the account of the eunuch Hermotimus, who extracted vengeance on Panionius, the man who castrated him and sold him into the court service of Xerxes, by forcing him to castrate his own sons and in turn be castrated by his sons.[45] Lucian of Samosata tells the story of a eunuch vying for a chair of philosophy in Athens who faced vituperation by one of his opponents, who claimed that it was "an ill-omened, ill-met sight if on first leaving home in the morning, one should set eyes on any such person." The opponent argues that eunuchs "ought to be excluded . . . from temples and holy-water bowls and all the places of public assembly."[46] Later Lucian describes the eunuch as "neither man nor woman but something composite, hybrid and monstrous, alien to human nature."[47]

One might have expected more respect for eunuchs in the setting of Greco-Roman cultic service, being that virgin priestesses were so highly respected. But religious castration was never a native practice among the purely Greek or Roman cults; it was an imported custom distinctive to Oriental cults that gradually infiltrated the Hellenistic world.[48] Hence, the personal sacrifice on the part of eunuch priests in these cults never managed to gain them much public respect. So while virgin priestesses were highly regarded in Greco-Roman culture, eunuch priests did not receive comparable respect but were instead prone to insults and maltreatment.[49]

Although they always faced a degree of public contempt, by Augustus's time eunuchs were used in the households of leading Romans, including the imperial court.[50] Claudius, Nero, Titus, and Domitian all had eunuch courtiers.[51] Herod the Great was very fond of eunuchs and had them not only managing his affairs of government but also bringing him supper and putting him to bed.[52] Josephus also had a eunuch as his son's tutor.[53] Despite the usefulness of eunuchs as household domestics, male castration was never a practice readily compatible with the ideals of Roman valor. By the end of the first century, Domitian (ca. AD 81) and Nerva (ca. AD 96) both enacted empire-wide prohibitions on the practice.[54]

Given the contempt toward eunuchs among Jews, Greeks, and Romans, for Jesus to use a eunuch to make his point about not marrying is truly surprising. Why would he use such an unsavory figure as an illustration? Jesus describes three categories of eunuchs; two were among those already distinguished in Judaism, but the third was unprecedented:

> There are eunuchs who have been so from birth [lit.: born that way from their mother's womb], and there are eunuchs who have been made eunuchs by men, and there are eunuchs who have made themselves eunuchs for the sake of the kingdom of heaven. (Matt. 19:12)

The first two categories consist of those made eunuchs involuntarily, as expressed through the passive verb, while the third, using the active reflexive verb, describes a class of voluntary eunuchs. It is the third category that Jesus wishes to highlight in light of his disciples' question, but he offers the other two categories for the sake of conceptual clarity. Had Jesus simply used the term *eunuch* to describe any individual who foregoes marriage, his listeners surely would have been confused, since they associated eunuchs only with the first two categories.

But even given that Jesus uses the eunuch to illustrate one who foregoes marriage for the sake of the kingdom of God, why would he choose such an unsavory figure to make his point? One reason relates to the broader use of the Greek word *eunouchos*, which, outside the New Testament, was used not only of men and castrated animals but also of fruits and plants that have no kernel or seed.[55] Dates without stones were called *eunouchos*, and a seedless melon was referred to with the related term *eunouchias*.[56] Domitian was accused of "eunuchizing (*eunouchizō*) the earth" when he passed a law forbidding the growth of vines.

The term essentially designated something devoid of reproductive seed. To "eunuchize" oneself was thus to deny oneself the right of reproduction of physical progeny. Therefore, in using the term *eunuch*, Jesus meant more than someone simply not marrying but rather one's setting aside the right of marriage and procreation. This is especially significant in light of the importance of offspring throughout the Old Testament and its association with covenantal blessing. Jesus is suggesting that there are *some* who will willingly give up the blessings of both marriage and offspring for the sake of the kingdom of God. Conversely, to be blessed in the kingdom of God no longer requires marriage and offspring.

Jesus' use of this term served an additional function of clearly distancing him from the Greco-Roman perspective on marriage; marriage was often declined simply on account of the troubles and stresses associated with having a wife and children.[57] But the connotation of making oneself a eunuch encompassed not merely abrogation of the formal commitment to marriage (in Greco-Roman style) but also *sexual abstinence*—something not generally associated with the marriage debate among the Hellenistic philosophical schools.[58] Thus, despite its unsavory associations, Jesus may have chosen the expression "made themselves eunuchs" because it conveys more fully the commitment being made. To eunuchize oneself entails more than simply not marrying but involves the sacrifice of one's right to marriage, procreation, and sexual relations, for the sake of the kingdom of God.

A third reason Jesus may have used the figure of the eunuch is hinted at in the reference to the "kingdom of heaven" (Matt. 19:12). As we noted earlier, eunuchs were known for their service in royal courts. The tradition dates back to the ninth-century Assyrians but was especially common under the Persian Achaemenean kings.[59] Though eunuchs are typically portrayed as royal domestics supervising the women's quarters (e.g., Est. 2:3), they also served in high-ranking roles as palace officials, statesmen, and military generals.[60] Mikeal Parsons sums up the eunuch's distinctive role:

> Eunuchs had great influence and power in the royal courts of Assyria and Persia because of their undivided loyalty to the reigning monarch. They were valued and needed because they had no family heirs (not, as in much popular thought because they posed no sexual "threat"). Only eunuchs could be trusted to stand outside the nepotism and intrigue created by the competition in the palaces among the many princelings. It was their lack of kinship heirs which made them the leading palace officials in Persian, Hellenistic, and Roman times.[61]

As Parsons points out, eunuchs were loyal because they had no family heirs. On the one hand, this ensured they were no threat to the king because they had no means of establishing their own dynasty. But it also meant that they were fully dependent on the king and the king's heirs since they had no heirs of their own to care for them in their old age. The eunuch staked his future in the survival of the king and his dynasty. If the dynasty was lost, so was the eunuch's future welfare.

The eunuch was also a model of devoted service because he was without the distractions of marriage and family. No personal family matters competed for his allegiances. He could afford complete, unhindered loyalty to his king and the king's concerns. The highest loyalty of the disciple of Jesus Christ is likewise to be to the kingdom of God (Matt. 6:33). Perhaps Jesus draws upon the figure of the eunuch to make his point precisely because the historical figure of the eunuch was a *paradigmatic model* of what such undivided loyalty to the king looked like in the ancient world.

It is remarkable that the Old Testament also gives us poignant examples of such eunuch-like devotion. As we saw in chapter 3, the most dramatic example is the figure of Daniel, who served as a eunuch in the court of Babylonian, Median, and Persian kings.[62] Despite Daniel's prominent rise to power, ultimately to second place in the kingdom (Dan. 6:1–3), he never comprised his devotion to the Lord through devotion to the earthly monarch in whose court he served. Nehemiah similarly risks his position as cupbearer before King Artaxerxes in order to follow the Lord in a mission to rebuild the walls of Jerusalem.

Jeremiah, as a prophet called by God to remain single without marriage or family (Jer. 16:1), also had access to the royal court of Judah. But unlike Daniel, Jeremiah knew from the very beginning that faithfulness to his prophetic call and service to the Lord was going to put him in a directly adversarial relationship with the royal court and that only God would ultimately rescue him (Jer. 1:17–19). Jeremiah recognized that faithfulness to his call was going to foster hostilities and repeatedly acknowledged to God, "To you have I committed my cause" (Jer. 11:20; 20:12).

There is another paradoxically eunuch-like Old Testament example in the figure of Joseph. This is argued in part by the Hellenistic Jewish writer Philo, who makes a number of perceptive observations in regard to the Genesis account of Joseph and Potiphar.[63] The irony of the Joseph situation is that it was Potiphar, not Joseph, who was designated by the Hebrew term *eunuch* (*saris*) in the Genesis account (Gen. 37:36; 39:1). Yet, as Philo observed, it was Potiphar who was married, and Joseph, the single man, who exhibited eunuch-like qualities in transcending his passions and resisting temptation to evil. Moreover, Joseph resisted the temptation to sexual immorality not merely because of his allegiance to Potiphar, but, more importantly, because it conflicted directly with his obedience to God (Gen. 39:9). As a result of his faithfulness, Joseph also eventually rose to become Pharaoh's deputy over the entire nation of Egypt, all the while maintaining his first allegiance to his own Lord and God.

Thus Daniel, Nehemiah, Jeremiah, and Joseph each in their distinctive way exhibited a positive example of eunuch or eunuch-like devotion to the Lord amidst their positions of power and access to the courts of powerful human kings.

Finally, Jesus may have found it fitting to appeal to the figure of the eunuch in respect to the marriage question simply because the eunuch is a redemptive figure. He is one who, according to Isaiah 56:3–5, has been given new hope of being restored into the eschatological covenant family of God and who will be given an inheritance within God's house and city with an eternal name better than sons and daughters. The Apocryphal Wisdom of Solomon makes the blessing implied in the Isaiah text explicit:

> Blessed also is the eunuch whose hands have done no lawless deed, and who has not devised wicked things against the Lord; for special favor will be shown him for his faithfulness, and a place of great delight in the temple of the Lord. (Wis 3:14 RSV)

The eunuch is blessed in his "faithfulness" to the Lord. He is blessed because he has an eternal inheritance in the temple of the Lord independent of children or family. He is a model of one lacking physical family yet being fully blessed, completely sufficient in the Lord to whom he is faithful. And if the despised eunuch has been redeemed and fully blessed, he is no longer a symbol of reproach and stigmatization. Rather, he is a positive model of undistracted and unfettered service to his Lord, all the while fully cognizant of his complete dependence upon the God he serves for the welfare of his future. Thus, he emerges not merely an example of one who has been redeemed from reproach, but one who becomes a positive model of emboldened dedicated service to God.

The Logic of Jesus' Response

Now that we have considered the figure of the eunuch in the ancient context and why Jesus may have appealed to the eunuch to make his point, we return to the logic of Jesus' surprising response to the disciples in Matthew 19:11–12. If we are correct in supposing the disciples' shocking conclusion was an attempt to get Jesus to qualify his words about marriage, then Jesus' response is also shocking—he conveyed tacit agreement with their conclusion. He says, "Not everyone can receive this saying, but only those to whom it is given."[64] The disciples had apparently uttered words beyond their understanding, and Jesus qualified their statement, showing on what grounds it indeed had validity.

The structure of Jesus' response in Matthew 19:11–12 consists of two qualifications with an extended explanatory clause supporting the first qualification:

Qualification 1:	"Not everyone can receive this saying, but only those to whom it is given."
Explanatory clause:	For there are three types of eunuchs . . .
Qualification 2:	"Let the one who is able to receive this receive it."

The Greek verb *chōreō*, translated "receive" in that dialog, typically connotes the idea of making room for something, holding or containing something in a physical sense (e.g., liquid, in John 2:6; or books, in John 21:25). But the word is also used figuratively of the ability to contain big or sublime ideas. Plutarch describes the group of senators who begged Cato that, "if they were not Catos and could not carry [*chōreō*] the large thoughts of Cato, to have pity on their weakness."[65] An aphorism of Pseudo-Phocylides records, "An untrained ear cannot grasp [*chōreō*] important teaching."[66] Josephus derided the historical Egyptians as those who were accustomed to erroneous ideas about the gods and "were incapable [*chōreō*] of imitating the solemnity of our theology."[67]

The examples suggest that the verb was used frequently on occasions in which an idea was so difficult or profound that it was beyond the full understanding of most. In Matthew 19, it is used to connote that indeed in some conditions it might be better not to marry at all. This also reinforces the conclusion that the disciples were not really serious about not marrying, because Jesus acknowledges the proposition is one not readily comprehended. In other words, the disciples had spoken truth beyond their understanding.

The two qualifications Jesus gives about the difficult idea are somewhat paradoxical. The first is that not all are able to contain or comprehend it, but only those to whom it has been given. In other words, some cannot comprehend it simply because they have not been given the means to do so. The understanding of anything and everything comes from God, and he reserves the right to choose those to whom he gives and those to whom he withholds (John 3:27).

The paradox that arises comes in the second qualification in the form of an imperative: the one who is able to grasp and comprehend it *should* grasp and comprehend it. Jesus suggests that it is a self-discerning process. It is given to me *if* and *only if* I can truly and wholeheartedly embrace it. But the imperative does not stop with the simple mental capacity to understand. The one who is truly able to comprehend it should also embrace it. To know what is good or better and not to do it is, in biblical terms, *not* to really know it (James 1:22; 4:17).

Finally, it is important that we not miss that Jesus differentiates between different kinds of eunuchs in his statement. The first two categories of eunuchs Jesus names are eunuchs involuntary, the third is voluntary. In our day there are some who remain single involuntarily while others do so voluntarily. As in Jesus' day, some today have congenital concerns that make marriage impossible or inadvisable. Others are single because of the lack of an available marriage partner.

However, just the condition of singleness is not what Jesus means by being a eunuch for the kingdom. A eunuch for the kingdom is voluntarily so for the sake of serving the King and the kingdom. Voluntary eunuchs are those who recognize that their assignment from God, whatever it is (and every Christian has one), can be better accomplished by remaining unmarried, whether for a select period or for a lifetime.[68]

This "service" covers a wide range of possibilities, from overseas mission assignments, to urban ministry, to a life devoted to Christian scholarship, to itinerant evangelism, to youth rehabilitation. At my former church there were single women who served as "pastoral nurses." They were free to attend, at almost any moment, the mesh of spiritual and physical needs of congregant shut-ins. Another church had volunteer "street pastors." They walked the city streets late on weekend nights to provide a Christian support brigade for the local police force. The eunuch for the kingdom is the one who voluntarily refrains from marriage and family so as to guard his or her freedom for the sake of serving the Lord in whatever way he should call.

Let us now sum up the whole of Jesus' logic in Matthew 19 with three propositions:

1) The idea that it may be better not to marry is a big idea that not all can embrace.
2) Though people may remain unmarried involuntarily (those born incapable of marriage and those not able to marry on account of the unavailability of a marriage partner), some will also willingly embrace foregoing marriage, children, and sexual relations for the sake of service to the kingdom of God.
3) Those who can embrace it should embrace it.

The practical challenge is in holding in proper tension Jesus' logic in these verses. We do so first by acknowledging that it is not better for everybody not to marry. Put positively, the prospect of remaining single and not marrying is a profound truth that not all can embrace. Second, those who can embrace singleness for the sake of the kingdom should do so. There is a genuine imperative to be heard. For some, remaining single for the sake of the kingdom is better than marriage, although for others, presumably most, it is not. The only way of determining the answer personally is through a process of self-discernment. The church must also practice such discernment, encouraging some toward marriage but not all, and likewise challenging those with the disposition to receive Jesus' challenge to embrace it for the kingdom.

Angels in Heaven

A second place where Jesus directly speaks to the question of marriage and singleness occurs in a response he gives to the Sadducees concerning their question about the resurrection of the dead. The pericope occurs in all three Synoptic Gospels (Matt. 22:23–33; Mark 12:18–27; Luke 20:27–40), but Luke's rendition is substantially more robust on the point of marriage and singleness in the resurrection. Jesus' words here would have been less shocking to his audience than what he had said about eunuchs, and some of the scribes even commend him for his words (Luke 20:39).

Apart from the Sadducees, there was already a strong current of belief in the resurrection within first-century Judaism (consider Dan. 12:2), and there is even some rabbinic corroboration for the expectation of a marriage-less resurrection.[69] Jesus' statements here are perhaps more difficult for those of us in the modern world, where relational intimacy, marriage, and the nuclear family are often given such elevated importance that it is difficult to imagine a resurrected existence without them.[70]

The context for Jesus' statements here is a question posed by the Sadducees concerning levirate marriage. The Sadducees were a sect that denied the resurrection (Luke 20:27), so their question is really no more than a carefully crafted attempt to construct an impossible conundrum for those who professed belief in it. The Sadducees propose a situation in which a woman had married a man with seven brothers. The man dies without children, and the woman, following the laws of levirate marriage

(Deut. 25:5), is given to the next brother, who then also dies without children. The pattern continues until all die, including the woman. So the Sadducees ask Jesus whose husband she will be in the resurrection, since she was married to all seven brothers.[71]

Jesus' response to the Sadducees' question is given by each of the three Gospel authors, shown in Table 5.1.

Table 5.1: Comparison of Jesus' Dialog on Marriage and Resurrection[72]

Matthew 22:30	Mark 12:25	Luke 20:34–36
For in the resurrection they **neither marry nor are given in marriage,** but are like **angels** in heaven.	For when they rise from the dead, they **neither marry nor are given in marriage,** but are like **angels** in heaven.	And Jesus said to them, "The sons of this age marry and are given in marriage, but those who are considered worthy to attain to that age and to the resurrection from the dead **neither marry nor are given in marriage,** for they cannot die anymore, because they are equal to **angels** and are sons of God, being sons of the resurrection.

Matthew and Mark simply state that in the resurrection there is no longer marriage. Luke, however, contrasts the "sons of *this* age" and those "worthy to attain to *that* age," who are also designated "sons of God" and "sons of the resurrection."[73] These he explains in a syllogism:

They neither marry nor are given in marriage
For they cannot die anymore
    Because
        They are equal to the angels
        They are sons of God
        They are sons of the resurrection

Though Matthew and Mark merely describe life in the resurrection as "like" (*hōs*) that of the angels, Luke clarifies the nature of the similarity: those worthy to attain to that age cannot die anymore, and metaphysically they shall be like angels as "sons of God." Paul refers to Christians in this life as "sons of God" (Rom. 8:14; Gal. 3:26) through adoption (Rom. 8:15; Gal. 4:5), although he also speaks of a yet future consummated sonship that will be realized in the redemption of our bodies (Rom. 8:19–23). But Luke is probably drawing on the long-standing identification of "sons of God" as supernatural beings, identified in the Old Testament as angels (see, e.g., Job 1:6; 2:1; 38:7).[74]

Luke's major point is that the metaphysical comparison with angels is to support the premise that those in the resurrection do not die anymore. The unstated logical link between marriage and death must be that marriage is necessary only for procreation, which, in turn, is necessary only on account of the mortality of humankind. Those who are "sons of the resurrection" are like angels, who do not die and in turn have no need for procreation or marriage.

What can be slightly disconcerting for us today is that the implication appears to reduce the necessity, and, in fact, the entire purpose of marriage, to nothing more than procreation for the sake of preserving the human race from extinction. There is no mention of the importance of relationship, of being created male and female, of help and mutual assistance between spouses, of the joys of human intimacy, or of the gospel witness of the new covenant modeled in marital faithfulness. Are we to envision life in the resurrection as not much more than an ascetic existence that does without all the created pleasures of this age?[75]

Indeed, the new heaven and new earth may lack many of the pleasures of this age, but that does not imply we will be living a life of denial or even giving a momentary thought to anything of this earthly existence that we have left behind. What we do know is that Jesus has promised he is preparing a place for us (John 14:2–3), where "we shall see him as he is" (1 John 3:2) and that "no eye has seen, nor ear heard, nor the heart of man imagined, what God has prepared for those who love him" (1 Cor. 2:9). The fact that there is no marriage in heaven speaks not to the paucity of our future existence but to the greatness of our God. For no earthly or human relationship we can or ever will experience will stand even as a momentary flicker of a candle in comparison to experiencing the blazing sun of our heavenly existence before the presence of our almighty God.

There is sometimes a tendency, especially among the idealistic young who presume to have most of their years yet before them, that singleness is a temporary period of one's life until one finds an eternal soul mate in marriage. This passage is a reminder that in the scope of eternity the opposite is actually the case; marriage is for a season and time, until, as the traditional marriage vow reads, "death do us part." It is as single and free individuals that we will stand before his throne and live for all eternity.

Jesus on Family

The New Family

In an age in which evangelical Christianity has been strongly identified with the politically active "family values movement," Jesus' statements in reference to family relationships sometimes seem surprising. On the one hand, for example, Jesus explicitly upholds the fifth commandment to "honor your father and your mother" (Ex. 20:12; Deut. 5:16), when speaking to the rich young ruler (Matt. 19:19; Mark 19:19; Luke 18:20); and he chastises the Pharisees for creating a loophole around the command and "thus making void the word of God" by their tradition (Mark 7:13; Matt. 15:6). Jesus responds by citing both the Decalogue and another more condemnatory reference from the law: "Whoever reviles father or mother must surely die" (Ex. 21:17; Lev. 20:9, AT). Ironically, while it is the Pharisees who accuse Jesus' disciples of not living "according to the tradition of the elders" (Mark 7:5), it is they who have departed from the most fundamental commandment of such tradition in not giving honor to their parents.

Other statements Jesus makes seem to redefine the very nature of family. The three Synoptic Gospels record a particular instance when Jesus was ministering to the crowd, and his mother and brother came to him and attempted to speak with him (Matt. 12:46–50; Mark 3:31–35; Luke 8:19–21). We do not know precisely what his family wished to discuss with him in the brief episode; however, Mark provides what may be a clue a few verses earlier. Mark places the episode early in Jesus' ministry, soon after he had called the twelve disciples. Jesus had entered a house, apparently for a meal, when a crowd gathered so that they could not eat (Mark 3:20). Apparently something of a furor developed, as Mark records that when his family heard about it, they went to seize him, for they were saying, "He is out of his mind" (v. 21).

At very least we can conclude that most of his immediate family did not (yet) believe in who he was—a fact that John makes explicit about Jesus' brothers (John 7:5). It would seem that his family was concerned about the notoriety and social disruption he was causing and wanted to have a word with him in hopes of settling him down. It is Jesus' pronouncement that is the point of the episode. After being told that his mother and brothers were outside seeking him, he looked at those around him and responded, "Here are my mother and my brothers! For whoever does the will of God, he is my brother and sister and mother" (Mark 3:34–35). Matthew emphasizes that Jesus was referring to his disciples in the statement.

Jesus' point is dramatic. In his disciples and in those to whom and with whom he was ministering is a new family that takes precedence over his physical family. The relational bond of Jesus with his ministry family was stronger than that with his physical family.

After being told by Jesus how hard it is for the rich to enter the kingdom of God, it is Peter, one disciple we know was married at the time of Jesus' ministry (Mark 1:30), who comments to Jesus, "See, we have left everything and followed you." Jesus responds:

> Truly, I say to you, there is no one who has left house or brothers or sisters or mother or father or children or lands, for my sake and for the gospel, who will not receive a hundredfold now in this time, houses and brothers and sisters and mothers and children and lands, with persecutions, and in the age to come eternal life. (Mark 10:28–30; cf. Matt. 19:28–29; Luke 18:29–30)

Surprising in Jesus' response is not just that he promises for any who leave house or family for his sake a future heavenly reward (cf. Matt 19:29: "inheriting eternal life"), but that they will have a hundredfold "now in this time." In other words, Jesus promises that whoever is forced by the call of the gospel to forsake home and family will also receive a new one, though "with persecutions."

Luke also adds "wife" to the list; that is, "house or *wife* or brothers or parents or children . . . " The point Jesus makes is not that following him necessarily means renouncing our family, but in case it should do so, one is not to let that be a hesitation from following him, since in following him one can anticipate new family relationships that supersede the old. The New Testament does not indicate that Peter permanently left his wife and family in order to follow Jesus,[76] but Peter himself felt like he had done so when he makes the statement to Jesus, "See, we have left all that is ours and followed you" (Luke 18:28, AT). The Greek verb translated "left," *aphiēmi*, in all three Gospels is also vocabulary used for divorce (e.g., 1 Cor. 7:11).

Luke is perhaps the strongest of the three Synoptic writers on the divided loyalties between one's physical family and one's new spiritual family in following Jesus. It is Luke that uses the language of "hate" to convey the magnitude of the contrast: "If anyone comes to me and does not *hate* his own father and mother and wife and children and brothers and sisters, yes, and even his own life, he cannot be my disciple" (Luke 14:26; cf. Matt. 10:37). Similarly, only Luke mentions Jesus' rebuke of the disciple who agrees to follow him but first wishes to return and say farewell to those at home (Luke 9:61–62).

Luke also makes explicit that Jesus' message brings not peace but potential division with families, "three against two and two against three" (Luke 12:51–53; also Matt. 10:34–36). It is the parable of the great banquet in Luke 14:15–24 that mentions marriage as one of the excuses for not attending: "I have married a wife, and therefore I cannot come" (Luke 14:20). Jesus' recurring message appears to be that the traditional commitments of marriage, home, and family never provide legitimate grounds for not responding to the call of discipleship. The ultimate bond of the *new family* through the gospel is even stronger than that of one's physical earthly family.

There are narrative episodes that also speak of the priority of the new family over the physical family but in more subtle ways.

> A woman in the crowd raised her voice and said to him, "Blessed is the womb that bore you, and the breasts at which you nursed!" But he said, "Blessed rather are those who hear the word of God and keep it!" (Luke 11:27–28)

One can readily identify with the woman's outburst. There is little more satisfying to a parent than to see a son or daughter turn out well. How all the more blessed is the mother of Jesus for bearing and raising him. As we have seen, children were, for the Old Testament Israelites, not only material blessings but covenantal blessing. Jesus seizes the moment here to offer a corrective. True blessing is ultimately not to be found in having children and a family (even having perfect children like Jesus!), but rather in truly hearing the word of God and keeping it. Therefore, the fount of true blessing is not to be found in the traditional values of having a great (physical) family, as good, satisfying, rich, and rewarding as that can be (and it can be!). Rather, true blessing is ultimately found in righteousness before God and in having a right relationship with him—it is what Jesus was about to offer and accomplish for sinful people through his atoning death on the cross. True blessing is righteous standing before a righteous God and sharing in the community of the saints in an eternal inheritance before his throne (Rev. 5:13). Here alone is where ultimate blessing is to be found.

Another surprising statement of Jesus' occurs when he is on the cross. John records that when Jesus saw his mother and the disciple "whom Jesus loved," presumably John himself, standing nearby, Jesus spoke to his mother, "Woman, behold, your son!" and to his disciple, "Behold, your mother!" The disciple then took her into his own home (John 19:26). The statement obviously points to Jesus' care for his mother. It is strange, given that Jesus had four brothers as well as sisters (Mark 6:3), that he committed Mary to the care of John. Jesus' point may well have been that the new familial bond between Mary and John as two disciples now superseded physical family relationships. It had become more appropriate for Mary to regard John as her son than her physical sons. The new family was taking precedence over the old.

A final episode that also may allude to the priority of the new family over the old family is the narrative in Luke 10:38–42, where Mary and Martha welcome Jesus into their home for a meal. While Martha was pre-occupied with preparations for the meal—fulfilling the domestic duties typical to the role of women—Mary was sitting at Jesus' feet, a role typi-cally reserved for men, listening to his teaching. Rather than affirming the traditional values and traditional roles, as Martha expected of Jesus when she complained, Jesus surprised her in commending Mary for choosing what is better, literally, "the good part." The tension here is between what exemplified the traditional role of a woman and what exemplified true discipleship.

Regardless of whether one is male or female, being a disciple of

Jesus and part of his new family takes precedence over the traditional responsibilities of the traditional family. The characterization of Martha as "distracted" (*perispaō*) and "anxious" (*merimnaō*) with domestic affairs anticipates Paul's discussion of singleness in 1 Corinthians 7:32–35, where similar vocabulary is used to contrast those who are married and those who are single. The married are anxious about the things of this world whereas the single person is anxious for the things of the Lord. Paul encourages them to remain single that they might serve the Lord "undistractedly" (*aperispastōs*). The contrast of competing anxieties and distractions Paul describes is embodied in the respective preoccupations of Mary and Martha.

Jesus as a Family Man

Was Jesus himself a "family man"? The answer depends on what we mean by "family." There is no record of Jesus ever having a wife or children. He appears to have embodied in his own life and ministry the "eunuch for the kingdom" that he describes in Matthew 19:12. Conversely, Jesus never denigrates the family and had a high view of marriage and respect for one's parents as divine principles to be obeyed. He continually invests himself in his "new family" of disciples. In many respects Jesus was a "family man" as he defined it.

Though Jesus never had wife or children, his life was never detached from his new family. Jesus had concentric circles of relationships. His innermost circle included only three disciples: Peter, James, and John. John in his Gospel refers repeatedly to "the disciple whom Jesus loved," which traditionally has been thought of as a reference to John himself.[77] The next circle were the twelve disciples, who accompanied Jesus during his ministry period in Galilee and traveled with him to Jerusalem (Luke 18:31). Luke 10:1 speaks of seventy-two others, who were apparently part of a yet wider social network.

Others appear relationally connected to Jesus on a less formal basis. Luke 8:1–3 indicates that a large group of women (including Mary Magdalene, Joanna, Susanna, and many others) also followed Jesus as he preached in the cities and villages of Galilee, ministering to him out of their own means. It was the women close to Jesus who mourned for him as he proceeded to the crucifixion (Luke 23:27), who looked on during the crucifixion (Mark 15:40), prepared the spices and ointments for his burial (Luke 23:56), and were first to witness his resurrection (Luke 24:1–11). Jesus' itinerant lifestyle also fostered occasions to develop close relationships with various individuals as hosts who extended hospitality to him. Some examples include Peter's mother-in-law (Matt. 8:14–15), Martha, Mary, and Lazarus (Luke 10:38; John 12:2), and Zacchaeus (Luke 19:5). Though Jesus lived a single life, it was rich in personal relationships with the new family to whom and with whom he ministered.

A genuine tension emerges in Jesus' perspective on family. Jesus inaugurates the presence of a "new family"—the spiritual family of those who believe on him and share in the bond and life of the Spirit. It is this family that is a foretaste of the eternal kingdom of God, and the relationships within it will ultimately supersede all our physical family relationships. Believers in Jesus Christ thus find themselves living with two families, a physical one resident only in the present age, and a spiritual one present now and also anticipating the age to come.

Neither can be ignored or neglected from the standpoint of our responsibilities. We are still called to honor our parents, love and nurture our marriages, and care for our children.[78] Amidst this tension, those who are single have an advantage of having fewer traditional family responsibilities to allow them comparatively greater investment in their spiritual family. Furthermore, as Christians we have the added assurance that whatever our physical family situation may be—good, bad, or nonexistent—we are never alone but are always part of another family, a family whose head has promised never to leave us or forsake us (Heb. 13:5).

Wrapping Up

This chapter has focused on three aspects of Jesus' teaching in the Gospels. We have looked briefly at his teaching on birth and new birth, on singleness, and on the family. We have devoted attention to these particular areas of Jesus' teaching, first, to demonstrate theological continuity between Paul's and Jesus' teaching on the nature of the new birth, and, second, to articulate Jesus' teaching on singleness within the context of what he says on new birth and new family.

There is, of course, an immediate correspondence between the new birth and new family in that the new birth defines who is a member of the new family. If it is new birth that defines one's membership in the new family and if being truly blessed of God is realized in being part of that new family, then marriage no longer plays the fundamental role in the new family of God as it did in the old covenant.

The logic of Jesus' affirmation of singleness thus follows in two respects. First, marriage is not fundamental in the building of God's people in the new covenant as it was in the old covenant. Second, singleness anticipates the age to come in which marriage itself will be obsolete. Singleness visibly heralds the coming of the new age.

There is a tension that we must maintain in what Jesus articulates. While singleness for the sake of the kingdom is a challenge to embrace by whoever can embrace it, it is simultaneously not a challenge that God gives to everyone. For those that can embrace it, Jesus uses the figure of a eunuch as a model of one who is completely loyal in undistracted service to the king. A life of singleness modeled in this way is testimony to the gospel itself as a pointer to the sufficiency of Christ for all things.

6

A *Charisma* in Corinth

Paul's Vision of Singleness for the Church

One of the fascinations of my youth was to play with a magnifying glass. Beyond discovering how to use a convex lens for its primary function of enlarging small text, I was quite amazed by the fact that a rather ordinary piece of glass could focus all the light passing through it into a single point. When I was a bit older and bought my first camera, I learned that using different lenses could radically affect how I see the image in the viewfinder. Telephoto lenses greatly magnify the center of view and block out the periphery. Wide-angle lenses, on the other hand, expand the whole field of vision by reducing the image at the center. Just as photographers use lenses to give perspective to a particular image, so we too have both implicit and explicit interpretive lenses that give perspective to our world.

For Paul and other New Testament authors, the life, death, and work of Christ is a pivotal lens through which they interpret the ethical code of the Old Testament. Some commandments, such as honoring father and mother, reappear in the New Testament largely unscathed (see Ex. 20:12; Deut. 5:16; Matt. 15:4; 19:19; Mark 7:10; 10:19; Luke 18:20; Eph. 6:2). Some are intensified by Jesus (e.g., adultery in Matt. 5:27–28). Others, such as the requirements for sacrificial sin offerings, are filtered out completely in light of the sacrificial effect of Christ's death (Heb. 10:12). As we saw in chapter 4, the fulfillment of God's covenantal promises to Abraham and his offspring were also interpreted by New Testament authors in light of the person and work of Christ (e.g., Gal. 3:16).

Awareness of Paul's christological lens is vital for making sense not only of Paul's theological developments, but also for his occasional writing to situations within individual churches. The most concentrated discussion Paul gives on the topic of singleness and marriage occurs in 1 Corinthians 7 to questions the church had written him. This one chapter contains the most direct instruction he offers on topics related to singleness, marriage, and divorce. What is striking in Paul's counsel to his Greco-Roman audience is that, while his perspective on sexuality and sexual ethics is so clearly rooted in the moral tenets of Old Testament law, his response on the question of marriage and singleness appears to be anything but a traditional Jewish perspective. What explains the difference is his christological lens through which he interprets the whole storyline of Scripture together with the very teachings of Jesus themselves to which he appeals.

What Makes 1 Corinthians 7 Such a Difficult Text

Jean Héring once commented on 1 Corinthians 7, "This chapter is the most important in the entire Bible for the question of marriage and related subjects." He adds, "It is strange to notice that in some Protestant discussions of marriage it is thought possible to ignore it completely."[1] Indeed, 1 Corinthians 7 is the longest sustained discussion of the subject of marriage and singleness in the New Testament. Yet despite expectations to find in the chapter practical instruction on the subject, most find it perplexing even to fully grasp what Paul is saying about the topic in the Corinthian context, let alone how the text might be applied in our time. As W. M. Ramsay once concluded, "There are not many passages in Paul's writings that have given rise to so many divergent and incorrect views as this chapter."[2]

What makes the chapter especially difficult becomes immediately apparent in the first verse. The NASB translation follows the Greek very literally in the wording:

> Now concerning the things about which you wrote, it is good for a man not to touch a woman. (1 Cor. 7:1)

It is clear from the opening words that what follows is a response to some previous correspondence to which we have no access, which presents the first difficulty. A second problem is the statement, "It is good for a man not to touch a woman." This appears to be some sort of euphemism. Is it a euphemism for sexual relations or for marriage? Are the man and woman mentioned generic or particular? A third critical difficulty is determining exactly whose view the statement represents. Are the words a quotation from the Corinthians' missing letter to Paul that Paul is merely restating? Or are the words Paul's own response? In either case, whose viewpoint is being represented? If it is expressing a Corinthian viewpoint, is it the view of the whole church or only a subset within it? English translations often venture some sort of interpretive judgment on these various difficulties. Consider the following two examples:

> Now concerning the matters about which you wrote: "It is good for a man not to have sexual relations with a woman." (ESV)

> Now regarding the questions you asked in your letter. Yes, it is good to live a celibate life. (NLT)

The ESV translators have added quotation marks (not present in the Greek) to indicate that what is being expressed in 7:1b is a direct quotation concerning sexual relations from the Corinthians' letter. The immediate implication is that some Corinthians, for ascetic or other reasons, are opposed to sexual relations. The NLT adds a "yes" to indicate that the words are Paul's response to the Corinthians' letter. Here the emphasis is on living a celibate life, suggesting that the Corinthians' primary interest in their initial letter to Paul may have concerned the status of being married, rather than sexual relations.[3]

The ESV interprets Paul's response very differently from the NLT. In one case, Paul appears to correct misguided Corinthian sexual asceticism (i.e., renunciation for the sake of spiritual gain); in the other, he appears to commend Corinthian aspirations to remain unmarried. Moreover, if our eventual interest is in distilling from Paul's response to the Corinthians some fundamental principles on the subject of singleness, the reconstruction of the situation in 7:1 can make a big difference. Does Paul begin the chapter by *restraining* overzealous Corinthians from disparaging sexual relations, or does he begin by *affirming* the value of singleness in the Christian life within certain constraints of sexual propriety?

A further complication to the question is that in 7:25–26 we find language parallel to that in 7:1. Paul introduces the two major sections of his discussion (7:1–24 and 7:25–40) with the same opening words, "Now concerning . . . ," an introductory expression that Paul will repeat in 1 Corinthians 8:1; 12:1; 16:1; and 16:12. In 7:26, we have again the distinctive "it is good for a man" language that is also present in 7:1b (cf. 7:8, "it is good for them"). Thus, both sections of the chapter begin with a similar expression and appear to cover primarily questions relating to singleness and marriage. But how do they relate to one another? Are they responding to one question or to two raised by the Corinthians? What we presume about how these sections of the chapter relate to one another substantially shapes how we understand the thrust of Paul's teaching on the topic.

The Prevailing Interpretation and Its Difficulties

Definitions

One of the difficulties we routinely face in making interpretive sense of 1 Corinthians 7 is defining the terms we use. A case in point is the term *celibacy*.

Traditionally "celibacy" (from the Latin *caelibatus*) was a term used to designate the state of being unmarried. The Roman *caelebs* was simply an *unmarried* man, whether never-married bachelor or widower or divorced. Today we more commonly use the term to designate abstention from sexual relations.[4] Richard Sipe's recent definition highlights well the ambiguity that has arisen:

> Celibacy is generally understood as a state of non-marriage and/or abstinence from sexual activity. Confusion results if religious celibacy is limited to this definition since one can be unmarried but sexually active or married and sexually abstinent. Christian celibacy demands greater specificity.[5]

To avoid confusion of meaning, our preference here is to use *singleness* to designate the state of not being married and *abstinence* to designate the state of remaining sexually inactive.

Another term that requires definition is *asceticism*, which we define as follows:

> Asceticism is the practice of abstention (either temporary or permanent) from the satisfaction of certain otherwise permitted creaturely desires or comforts, for the sake of the positive pursuit of a spiritual ideal or goal.

Typically, asceticism involves abstention from bodily sensual indulgences such as sexual relations and the comforts of wealth and fine living. It may include austerity in food and drink, bodily necessities that cannot be completely renounced but can be tempered of excessive indulgence. Ascetic abstention from sexual relations typically results also in the renunciation of marriage and family, although couples already married can also practice an ascetic abstinence from relations and still remain married. Asceticism involves the renunciation of one or more normally good things for a specific purpose—the pursuit of a spiritual ideal or goal. Fasting for the sake of devoting time to prayer or being reminded of one's spiritual needs is an ascetic exercise. On the other hand, fasting for weight loss or health benefits is not an ascetic exercise. When we speak of the Corinthians as being "ascetically motivated," we are suggesting that they advocate the denial of sexual relations for the specific purpose of pursuing a spiritual ideal or goal.

Summarizing the Prevailing Interpretation

The predominant view of most modern commentators is that in 1 Corinthians 7 Paul is responding to an ascetically motivated group in Corinth. The precise motivating factor for the Corinthians' asceticism varies from scholar to scholar. Popular suggestions include (1) it was a way to new depths of personal holiness and spiritual maturity;[6] (2) it was the influence of Gnostic dualism;[7] (3) it was their own brand of "spiritualized eschatology" arising from their "present pneumatic existence";[8] and (4) it was just "in the air" in first-century Corinth.[9] Perhaps the most popular conjecture is that the Corinthians believed they were already living a post-resurrection life, similar to angels.[10] The Corinthians' disposition against all sexual relations was causing them not only to reject marriage but also to abstain from relations within marriage, and in some cases to even divorce their spouses in order to vigorously pursue a new life in the Spirit.

It is important to observe that actual evidence in the chapter that the Corinthians were ascetically motivated is extremely thin. The primary evidence in the text that the Corinthians were predisposed against all sexual relations and therefore also against marriage and marital relations is the ascetic-sounding statement in 7:1b, "It is good for a man not to touch a woman," which many scholars interpret as reflecting the viewpoint of the Corinthians writing to Paul. Most of the other apparent evidence for Corinthian asceticism can be explained other ways.[11]

But do we know that the statement of 7:1b necessarily reflects the opinion of the Corinthians rather than of Paul? The basis for suggesting it generally follows some form of the following deductive line of argument:

1) The statement in 7:1b, "It is good for a man not to touch a woman," is a statement reflecting either Paul's viewpoint or the Corinthians' viewpoint.
2) As the statement seems to affirm the goodness of *not* having sexual relations, it appears to promote an ascetically motivated lifestyle.[12]
3) It cannot reflect Paul's viewpoint for the following reasons:
    a) The statement practically contradicts Genesis 2:18: "It is not good that the man should be alone."[13]
    b) The statement runs counter to Paul's Jewish heritage, to Jesus, and to Paul's theological assumptions and explicit statements.[14]
    c) The statement violates Paul's subsequent affirmation of conjugal relations within marriage in 1 Corinthians 7:2–5.[15]
    d) Paul does not evidence an ascetic worldview, especially with regard to food and drink (e.g., 1 Cor. 9:19–23; 10:25–26). He has a very high view of marriage (e.g., Eph. 5:22-33) consistent with his Jewish heritage.[16]
4) It must therefore reflect the Corinthians' viewpoint, and they must be the ones promoting an ascetic lifestyle.

It is important to see how heavily the so-called evidence for the Corinthians' asceticism rests upon the assumption that the statement in 7:1b cannot be attributed to Paul. There is really no positive evidence from the text that the Corinthians themselves were predisposed *against* sexual relations, something necessary if they were truly ascetics. It is essentially a logical deduction from what we presume to be true about Paul.

Problems with the Ascetic Reconstruction

One of the main difficulties in positing a theory that the Corinthians wrote to Paul from any sort of negative disposition toward "touching a woman" in sexual relations is that virtually all the other evidence we have about the Corinthians from Paul's correspondence with them suggests that they had quite the opposite disposition. This is evident not only in 1 Corinthians itself but in the whole progression of the Corinthian correspondence.

In 1 Corinthians 7:2, for example, immediately after the maxim, "it is good for a man not to touch a woman," Paul responds, "But on account of cases of immorality, each man should have his own wife, and each woman her own husband" (AT). Even a casual reading suggests this is a very strange way to respond to ascetics who were disparaging all sexual contact whatsoever. Paul makes other references in the chapter to their apparent struggle with immorality. In verse 5 he references Satan's tempting them because of their lack of "self-control"; in verse 9 he again mentions their inability to "exercise self-control"; and in the same verse he asserts, "it is better to marry than to burn with passion." Paul gives us clear evidence of the struggles they had with sexual immorality.

Elsewhere in the letter Paul makes reference to a range of inappropriate, sexually licentious behaviors. In 1 Corinthians 5:1–13, Paul finds it necessary to call for discipline over a kind of sexual immorality that is "not tolerated even among pagans" (v. 1). And in 1 Corinthians 6:8–9 (NASB) Paul lists ten types of people who will not inherit the kingdom of God. Four of these ten are those who practice sexual sin: "the sexually immoral," "adulterers," "effeminate," and "homosexuals."[17] Here we get a strong hint of the range of immoral sexual behavior that was common in the Corinthian world, which, in 1 Corinthians 6:11, Paul makes clear that *they too* had practiced.

Paul condemns the Corinthians' practice of patronizing prostitutes (1 Cor. 6:12–20). He cites Genesis 2:24 with the implication that the act of sexual union itself is part of God's joining of a man and woman in marriage and cannot be inappropriately stripped of its context. In 1 Corinthians 6:18 he concludes his discussion with a direct imperative: "Flee from sexual immorality." Paul's use of such an imperative can only suggest that the use of prostitutes was a common problem among his congregants.

In 1 Corinthians 10:7–8 Paul again directly warns them against indulging in immorality in the pattern of the Israelites at Sinai with the golden calf (Ex. 32:5–6) and at Peor with Baal (Num. 25:1–9). The implication is that Paul is addressing the Corinthians' participation in pagan idol feasts, which also included ample feasting and sexual revelry. Paul insists that the punishment of the Israelites serves as a warning; it is for "our instruction" (1 Cor. 10:6, AT).

Sexual immorality appears to have been a persistent pattern within the Corinthian congregation even before Paul wrote the letter we know as 1 Corinthians. In 1 Corinthians 5:9 Paul speaks of a previous letter he had written to the Corinthians in which he had warned them not to associate with "sexually immoral people," but he clarifies in 5:10–12 that those to be avoided are the sexually immoral within the church, not those outside of it. Sexual immorality remains an issue in 2 Corinthians, where Paul later speaks of mourning over the many who sinned earlier and "have not repented of the impurity, sexual immorality, and sensuality that they have practiced" (2 Cor. 12:20–21). The Greek word for *sensuality* (*aselgeia*) is also translated elsewhere in the New Testament as "licentiousness," "lasciviousness," and "debauchery" and paints as polarized a picture to the ideals of asceticism as is possible to convey.

Even in the non-canonical letter of *1 Clement*, written to the Corinthians several decades later, we find the author upbraiding the Corinthians for "unchaste embraces" along with "abominable desire" and "detestable adultery."[18] Evidently, the church's struggle with issues of sexual immorality persisted beyond Paul's involvement with it.

Given the extensive evidence of the church's persistent and pervasive problems with sexual immorality, the likelihood that the church simultaneously had within it a major movement of sexual asceticism seems remote. Nevertheless, it is typically posited that there were two different groups in Corinth, one licentious and another ascetic, and that Paul was addressing the licentious group in 1 Corinthians 6 and the ascetic group in 1 Corinthians 7. However, even assuming that two such groups representing such diametrically opposed ideologies and lifestyles could have coexisted within the same modestly sized Corinthian congregation,[19] we immediately encounter two further problems.

First, there is no evidence in the letter itself that Paul made a sudden switch to a different audience at the beginning of chapter 7. Elsewhere in the letter, Paul indicates when a viewpoint or behavior is characteristic of some but not all the Corinthians (e.g., 1 Cor. 4:18; 8:7; 15:12, 34), but in 7:1 he simply addresses them as a unified whole.

Second, as we have noted, numerous references to their immorality occur in chapter 7, beginning with his reference to their sexual immorality in verse 2. The same Greek word, *porneia*, likely links the "cases of sexual immorality" he reports in 7:2 with his admonition to them to "flee from sexual immorality" four verses earlier (6:18). This suggests continuity in the audience from chapter 6 to chapter 7.

A view gaining popularity today is the possibility that the ascetic movement was precipitated by the women in the congregation, while the men were engaged in sexual immorality.[20] Based on details in the text, this possibility also seems remote.[21]

In sum, the evidence of the text repeatedly paints a picture of a congregation struggling with sexually immorality, be it fornication, prostitution, adultery, or homosexuality, whether secular or cultic. There is little basis to suggest that Paul begins responding in verse 1 to a group of ascetics that is advocating abstinence from all sexual relations. It appears far more likely that the Corinthians in chapter 7 were no different from those being addressed everywhere else in the Corinthian correspondence.

A Further Look at 1 Corinthians 7

We have seen so far that 1 Corinthians 7 is a difficult text and that the prevailing ascetic reconstruction may not be the best interpretive fit for understanding the text. There is a better way to pull together the details of the text, and it provides a clearer picture of Paul's vision of singleness as a spiritual gift for the church.

The Corinthians' Disposition

Corinth and the Corinthians

Most indications we have from the text suggest that the Corinthians among whom Paul founded his young church were fairly typical urban residents of the early Imperial Corinthian colony. Along with Rome, Alexandria, and Syrian Antioch, Corinth was among the largest and most influential cities of the Empire, with perhaps as many as 100,000 residents.[22] As a critical transport hub between Rome and the eastern Empire, Corinth was an ethnic mix of Roman settlers, native Greeks, and immigrants from all around the Mediterranean world.

We see evidence for the diversity in the Corinthian congregants in the names of various people mentioned in the letters, which include Roman names (e.g., Gaius, Crispus, and Lucius) and Greek names (e.g., Achaicus, Erastus, and Stephanus).[23] There is also evidence to suggest there were at least some Jews in the church. Crispus, the ruler of the synagogue, and his household were part of it (see Acts 18:8). Other evidence includes Paul's reference to Jewish history: "our fathers" in the wilderness (1 Cor. 10:1–5) and the term "unclean" in 7:14. But the nature of the major concerns (e.g., immorality and food sacrificed to idols) and a few direct references in the letter (6:11; 12:2) point to a predominantly Gentile membership.[24]

The Corinthians reflected a spectrum of mainstream Greco-Roman society. Paul describes them this way: "Not many of you were wise according to worldly standards, not many were powerful, not many were of noble birth" (1 Cor. 1:26). Though likely the social elite classes were not represented among Paul's infant Corinthian church, indications from the letter itself reveal that there was still some social stratification among the believers. Notable here are the tensions between those of a wealthier and more influential social standing and those of comparatively lower social status (1 Cor. 11:17–22), as well those of comparatively greater educational standing and those of less (8:7–13; 12:21–26).

The Corinthian congregants also appear to have been socially well-integrated with their non-Christian neighbors.[25] They availed themselves of the secular civil authorities to settle their disputes (1 Cor. 6:1–6); they were invited to dinner engagements in the homes of unbelievers (10:27), and, conversely, it is possible that their unbelieving friends dropped in during their meetings from time to time (14:24–25). Some of the Corinthian Christians may have attained wealth through business dealings and continued to maintain those business relationships (7:30–31), and Paul encouraged them to maintain existing marriages with unbelievers but not to seek out further unions (7:12–13; 2 Cor. 6:14). Some may even have been participants in the parties and feasts at the dining rooms of pagan temples (1 Cor. 8:10). Far from embracing the principled ideals of ascetic denial through a countercultural separation from society, the clues of the text point to the likelihood that the Corinthians were quite socially integrated with the pagan world around them, and at times so much so that they failed to distinguish themselves as Christians (e.g., 5:9–13).

The Greco-Roman View of Marriage

If the Corinthian church to which Paul wrote was fairly representative of the Greco-Roman culture in the early Roman Empire, what would their disposition toward marriage likely have been, and what might have prompted them to write to Paul? While it is impossible to know exactly the circumstances that prompted them to write, we can construct some reasonable possibilities from what we know of the Greco-Roman world and from the text itself.

From a Greco-Roman perspective, the purpose of marriage is summed up well by the famous dictum attributed to Demosthenes:

> For this is what living with a woman as one's wife means—to have children by her and to introduce the sons to the members of the clan and of the deme, and to betroth the daughters to husbands as one's own. Mistresses we keep for the sake of pleasure, concubines for the daily care of our persons, but wives to bear us legitimate children and to be faithful guardians of our households.[26]

Note that Demosthenes distinguishes between "living with a woman" and "wife." A man could live with a woman not his wife on a permanent and intimate basis. If a man wanted a wife, he had to find a respectable woman, which he did typically through connections to her father or legal guardian, in order to obtain legitimate children. Having children, in turn, established a man's household within the city, giving him added civic status. It also provided a man both heirs to manage his estate and responsible parties to care for him in old age. Beyond providing a man with legitimate heirs, the wife's primary function was to manage the man's household and domestic affairs.

Demosthenes also describes three classes of women that men could access for sexual relations: mistresses, which included women ranging from personal courtesans to street prostitutes; concubines, which included female household slaves; and the wife, whom the man needed only to produce legitimate heirs.

Xenophon similarly expressed the distinction between marriage and sexual fulfillment:

> Of course you don't suppose that lust provokes men to beget children, when the streets and the stews [brothels] full of means to satisfy that? We obviously select for wives the women who will bear us the best children, and then marry them to raise a family.[27]

The satisfaction of lusts could be obtained from the street, while a wife was selected from a reputable family as a woman suitable for bearing legitimate heirs and managing a man's household. Plutarch, in his *Advice to Bride and Groom*, cautions the young bride that if her husband in his private life "commit some peccadillo with a paramour or a maidservant, [she] ought not be indignant or angry." Rather, she should reason that it is out of respect for her that her husband indulges his "debauchery, licentiousness, and wantonness with another woman."[28]

There were also voices calling for moral reform in Greco-Roman society. Much earlier, in the second-century BC, Polybius had decried the low birthrate in the whole of Greece, which he attributed to men who "had fallen into such a state of pretentiousness, avarice, and indolence that they did not wish to marry, or if they married to rear the children born to them."[29] Antipater of Tarsus, writing in the same period, complained about the lawlessness and frivolity in the cities:

> Even marrying is reckoned to be among the most irksome things. They consider the young bachelor's [life] godlike because it gives them license for licentiousness and enjoyment of various sordid and cheap pleasures [note: there is a wordplay in the Greek between "bachelor" and "godlike"].[30]

In the early Roman Empire, Livy decried a similar relaxation of discipline and the decline of morals when he spoke of "the downward plunge which has brought us to the present time, when we can endure neither our vices nor their cure."[31] Expressions of similar sentiment were quaffed in the late Republic and early Empire by Sallust, Horace, and Cicero, while Quintillian, following Antipater, also notes a similar verbal connection in Latin between "bachelors" (*caelibes*) and "gods" (*caelites*).[32] A remnant of this verbal association persists even into modern English in the similarity of "celibate" and "celestial."

Stern Stoic moralists also emerged, such as Hierocles and Musonius Rufus, who argued that sexual relations should only occur within marriage for the purpose of begetting children and simultaneously elevated the purpose of marriage to include not just procreation, but companionship, mutual love, and shared devotion.[33] But that the moralists needed to call their peers to reform is further corroboration that the prevailing disposition of society was otherwise.

Augustus, as emperor, also recognized the problem and danger that a falling birthrate could have upon the strength and future of the newly consolidated Roman Empire, and he quickly assumed the mantle of moral reformer.[34] In 18 BC Augustus enacted legislation, called *Lex Julia de Maritandis Ordinibus*, which was intended to encourage marriage and the production of children. It contained thirty-five chapters of combined carrot and stick provisions. [35] The legislation bestowed various financial and status benefits on those who married and had three children and corresponding penalties upon those who did not. The result was mixed at best, and according to Dio Cassius in AD 9 Augustus was confronted in the Roman forum by a crowd of knights urging its repeal.[36] When Augustus separated the married knights from the unmarried, he was grieved to find far more unmarried than married. After an extended speech castigating the unmarried knights for failing to perform their "duty" by marrying,[37] he deployed a further round of marriage legislation, which increased the rewards given to those with children. Ironically, Dio notes that even the consuls who framed the marriage legislation for Augustus were themselves both childless and unmarried, and he comments, "From this very circumstance the need for the law was apparent."[38]

Hesiod and the Creation of Woman

What lies at the root of the apparent Greco-Roman ambivalence toward marriage may run as deep as the Greek creation myths that helped give shape to what they thought and presupposed about marriage itself. Modern Western culture, for all its ills, remains shaped in some fundamental ways in how it thinks about marriage by the creation account in Genesis 2:18–24. Marriage, according to Genesis, is a *good* thing for human beings. God observed that it is "not good" for the man to be alone (v. 18) and that there was not a "helper" fit for him (v. 20). God created the woman from the man's rib (v. 22), and the man is glad upon encountering her: "This *at last* is bone of my bones and flesh of my flesh" (v. 23). The etiology concludes with a pronouncement of the institution of marriage: "Therefore a man shall leave his father and his mother and hold fast to his wife, and they shall become one flesh" (v. 24). Even with the erosion of the hold that Christian values and ideals once exercised upon Western culture as a whole, Genesis remains our creation story, and marriage remains something *good* and desirable for human beings.

But Genesis was not foundational to the Greco-Roman world or to that of most Corinthians. Their marriage etiology likely came from the creation mythology of the Greek poet Hesiod (eighth century BC). Hesiod's account of the creation of woman is considerably different from the account in Genesis. In a series of tit-for-tat deceptions between the supreme god Zeus and the lesser god Prometheus, Prometheus steals fire from Zeus (which Zeus had hidden from human beings) in a giant fennel stalk and gives it to mankind.[39] This deception of Prometheus's enrages Zeus so that "immediately he contrived an evil for human beings in exchange for fire."[40] He has Hephaestus forge from the earth "the semblance of a reverend maiden" and has Athena adorn her with "silvery clothing" and place around her head "budding garlands that arouse desire."[41] Hesiod describes Zeus's presentation of his counter deception:

> Then, when he [Zeus] had contrived this beautiful evil thing in exchange for that good one [i.e., fire], he led her out to where the other gods and the human beings were . . . and wonder gripped the immortal gods and the mortal human beings. For from her comes the race of female women: for of her is the deadly race and tribe of women, a great woe for mortals, dwelling with men, no companions of baneful poverty but only of luxury.[42]

Hesiod describes the woman as a "beautiful evil," literally *kalon kakon,* a "good-evil." Woman is the progenitor of the race of females—a "deadly race" and "great woe for mortals." The dilemma for the man is clear: she is both beautifully attractive and simultaneously a great economic distress because she will not live with simple poverty but demands luxury.

Hesiod then contrasts the alternative evil:

> And he bestowed another evil thing in exchange for that good one; whoever flees marriage and the dire works of women and chooses not to marry arrives at deadly old age deprived of assistance; while he lives he does not lack the means of sustenance, but when he has died his distant relatives divide up his substance.[43]

Hesiod points here to the two woes of the one man who chooses to remain single and not marry: he has no one to care for him in old age and no heirs to pass on his estate. He concludes by observing that for the man who obtains a truly "cherished wife . . . well-fitted in her thoughts," for him the evil is balanced with the good. On the other hand, the one who obtains "the baneful species" must live with "incessant woe in his breast, in his spirit and heart, and his evil is incurable."[44]

In contrast to the biblical perspective in which the wife is created as a helper for the man and as an economic asset, Hesiod views the wife strictly as an economic liability. Elsewhere Hesiod gives advice to his brother Perses regarding how to be an economically successful farmer:

> I bid you take notice of how to clear your debts and how to ward off famine: a house first of all, a woman, and an ox for plowing—the woman one you purchase, not marry, one who can follow with the oxen—and arrange everything well in the house, lest you ask someone else and he refuse and you suffer want, and the season pass by, and the fruit of your work be diminished.[45]

For strictly economic advantage a female slave was preferable to a wife. The slave was always available and did exactly what she was told to do (even following the oxen!), while a wife, as Hesiod also warns, would guilefully cajole a man while she deceptively "pokes into your granary" and helps herself.[46]

The best hedge against the threat of devastation through famine (a frequent occurrence in Greece) was to have servant help rather than a wife who might not. Hesiod later does recommend that his brother marry, but only when he is in a "good season," that is, already economically established at around thirty years of age. Even then, he is to choose carefully, selecting a young and malleable virgin, because a bad wife "singes her husband without a torch" and "gives him over to a raw old age."[47]

Just as the creation account in Genesis has been influential among Judeo-Christian traditions in seeing marriage as something fundamentally good and beneficial, so too Hesiod's perspective—that marriage is fundamentally a dilemma for man—reverberates through Greco-Roman thought. Central to the dilemma is that, on the one hand, the woman is something inherently good; she provides heirs for inheriting and managing a man's estate and caring for him in old age. On the other hand, she and the children she brings are an economic liability for the man, and she is a potential source of trouble and stress to his heart.

The Greco-Roman Marriage Dilemma

Whatever the legacy of Hesiod's mythology, the dilemma of marriage emerges as a recurring ethical question discussed and debated throughout the history of Greco-Roman philosophical thought. We see evidence of it among the earliest Greek pre-Socratic philosophers. Additionally, it was a question entertained among all the major Socratic schools and a perennially debated topic in Greco-Roman rhetorical pedagogy.

The pre-Socratic philosopher Thales (ca. 585 BC) refused to marry because he did not desire to subject his life to "unnecessary pains."[48] Antiphon (fifth century BC) described marriage as a "great contest" for a man. If the wife turned out to be unsuitable, there was little recourse, as divorce made potential enemies of all one's relations.[49] Even if a wife proved to be a woman after a man's own heart, what is necessary for health and livelihood doubled his distresses amidst the pleasure.[50] Democritus (460–357 BC) similarly advised against having children: "It does not seem to me to be necessary to have children; for in acquiring children I see many great dangers and much grief, and few blessings and those meagre and weak."[51]

A contrary point of view was espoused by Xenophon (430–354 BC), a contemporary of Socrates who argued that the gods coupled together male and female for "a perfect partnership in mutual service" in order that they may have children for the preservation of the species and for support in old age.[52] Having a wife was thought to be an advantage, since, having her to run his domestic affairs, he was able to enjoy more free time.[53]

Each of the major Socratic schools addressed the ethical question of whether it was better for a wise man to marry or to remain single. Although Plato himself remained unmarried, he advised that a wise man would both marry and take part in public affairs.[54] But Plato also recognized that not every man was predisposed to marry, so he advised the prudent lawmaker to enact marriage laws in the state declaring that any man not married by age thirty-five "shall pay a yearly fine . . . lest he imagine that single life brings him gain and ease."[55]

Aristotle considered marriage and family to be external goods that contribute to achieving the true happiness that comes through the exercise of one's faculties in conformance with virtue.[56]

The Stoics built an essentially cosmological argument for the necessity of marriage. The universe is built upon cities, and the fundamental building block of the city is the family unit. Therefore, the intended pattern of nature is that humans should marry and have families.[57] The Stoics also argued that marriage was advantageous not only because the wife could help with the management of a man's domestic affairs but also because she could be a comfort to her husband in his distresses and problems and restore and refresh him with unaffected enthusiasm.[58]

Plato, Aristotle, and the Stoics were on one side of the marriage question, while the Cynics and the Epicureans were on the other side. The Cynics rejected both political involvement and marriage, believing that neither was helpful or advantageous for the wise man's pursuit of the virtuous life.[59] The Epicureans also rejected marriage as beneficial for the wise man, but for a different reason.[60] Epicurus and his followers argued that happiness was ultimately achieved only through a tranquil life characterized by the absence of pain in the body and trouble in the soul.[61] Since marriage, family, and political life brought many drawbacks and were potential sources of stress and anxiety, the wise man was generally better off avoiding them.[62]

Under the Roman Empire whether to marry was a standard topic of debate among philosophers. Dio Chysostom (AD 40–120) describes philosophers as men who "deliberate and legislate" about a range of issues including marriage, the duties of citizenship, and the setting up of households.[63] Perhaps the best evidence that the marriage question was much debated in the Roman period is its prominence in surviving books of *progymnasmata* or "preliminary exercises" used to train students in the rhetorical skills of oration and speech making. There we find references to the marriage question from the sophist Aelius Theon (first century AD) and Quintillian (AD 35–100) and later examples from Hermogenes of Tarsus (second century AD), Aphthonius the Sophist (fourth century AD), and Nicolaus the Sophist (fifth century AD).[64]

Conclusion: What Was the Corinthians' Question?

We can expect that the Corinthians had heard a number of viewpoints on the question of whether to marry and likely had different views themselves. For some, marriage was perhaps a matter of political duty. Corinth was a Roman colony and marched to the drumbeat of the Imperial order, and Augustus's marriage legislation was the law of the land. Others, perhaps especially ethnic Greeks, may have had more antipathy for the Empire and saw in Paul's gospel the inauguration of a coming new order in the kingdom of God.

Marriage implied assuming the responsibility to provide for children, an economically risky commitment in an urban context where food had to be purchased on the erratic open market. Poorer men in the congregation who had likely come to Corinth looking for work may well have struggled to survive on their own, let alone provide for a wife and family. In addition, wives could be irksome and troublesome and were hardly necessary for the pleasures of intimacy. Sexual outlets permeated the city's poor neighborhoods, and those of greater means had servants around and could afford personal courtesans.

For the Corinthians whether to marry came down to a tradeoff between personal and economic freedom and civil duty and responsibility. The philosophically oriented Corinthians no doubt saw the question as an important one to bring to Paul, their founding teacher. Moreover, Paul was single himself. As we shall see, their circumstances made the question a critical one to bring to Paul—at that present time more than ever.

Paul's Disposition in His Answer

Four Strands

Though Paul recognizes that he has the Spirit of God as he responds to the Corinthians (1 Cor. 7:40), it is also apparent that his perspective is informed by a few distinguishable strands that weave together in his response. The first of these is the high view of marriage and sexuality given in the Old Testament law. Paul is aware from Genesis 2:24 (which he cites a few verses earlier, in 1 Cor. 6:16) that since the sexual union symbolizes the marital union, which, according to Jesus, is given by God (Matt. 19:6), the act is not appropriate for any context outside of marriage.

The second strand is Paul's christological lens through which he recognizes that the new-covenant people of God are fully blessed through the single provision of God's offspring in Jesus Christ. They no longer look to the material blessings of marriage and family as tangible evidence of God's covenantal blessing in the pattern of the Sinai covenant. Hence, for Paul, marriage was neither a divine command nor necessary for divine blessing—one could remain as one was called, in either the single or married state.

The third strand is the preserved oral traditions of Jesus' words from the Gospels on marriage, singleness, and divorce. Paul makes direct reference to having a command from the Lord when he directs the married not to divorce (1 Cor. 7:10–11). This contrasts with his having no command from the Lord when giving his instruction on mixed marriages (1 Cor. 7:12–16) and then again in his instruction to the virgins and widows (1 Cor. 7:25–40), where twice he makes reference to his own judgment (vv. 25, 40). Paul's prohibition from the Lord on divorce (7:10–11) so closely aligns with the statement of Jesus' recorded in the Synoptic Gospels (Matt. 5:32; 19:9; Mark 10:11–12; Luke 16:18) that it is all but certain that Paul had access to the circulating Gospel tradition.

Since Jesus' pronouncement on divorce (Matt. 19:9) was given in the immediate context of the eunuch *logion* (Matt. 19:12), there is a strong likelihood that Paul was also familiar with Jesus' challenge on being a eunuch for the kingdom of God. That Paul in 1 Corinthians 7:25 expressly states that he has no command from the Lord on the subject of singleness may reflect the fact that Jesus did not give an absolute command regarding singleness in Matthew 19:11–12 but rather presented a challenge to those "who can receive this saying." Paul might have been seeking to guide his Corinthian congregants in applying Jesus' qualified challenge in their particular situation.[65]

The fourth strand is Paul's commitment to being a Jew to the Jews and a Gentile to the Gentiles (1 Cor. 9:20–21). Paul was not hesitant to rally aspects of the indigenous culture that could be beneficial for the furtherance of his message or the advancement of Christians' discipleship. In 1 Corinthians 15:33 he cites the Greek comedy writer Menander, "Bad company ruins good morals,"[66] to shame them from associating with those who deny the resurrection. In 1 Corinthians 7 Paul enters directly into the Greco-Roman world of the marriage question and responds in terms that Greco-Romans would resonate with and understand.

Paul's Priority

Paul in his mission to the Gentiles stood in the pivotal transition point where Christianity was breaking out from being merely the faith of a group of Jews to a faith inclusive of both Jew and Gentile, based on the proclamation of God's reconciliation in the atoning work of Christ. In Acts 15:19–20 the Apostolic Council in Jerusalem ruled that while Gentile believers should not be burdened with the whole law of Moses, four things were still required of them, including abstaining from things polluted by idols and sexual immorality. Not surprisingly, both those topics feature prominently in 1 Corinthians, and, as we have seen, the Corinthians' problems with sexual immorality pervade all of Paul's correspondence with them.

Thus, we can posit that there was somewhat of a mismatch between the central concern of the Corinthians in writing to Paul and Paul's central concern in his response. Whereas the Corinthians were primarily interested in the practical question of the necessity of marriage, Paul was primarily concerned with the issue of sexual propriety. Moreover, the question of marriage was also directly related to presumptions the Corinthians had about allowable sexual behavior. Paul needed to correct their fundamental dissociation between sexual activity and the purpose of marriage. Whereas the Greco-Roman Corinthians saw no connection between the domain of one's sexual activity and marriage, for Paul they were inextricably linked. Paul had to correct this fundamental blind spot in their thinking before he could address their question on their terms.

Making Sense of the Text

With this in view, we can consider a plausible reconstruction of the logic of Paul's response to the Corinthians' question.

The Unity of the Chapter

The structure of 1 Corinthians 7 can be depicted in the following outline:

1. Preliminary matters: the marriage question is not unrelated to sexual propriety! (vv. 1–7)
2. Paul's general advice on the marriage question (vv. 8–16)
   a. To the unmarried and widows (vv. 8–9)
   b. To those in believing marriages (vv. 10–11)
   c. To those in mixed marriages (vv. 12–16)
3. Segue: Remain as you are called (vv. 17–24)
   a. Remain as Jew or Gentile (vv. 18–19)
   b. Remain as slave or free (vv. 21–23)
4. Paul's specific advice to the not-yet married: Remain as you are (vv. 25–40)
   a. Three reasons to remain single (vv. 26–35)
      i. Those who marry will have worldly troubles (vv. 26–28)
      ii. The existence of the cosmos does not depend on marriage (vv. 29–31)
      iii. Singleness is an opportunity for undivided service to the Lord (vv. 32–35)
   b. Special circumstances (vv. 36–40)
      i. The betrothed (vv. 36–38)
      ii. The widows (vv. 39–40)

We can see immediately that the chapter is generally unified around the question, whether or not to marry, with only two major exceptions: verses 1–7, which focus upon sexual relations and marriage, and verses 17–24, which focus upon living as one is called in two specific circumstances. The first of these (vv. 1–7) actually functions as a preliminary discussion for Paul, while the latter (vv. 17–24) is a segue discussion introducing a principle with two illustrations that anticipates Paul's major discussion in 7:25–35.

There remains a major interpretive question concerning the fundamental relationship between the two major sections of the chapter, which are introduced with the expression "Now concerning . . . " (7:1–24 and 7:25–40). Do the two sections represent two different questions from the Corinthians' letter? Or is Paul responding to two different audiences (i.e., the married in 7:1–24 and the "virgins" in 7:25–40) but addressing the same question?

The simplest answer may be the most probable, that 1 Corinthians 7 addresses a single question raised by the Corinthians—Was getting married wise in light of the difficult circumstances confronting them?—and that Paul responds to their question directly in verses 25–40. But before he does so, he has a greater concern—infidelity and immorality within the congregation. Such infidelity includes some unmarried men involved with multiple women but married to none; married men looking for sexual gratification outside the marital bond; and wives, fed up with their husband's exploits, contemplating divorce and remarriage in hopes of finding a better man. Paul, having just directly addressed the problem of immorality (6:12–20), uses the occasion of their question to correct their misguided views of the relationship between sexuality and marriage (7:1–16) before answering their question directly (7:25–40).

The Question Raised in 1 Corinthians 7:26

One of the details in the text that seems to support this interpretation is the recurring appearance of the "it is good" language. The reference appears four times in the chapter in three critical locations (when translated literally):

7:1b: "It is *good* for a man not to touch a woman"

7:8: "It is *good* for them [the unmarried and widows] if they remain as I am"

7:26: "I think that this is *good* . . . that it is *good* for a man to remain thus"

194

The pattern of the similar "it is good" (*kalon*) vocabulary seems to be more than accidental. From the Greco-Roman perspective, the "good" language recalls the classical Greco-Roman marriage question. Hesiod presents the woman to the man as a "good-evil," a debatable entity, and from then on philosophers debated whether marriage was indeed "good" or "advantageous" (the latter *symphoron* vocabulary is used by the disciples in Matt. 19:10 and by Paul in 1 Cor. 7:35) for a man to marry. From the Jewish perspective, the "good" language also recalls the marriage-related concern of Genesis 2:18, that "it is *not good* for the man to be alone." The statements of 1 Corinthians 7:8 and 7:26 are especially similar. Both primarily address the unmarried; 7:26 addresses the "virgins," while 7:8 addresses the wider class of the "unmarried" and "widows." Both emphasize that it is good to remain in one's current state,[67] the basic principle Paul will emphasize in the segue section of 7:17–24 (see esp. vv. 17, 20, 24).

Two peculiarities are apparent. First, the language in 7:1b is noticeably different. Whereas the thrust of the main discussions that emerge in 7:8 and 7:25 (and the segue between them) address whether it is "good" to remain in one's marital state or to change it, the sexual euphemism "touching a woman" appears in 7:1b. Second, the syntax of Paul's statement in 7:26 is very awkward. The full sentence literally reads as follows:

> "I think then that this is good, on account of the present crisis, that it is good for a man to remain thus."

The best way to make sense of this awkward syntax is to say that Paul, with the first "good," is giving his judgment on the Corinthians' statement, "It is good for a man to remain thus." Otherwise it makes no sense that he so distinctly would have separated his judgment of the statement from the statement itself. A further clue that Paul is citing the Corinthians' statement is the presence of the word "that" (*hoti*), a standard Greek word used to introduce a citation.[68]

In fact, a number of factors suggest that the kernel of the discussion, both the original question asked of Paul and his answer to it, is presented in 7:25–26, not in 7:1–2. First, as we have just seen, the syntax of the sentence and the direct discourse marker both point to the likelihood that "it

is good for a man to remain thus" is a quotation from the Corinthians' letter. Neither feature is present in 7:1–2. Second, the statement "it is good
for a man to remain thus" concerns the question of marriage in keeping
with the classical Greco-Roman marriage dilemma (unlike the phrasing
of 7:1b), a question that the Corinthians were likely to have asked Paul.
It is the question that strikes at the very heart of the central discussion of
the chapter as a whole. Third, the extended qualification that Paul gives
in 7:25 ("one who by the Lord's mercy is trustworthy") before answering
their question suggests that the answer he is about to give is especially
important to the Corinthians. Fourth, the reference to the "present crisis"
in 7:26 points to the probable trigger that spurred the Corinthians to
raise the question with Paul. Fifth, Paul's immediate response (7:27–28)
to their question speaks directly to concerns germane to their world of
the classical marriage dilemma—Paul wishes to spare them the worldly
troubles that marriage brings.

The Point of 1 Corinthians 7:1b and 7:1–7

If the theory is correct, that the kernel of the original Corinthian question appears in 7:25–26, then it remains to explain the odd euphemism
of 7:1b and the reason Paul begins with it rather than with the question
the Corinthians had asked him. Before Paul can address the Corinthians
on their terms, he must first address a critical blind spot in the presup-
position that underlies their question, namely, that the marriage question
is independent of one's sexual behavior. Indeed, for Paul, it is precisely
the Corinthians' immorality, inside and outside of marriage, that is the
foremost problem, and the one he must address in relation to their question before he can respond to their question in the way they intended it.

The point Paul needs to make is that marriage alone is the
divinely sanctioned domain for the exercise of one's sexual expression.
Nevertheless, in the light of the sufficiency of Christ in the new covenant
and Jesus' own words, Paul wishes to clarify that it is good for a person to
remain single and not marry, but if and only if that person can also remain
sexually chaste. Rather than express the point in a wordy expression
such as, "It is good for a man not to marry, if and only if, he also remains
sexually abstinent," Paul simply condenses his statement into the more

elegant euphemism that conveys the same point: "It is good for a man not to touch a woman." In other words, it is good for a man to refrain from marriage by refraining from all sexual contact with a woman.

It is beyond our scope here to provide a verse-by-verse interpretation of the details of 1 Corinthians 7, but we can offer a few observations regarding how the preliminary section, verses 1 through 7, makes good sense with our reconstruction of Paul and the Corinthians.[69] A minimally interpretive translation of the section can be rendered as follows:

> Now concerning the matters about which you wrote, it is good for a man not to touch a woman. But on account of cases of immorality, each man should have his own woman and each woman her own husband. To his wife the husband should fulfill his obligation, and similarly the wife to the husband. The wife does not have right over her own body, but the husband does; in the same way also the husband does not have right over his own body, but the wife does. Do not deprive one another, except by agreement for a time, in order that you might devote yourselves to prayer; and then come together again in order than Satan might not tempt you on account of your lack of self-control. But this I speak as a concession, not as a command; I desire all men to be also as I am, but each has his own spiritual gift from God, one in this way, another in that way. (1 Cor. 7:1–7, AT)

The Corinthians had asked Paul's view on the wisdom of refraining from marriage, especially in light of the "present crisis" they were facing, and Paul gives a very surprising response. He suggests that, in principle, it is good for them not to marry, but only if they also can assume responsibility for complete control of their sexual lives. Paul immediately qualifies his statement, well aware of the prevailing disposition of the Corinthians toward sexual activity apart from marriage. He must first remind them in no uncertain terms that marriage, and only marriage, is the divine provision for the exercise of sexual activity.

The language of verse 2 bears out the likelihood of this interpretation. The text reads, literally, "but on account of *porneias*." The plural *porneias* suggests that multiple actual cases are in view (so NRSV; cf. NLT: "so much sexual immorality"), and there is no textual reason to read this as a reference only to *temptation* to immorality, as some translations render (e.g., RSV, ESV), in which case we would expect Paul to have used the singular.[70] The strange reference to "one's *own* woman" (7:2) probably does not reflect temptations toward polygamy, which was rare in the Greco-Roman context, but rather the situation of not having a specific "woman" at all. Men, especially the unmarried, who had sexual access to concubines, slaves, courtesans, and prostitutes, did not necessarily think in terms of a particular woman as their own.

Paul's call in light of the Corinthians' disposition to immorality is for each man and woman to have their own mate. This call or command in verse 2, as well as the subsequent imperatives he gives in verses 3 and 5 to be faithful in conjugal relations, Paul further qualifies: "But *this* I speak as a concession not as a command" (v. 6, AT).[71] It is critical to see that Paul neither suggests that it is good for all to remain single (and to be sexually abstinent) nor instructs that all ought to marry and have relations. He is saying that it is good for a person not to marry and to remain sexually chaste, but he concedes that if they cannot remain sexually chaste as single, they ought to marry and maintain a healthy conjugal relationship with their spouse. This is precisely the logic given in 1 Corinthians 7:7.

Paul's surprisingly strong language in 1 Corinthians 7:3–5 requiring husbands and wives to respect one another's conjugal rights and maintain regular relations need not imply that the husbands (or wives) were ascetically disposed. Rather, it seems better explained by the tendency within Greco-Roman culture to neglect marital relations once a man had his desired number of children when other sexual avenues were readily available. Hence husbands especially must recognize the wife's rights to regular marital relations.[72]

This understanding makes better sense of Paul's concern with their "lack of self-control" (*akrasia*) in 7:5, which was an extremely strong charge to make against anyone in the Greco-Roman culture (because they regarded temperance and self-control as cardinal virtues), let alone against ascetics chiefly defined by the exercise of such self-control.[73]

Singleness as a Charisma in 1 Corinthians 7:7

Verse 7 offers a rationale to support Paul's claim in verse 6 that his directive in verses 2–5 is to be understood not as a universal command but as a concession to their lack of self-control. This is because, while he desires all men to be as he is, each one has his own "spiritual gift" (*charisma*) from God. The verse expresses a fascinating tension that should not be missed. On one hand, through use of the present-tense Greek verb for "I wish" (*thelō*), Paul expresses a desire for something that is able and ought to be realized.[74] Paul wishes and invites all human beings to be as he is. On the other hand, Paul qualifies his wish with the adversative "but," (*alla*), that "each has his own spiritual gift from God," with the implication that the ability to live single and continent is ultimately only a provision from God.

The human-divine tension there is similar to the paradoxical response that Jesus gave to the disciples regarding marriage: "Not everyone can receive this saying, but only those to whom it is given. . . . Let the one who is able to receive this receive it" (Matt. 19:11–12). What we can conclude from both Matthew 19:11–12 and 1 Corinthians 7 is that singleness, like salvation itself, is an open call to live a distinctive life for the sake of the kingdom of God, and those who have a sense of their innate ability to respond to the call *should* do so.

Two further questions are raised. First, is Paul suggesting that both singleness and marriage are spiritual gifts? Second, is the spiritual gift of singleness here in 1 Corinthians 7 of the same type as gifts listed elsewhere in Paul's taxonomies of spiritual gifts (e.g., Rom. 12:4–8; 1 Cor. 12:4–31; Eph. 4:11–16)? These questions are more interrelated than they first appear because they both beg the question of what Paul actually means by a "spiritual gift" of singleness.

Paul's statement in 1 Corinthians 12:7 is perhaps the closest we come to a definition of a *charisma*: "To each is given the manifestation of the Spirit for the common good." There are three essential points here about a *charisma*, or spiritual gift. First, a *charisma* is selective, that is, a particular gift is given selectively, not generally. Second, a *charisma* is a manifestation of the Spirit. The connotation of the Greek word for "manifestation," *phanerōsis*, in the classical world was one of astronomical appearance—something becoming visible.[75] A spiritual gift, therefore, is a divine enablement in which the Spirit is revealed among the people of God. Third, it is for the mutual advantage or common good of the body of Christ as a whole. A spiritual gift is not a talent or bestowment for one's personal benefit but a divine enablement given for the mutual benefit of strengthening the substance and mission of the church.

Though Paul does not explicitly refer to singleness as a *charisma* apart from 1 Corinthians 7:7, it seems to fit well with the description of 1 Corinthians 12:7. In 7:7 he emphasizes that singleness is not given to all but that "each one" has his or her own spiritual gift from God. Paul does not elaborate in this verse how singleness serves the common good, but he gives some hints later in the chapter, where the implication is that its essence is a freedom for dedicated service to the kingdom of God (e.g., vv. 28, 32–35), a theme that parallels Jesus' description of becoming a eunuch for the kingdom of God (Matt. 19:12). In view of both Paul's and Jesus' statements, we can define the *charisma* of singleness this way:

> The *charisma* of singleness is a Spirit-enabled freedom to serve the King and the kingdom wholeheartedly, without undue distraction for the longings of sexual intimacy, marriage, and family.

The essence of the gift is a freedom that transcends the innately human desires for marital intimacy and family life, desires which are good and normal and part of how God has designed us as male and female for the present age. The definition does not imply that those with the gift of singleness are asexual individuals with no interest in marriage or family life. But it is suggesting that they experience a genuine freedom that allows them to serve God with a whole heart, irrespective of whether they ever experience the fulfillment of marital intimacy and family life. It is this freedom that Paul experiences and, according to 7:7, desires that the Corinthians might also have.

Conversely, the gift of singleness is not simply the situation or status of being unmarried. Unless one marries the day after puberty, one will inevitably live part of his or her life as a single person. There are some who may have to live their entire lives as single people, without the gift of singleness—not ever finding a suitable mate. As we noted earlier, Jesus recognized that some are eunuchs not because they chose to be but because of factors outside their control. However, those who have the gift of singleness can remain single by choice.

Paul is not suggesting that both singleness and marriage are spiritual gifts. Marriage remains the norm for most of us because of the way we have been created. It is good, and it is a gift of God, just as all good things are gifts of God (James 1:17). But marriage does not entail a special manifestation of the Spirit for edifying God's people and serving the kingdom of God. The *charisma* of singleness is something more—it is a divine enablement with a specific purpose. Moreover, suggesting that marriage is a gift complementary to singleness leaves those who are single involuntarily in an ambiguous state. They do not have the "gift" of marriage, but neither do they have the "gift" of singleness, as their desire is to be married. Paul recognizes that while some have the gift of singleness, others have different gifts, apportioned by the Spirit according to his will (1 Cor. 12:11), such as those listed in 1 Corinthians 12:8–10.

Does Paul's Claim in 1 Corinthians 7:1b Contradict Genesis 2:18?

As we discussed above, one of the principle objections commentators have raised to the likelihood that the statement, "It is good for a man not to touch a woman" (7:1b), is Paul's rather than the Corinthians is that the language recalls Genesis 2:18, "It is not good that the man should be alone," which appears to express a contrary view.[76] The objection is articulated succinctly by Simon Kistemaker:

> On his own authority, Paul could not have advocated celibacy for everyone, for he would be contradicting God's utterance: "It is not good for the man to be alone" (Gen. 2:18). Then Paul would be against procreation (Gen. 1:28), God's covenant blessings from generation to generation (Gen. 17:7), and the growth of the church.[77]

Paul surely was not advocating celibacy for everyone; his statement was carefully qualified. But assuming he was affirming that living an abstinent single life is good for all those able do so, he was not in contradiction with Genesis. Paul is not affirming that it is good to be alone but only that, in appropriate circumstances, it is good not to marry. Conversely, when Genesis 2:18 affirms that it is *not good* to live alone, marriage is given as a provision. But this does not imply that marriage was designed to be the sole provision for one's aloneness. We recall that Jesus was a single man but not a man alone, one devoid of family and relationships.

Although Paul may have had some extended time of solitude imme-diately after his conversion,[78] he, like Jesus, was a man immersed in new family relationships. We are struck by how many different companions, partners, co-laborers, and underlings are mentioned from the period of his Gentile ministry.[79] His use of family language is robust as he addresses those in his church constantly as "brothers" (Rom. 1:13; 1 Cor. 3:1; Gal. 4:12; Phil. 1:12; 1 Thess. 1:4), and "sisters" (Philem. 2), "children" (Gal. 4:19; 1 Cor. 4:14), "legitimate sons" (1 Tim. 1:2; Titus 1:4), and "kins-men" (Rom. 16:7). He speaks especially affectionately of Timothy, who "as a son with a father . . . has served with me in the gospel" (Phil. 2:22). Timothy is instructed to treat old men as fathers, young men as brothers, older women as mothers, and younger women as sisters (1 Tim. 5:1–2).

There are numerous indications in the New Testament of the deep spiritual intimacy Paul shared with his converts and fellow believers. To the Thessalonians he writes:

> So, being affectionately desirous of you, we were ready to share with you not only the gospel of God but also our own selves, because you had become very dear to us. (1 Thess. 2:8)

Similarly, he "yearns" for the Philippians with the "affection of Christ" (Phil. 1:8); he longs to visit the Romans so to be "refreshed" by their company (Rom. 15:23, 32); and he weeps and embraces the Ephesian elders (Acts 20:37) upon his departure from Miletus. Though Paul did not have his own wife and family, he experienced profound familial inti-macy within the spiritual family of God in which he had utterly invested himself.

As men free to invest all their time and energy in advancing the kingdom of God, neither Paul nor Jesus lived a life alone. This is not to suggest that the relationships that come through the new family of God are a substitute for a spouse, a way to fill the relational gap of not having a spouse and family. There is something unique in God's joining man and wife in "one flesh" that is never replicated in other types of human relationships. In remaining single, one sacrifices such physical intimacy.

But intimacy has other dimensions, beyond the physical. A bond of spiritual unity as brothers and sisters in Christ can emerge through a oneness of mind in corporate prayer and worship, a shared eternal hope, and a common mission of proclaiming the gospel and making disciples that also powerfully transcends human day-to-day experience. The freedom and flexibility of the single life will often open access to levels and opportunities of spiritual intimacy with other believers that those who are married do not have available in the same way and to the same degree.

Paul's General Response to Their Question in 1 Corinthians 7:8–16

After establishing that control of one's sexual behavior has a direct bearing upon the issue of marriage, Paul gives a response to their question by addressing both the married and unmarried. In 1 Corinthians 7:8–9 Paul gives a response to the unmarried generally, which includes the divorced and widowed, about whether to marry. He may have singled out widows because they represented a significant sector of the congregation. His advice here is a direct application of his fundamental principle given in 7:1b:

> Now I say to the unmarried and to the widows, it is good for them if they remain as I am. But if they are not able to exercise self-control, they should marry, for it is better to marry than to burn. (1 Cor. 7:8–9, AT)

This passage reinforces that 7:1b is probably Paul's formulation rather than a restatement of a question posed by the Corinthians, as it is essentially the same point expressed earlier (i.e., it is good to remain unmarried if and only if one can exercise self-control), but here he includes the explicit "I say." There is a double reference to their sexual incontinence with the verbs "exercise self-control" and "burn," a euphemism for sexual passion.

Paul then gives a general word to those in a believing marriage (vv. 10–11) and those in mixed marriages (vv. 12–16). Here his charge to the married reiterates Jesus' command against divorce. His extended discussion is intended to address the special situation of existing marriages to unbelievers in light of his strong condemnation against having any sexual contact with prostitutes in 1 Corinthians 6:15–18. Though one joined to the Lord should not be joined to a (presumably unbelieving) prostitute, a Christian should not divorce an unbelieving spouse who consents to live with him or her.

Paul's Vision: Singleness as Charisma for Corinth

We have argued that there is good reason to believe that the actual kernel of the Corinthians' question to Paul about marriage and his response is given in 1 Corinthians 7:25–26, which he then develops more fully in 7:27–35. Before we look at that, we need to consider three underlying issues: (1) the purpose of the segue in 7:17–24; (2) the identity of the "virgins" in 7:25; and (3) the identity of the "present crisis" mentioned in 7:26.

First, then, is Paul's segue in 7:17–24 that he gives before returning to the Corinthians' original question in 7:25–40. In 7:25–40 he uses two illustrations to make a single point—that Christians need not change the condition in which they were called to Christ (7:17, 20, 24). The point is that one has full status within the family of God irrespective of social categories. The Gentile need not be circumcised to become a Jew (vv. 18–19). The slave need not be concerned about obtaining his freedom (vv. 21–22) although he or she is free to take advantage of opportunities for freedom. The illustrations anticipate Paul's response to the marriage question; namely, that the Christian who has not married need not get married for the sake of improving his or her status within the community (v. 27). Given the imperial marriage legislation, which compelled individuals to marry through a system of rewards and enhanced status, there is little doubt that, in a Roman colony such as Corinth, there was substantial societal pressure to marry, have children, and be politically active. Contrary to Augustus, Paul emphasizes that in the family of God, one's status is not improved through marriage.

Second, the precise identity of the "virgins" addressed in 7:25–40 poses one of the greatest exegetical difficulties in the chapter. The principal problem is that the word *virgin* has been used a number of different ways in the passage. Paul appears to use the term to refer generically to never-married males and females in verse 25, specifically to unmarried females in verses 28 and 34, and specifically to betrothed females in verses 36–38. The natural tendency is to attempt to read all the references as a single group. However, it seems necessary to let Paul's context in each case govern the meaning rather than to force a single interpretation for all six instances.[80]

There is no lexical justification to presume that when Paul begins his discussion in 7:25, "Now concerning virgins . . . " (NASB), he is referring to betrothed individuals. The Greek word for *virgin*, *parthenos*, never in itself designates an engaged person without some further designation or contextual clue (i.e., Luke 1:27, "a virgin betrothed").[81] In the three references to virgin in 7:36–38 Paul includes a personal or reflective pronoun, "his" or "his own," indicating that in this case the virgin "belongs" to the man as his particular betrothed virgin.[82] No such indicator appears in 7:25–34. The default is to understand *parthenos* as simply a never-married female, which appears to fit the context of verses 28 and 34.

In verse 25, however, he uses the term "virgin," *parthenos*, as a topical marker to introduce the topic for discussion. Since he is returning to the question of whether it is fitting and beneficial to marry at all, and since Paul's response to this question hinges on one remaining sexually abstinent (i.e., remaining a *parthenos*, whether male or female[83]) as he has just clarified in 7:1–7 and also in 7:8–9, he simply calls them what he presumes they must be—namely, virgins—before he gives his response. In the use of this one word, he subsumes his entire earlier discussion (7:1–7) without having to refer directly to it.

The third interpretive conundrum concerns the identity of the "present crisis" mentioned in the middle of Paul's response to the Corinthians in 7:26:

> Now concerning the virgins, I do not have a command from the Lord, but I give my opinion as one, who by the Lord's mercy is trustworthy. I think then that this is good, on account of the present crisis, that it is good for a man to remain as he is. (1 Cor. 7:25–26, AT)

Commentators have long debated the exact nature of the "crisis" that is referenced in Paul's response. In short, some scholars have viewed the crisis as an apocalyptic reference to the impending great end-time tribulation,[84] while others have argued in favor of a temporal phenomenon imminently facing the Corinthians.[85]

The exegetical question is important because of its implications. Is Paul advising the Corinthians against marriage solely because he believed the end of the world was so near that having children was pointless? And, if so, how would he advise the church two thousand years later?[86] But in light of Paul's theological bedrock and the explicit challenge of Jesus to becoming eunuchs for the kingdom, Paul's advocacy of singleness has far more to do with making the most of the opportune time (1 Cor. 7:29) than with precise timetables of the *parousia*.

Paul, however, nowhere else uses the word *crisis* (Greek *anankē*) in an eschatological sense.[87] In a secular context the word was most commonly associated with either the siege of a city or a food shortage or famine.[88] The only place in the New Testament where the term is used in any kind of eschatological context occurs in Luke 21:23, where the siege of Jerusalem is described, but even there it fits the common understanding of a temporal crisis. Thus, it appears most likely that here Paul is referring to some sort of temporal economic crisis confronting the Corinthians, most probably a food shortage.[89] The crisis most likely served as a catalyst for the Corinthians to bring to Paul the question of the wisdom and necessity of marriage.

Living a Simpler Life (1 Corinthians 7:27–28)

After agreeing with the Corinthians' disposition not to marry in light of their particular circumstances Paul then elaborates:

> Are you bound to a wife? Do not seek to be free. Are you free from a wife? Do not seek a wife. But if you do marry, you do not sin, and if a virgin marries, she does not sin. But such as these will have trouble in the flesh, and I want to spare you that. (vv. 27–28, AT)

Two factors from the Corinthians' experience inform Paul's immediate response to their question. The first is evident in the balanced statements in verse 27 that those "bound" should not seek to be "free," while those "free" should not seek to be married. Just as the circumcised has no greater status than the uncircumcised, the free has no greater status than the slave; so too in God's economy and *contrary* to the goals of Augustus's marriage legislation, the married person has no greater status than the unmarried. Despite the intense social and political pressures to marry, the Christian's status in Christ is not improved through taking up the responsibilities of marriage and family.

A second factor Paul appears to be addressing is the classical Greco-Roman marriage debate. He counsels that the wise choice of action, especially in circumstances of distress or crisis such as they were experiencing, was to remain just as they were. Paul clarifies that he is advising, not insisting, that they remain single. To marry is not a sin—one is perfectly free to do so—but one should never feel compelled to do so. The phrase, "worldly troubles," literally "tribulations" (*thlipsis*) "of the flesh" (v. 28), speaks directly to the familiar issues of the marriage debate.

Epictetus, for example, speaks of the burden of responsibilities that falls upon the married man. He must "show certain services" to his father-in-law and the rest of his wife's relatives. He must act as a nurse for his family and provide for them. "He must get a kettle to heat water for the baby, for washing it in a bath-tub; wool for his wife when she has a child, oil, a cot, a cup (the vessels get more and more numerous)."[90] Paul's response resonates in some sense with the difficulties associated with married life, which the ancients knew well. The single life is in many respects a simpler life, and Paul wanted to spare them from unnecessarily assuming the burden of worldly troubles.

Living a Sufficient Life (1 Corinthians 7:29–31)

Although the crisis of 1 Corinthians 7:26 likely fits best with the temporal world of the Corinthians and whatever about it prompted them to raise the question about marriage to Paul, we do find an eschatological argument in 7:29–31:

> I say this brothers, the time has been shortened. From now on, those who have wives should be as those who have none, and those who weep as not weeping, and those who rejoice as not rejoicing, and those who buy as not possessing, and those who use the world as not making full use of it, for the form of this world is passing away. (AT)

The Stoics with whom Paul dialoged in Athens (Acts 17:18) had argued the necessity of marriage on cosmological grounds. The social universe depended on cities, which in turn depended on family units, which in turn depended on marriage.[91] Human beings had a duty to marry for the sake of preserving the world and its institutions. Paul counters the Stoic argument by appealing to a more expansive cosmology. The survival of the world is not dependent on human marriage since the very form of the present world is already passing away in anticipation of the coming eternal kingdom of God. Something greater than the present age had broken into history, and Christians were to herald its coming.

The cosmological horizon of the Christian subsumes the present age into the eternal one. This means that the plans and purposes of the present age are subsumed into the plans and purposes of the anticipated eternal kingdom of God. This is not a denigration of the present world but a radical relativizing of the current age in light of the eternal age, recognizing that one's true sufficiency and fulfillment will be realized ultimately only in the coming age of the King and the kingdom.

From the standpoint of Paul's expanded cosmological horizons, singleness is no longer to be considered a liability because it does not further the physical race of humankind. Rather, it can be viewed as a cosmological asset and visible sign of the coming new age. However, the fact that individuals may be single and Christian does not necessarily make them vibrant witnesses of the new age. When people choose to remain single for the sake of the kingdom of God because they recognize that their true sufficiency is found only in their relationship to Christ and the coming of his kingdom, and they orient their lives around this conviction, they become in their singleness visible signs of the coming new age.

They serve as signs because the world does not have a category for this kind of intentional singleness. Singles who live with this conviction provide a powerful testimony to the sufficiency of Christ for all things—to those both inside and outside the church. This is a component of the spiritual gift or *charisma* of singleness.

Living a Life of Serving (1 Corinthians 7:32–35)

Paul shifts to a third argument, this one replete with language of the classical marriage debate: [92]

I desire you to be free from concern. One who is unmarried is concerned for the things of the Lord, how he might please the Lord. But the one who is married is concerned for the things of the world, how he might please his wife, and he is divided. And the unmarried woman or the virgin is concerned for the things of the Lord in order that she may be holy in body and in spirit. But the one who is married is concerned for the things of the world, how she may please her husband. I say this for your *own* benefit, not that I might lay a noose upon you, but to foster what is above reproach and enables constant service to the Lord without distraction. (1 Cor. 7:32–35, AT)

Those on both sides of the marriage question acknowledged that marriage incurred cares and concerns not present among those who did not marry. This perception was reinforced by comic playwrights such as Menander, who readily intoned that having wife and children "brings many cares in life."[93] Paul's desire (v. 32) that they be free from concern recalls his desire for them to be as he is (v. 7).

The way in which he desires them to be like him is in being free from concern. In subsequent verses he describes this concern as for the "world," but more specifically it is concern for meeting the needs of a spouse. So Paul advises them not to marry in order to spare them worldly trouble (v. 28). The Cynics avoided the troubles and concerns of marriage in order to devote themselves to the pursuit of virtue. The Epicureans avoided the troubles and concerns of marriage for the sake of living a more tranquil life. But Paul responds to the Greco-Roman marriage question by invoking the eunuch image of Jesus—he advises them to be free from worldly concerns in order to direct that concern to the Lord, that is, to the service of the King and his kingdom.

Paul concludes by expressing his desire to foster in them what is above reproach and enables constant service to the Lord without distraction (v. 35). The first of these terms, "above reproach" (*euschēmōn*), usually means living honorably and respectably (e.g., Mark 15:43; Acts 13:50), but Paul conveys a slightly different meaning here. A clue as to how he uses it here is found in how he uses it in Romans 13:13, where it stands in direct contrast to (among other things) walking in sexual immorality and sensuality. With this term Paul is again calling them to complete integrity in the conduct of their sexual behavior.

The second term, "constant service" (*euparedros*), is not found elsewhere in the New Testament,[94] but its root connotes "sitting beside,"[95] and a sense of constant attendance in the context of devoted service fits well. The picture is of one who sits beside the Lord, ready and waiting in his service. Paul probably could not have used a more apt word to describe the relationship of a eunuch to his king. The third of these terms is *aperispastōs*, which carries the sense of being "without distraction," as described in 7:32–34.

This triad of terms probably gives us the most accurate understanding of Paul's vision of the gift of singleness in operation. He envisions those who are above reproach in their sexual conduct, undistracted by spouse and family, and ready and waiting at the service of their Lord.

The vision Paul offers is genuinely paradoxical. He employs language that conveys being free from the concerns of marriage, spouse, and children. It is something he desires for their benefit, not to shackle them, simply trading one noose for another (v. 35). However, the freedom he has in mind is for the express purpose of constant service to the Lord, just as a eunuch was always at the beck and call of his king. It is a freedom to serve. It is this freedom that Paul relishes and desires, with every ounce of his being, that the Corinthians too might experience.

Wrapping Up

Despite its occasioned nature, Paul's response in 1 Corinthians 7 provides a fitting capstone to a biblical theology of singleness. Most likely the Corinthians that Paul was addressing were not exuberant ascetics but representative of an immature church entrenched in the secular thinking of the day and thus questioning their teacher on the wisdom and necessity of marriage, especially amidst adverse circumstances. Paul, in his response, had to navigate the difficult tension between the biblical worldview and that of his neophyte church. While preserving the high view of marriage and sexuality reflected in the Old Testament law, Paul was able to entertain the question from the perspective of the classic marriage debate familiar to his Corinthian audience.

His answer first had to address a critical blind spot in their assumptions. The question of whether to marry was not independent of the issue of sexual continence but related to it. Conversely, marriage was neither a means of enhancing one's status nor required for the purpose of preserving the social cosmos. Nor was it required as an expression of obedience to the Old Testament law or manifestation of covenantal blessing, since in the new covenant one is fully blessed in union with Christ independent of marriage, family, or possessions. In the sufficiency of Christ, one can remain in whatever condition he was called.

But marriage is a provision of God for maintaining sexual continence. That is why Jesus' call to be a eunuch for the kingdom was not given to all, but only to those who can willingly receive it in a life of sexual purity. The capability to remain single is thus to be regarded as a spiritual gift, and it is characterized by three predominant features: a life of simplicity free from the stresses of spouse and family; a life that finds sufficiency in the blessings of Christ alone apart from the experiences of sexual intimacy, marital companionship, and physical family; and a life ready and free for service to the King in whatever way he should call.

Epilogue

Christianity is distinctive from its monotheistic sibling faiths of Judaism, Islam, and Mormonism in its affirmation of singleness. While on the one hand Christianity, like the others, affirms a high view of marriage and family and a high sexual ethic, understanding sexual relations as something designed by God for and within marital union, it differs from the others in distinctly affirming both singleness and marriage as something good within the new family of God. The reason for this difference has its roots in what makes Christianity fundamentally different from its sibling faiths, namely, its affirmation that Jesus Christ has come in human history as God's offspring and that through him come all the blessings of the new covenant.

Jesus Christ is the fulfillment of the promised seed of Abraham, and in him are Abraham's true offspring, heirs of the eternal inheritance promised by God. Since all the blessings of the new covenant are realized through our reconciliation to God through Christ, marriage is no longer a fundamental marker of covenantal blessing as it was in the covenant of Sinai. Singleness lived to the glory of God and the furtherance of his kingdom testifies to the complete sufficiency of Christ for all things. The Christian is fully blessed in Christ, whether he or she is married or single, rich or poor, in comfort or duress. The distinctive calling of singleness within the church testifies to this truth.

Paul distinguishes the spiritual gift or *charisma* of singleness by three elements. First, it is characterized by one who, by the grace of God, lives a continent life apart from marriage, that is, above reproach in the sexual arena. Second, it is distinguished as a life free from the distractions of a spouse and children, a life characterized by freedom and simplicity, which testifies to the complete sufficiency of Christ. Third, it is a life enabled for constant service to the King and the kingdom. It emulates the model of the eunuch who is ready and waiting to serve the king whenever and however he is called.

The macro-trend in Western society indicates that the institution of marriage is in steady decline. This largely reflects the continued waning influence of Judeo-Christian presuppositions in the wider public sphere, i.e., the fundamental presumption that marriage between a man and a woman is something good and to be cherished. From the limited data I have examined from the ancient world, the macro trend of the West is moving much closer to approximating the marriage and sexual behavior patterns of pagan Roman culture—patterns characterized by a wider variety of living arrangements and a dissociation between marriage and the locus of one's sexual behavior. Thus, the distinctively biblical-Christian view of singleness and marriage needs to be articulated again to an increasingly pagan wider world.

This re-articulation should draw people to the positive vision the Christian Scriptures provide for *both* marriage and singleness as well as for human sexuality: Christian marriage is a testimony of the utterly faithful and unchanging love of God for his people in a permanent covenant relationship with him;[1] Christian singleness is a testimony to the complete sufficiency of Christ for the present age and gives visible witness to the hope of our eternal inheritance yet to come; and Christian sexuality is an expression of the exclusive unity and oneness in the bond of the marriage relationship.

Within the church this message is also in need of fresh articulation. Our youth are subject to an endless barrage of confusing messages concerning relationships and sexuality. Our culture idolizes the never-satiated lusts for sexual intimacy and the trappings of material comforts. To this end the Christian church needs to be intentional in teaching the biblical vision for both Christian singleness and Christian marriage. This entails not "Christianizing" the pervasive relational and material lusts of our culture into a preoccupation with building perfect families and exquisite homes. What is needed is a vision for promoting lifestyles in accordance with the fundamental tenets of the gospel, that the kingdom of God is at hand and that consummate satisfaction is to be found ultimately only in being reconciled to our God in Jesus Christ.

In accordance with this, the church should encourage all those who can to receive the challenge of both Jesus and Paul to remain single and free for the kingdom of God as a visible testimony of Christ's sufficiency in the present age and the true inheritance yet to come. Similarly, the church should again articulate within its ranks Paul's admonition that the choice to remain single is not independent of one's sexual behavior. Sexual union was ordained by God to be a physical expression of marital union, and the two go together necessarily and exclusively. Christian marriage is thus a holy and blessed alternative to Christian singleness, testifying to the exalted covenantal union of God with his people and modeled after the relational intimacy of that union.

The excessive value the Western world has placed on individualism fosters a psychological tendency to associate singleness with living alone. This is a tendency the church should resist. Christian singleness is not a denial of the underlying principle of Genesis 2:18, that it is not good to be alone. Neither Jesus nor Paul as single men was devoid of relationships. On the contrary, their relationships flourished in both number and depth by the freedom and flexibility their singleness afforded them.

There are many possible living arrangements for single Christians. As a single adult, I have lived alone in a house, with roommates, as part of a community of singles, as part of another Christian household, and with elderly parents. Of all these arrangements, living alone was least satisfying for my personal and spiritual welfare. The flexibility and simplicity of singleness can be a strategic asset for building quality and substantive relationships within the family of God—living arrangements are an opportunity to leverage this asset.

Like Christian marriage, Christian singleness lived in its fullest expression is a powerful testimony to the gospel. In the unchanging commitment of love and submission expressed between husband and wife, Christian marriage testifies to God's faithful covenantal love toward his people and their submission and reception to his sovereign love. Christian singleness is a testimony to the supreme sufficiency of Christ for all things, testifying that through Christ life is fully blessed even without marriage and children. It prophetically points to a reality greater than the satisfactions of this present age by consciously anticipating the Christian's eternal inheritance in the kingdom of God. Christian singleness lived as testimony of this gospel truth is a redeeming singleness.

Bibliography

Allison, Dale. *Matthew: A Shorter Commentary*. London: T & T Clark, 2004.

Arnold, Bill T., and Bryan E. Beyer, eds. *Readings from the Ancient Near East: Primary Sources for Old Testament Study*. Grand Rapids, MI: Baker, 2002.

Balch, David L. "1 Corinthians 7:32–35 and Stoic Debates about Marriage, Anxiety and Distraction." *JBL* 102 (1983): 429–39.

Balz, Horst, and Gerhard Schneider, eds. *Exegetical Dictionary of the New Testament*. 3 vols. Edinburgh: T & T Clark, 1990–1993.

Barclay, John M. G. "Thessalonica and Corinth: Social Contrasts in Pauline Christianity." *JBL* 47 (1992): 49–74.

Barna, George. *Single Focus: Understanding Single Adults*. Ventura, CA: Regal, 2003.

Barrett, C. K. "The Allegory of Abraham, Sarah, and Hagar in the Argument of Galatians." In *Essays on Paul*, 154–70. Philadelphia: Westminster, 1982.

———. *A Commentary on the First Epistle to the Corinthians*. 2d ed. London: A & C Black, 1971.

———. *The Gospel According to St. John: An Introduction with Commentary and Notes on the Greek Text*, 2d ed. Philadelphia: Westminster, 1978.

Bartchy, S. Scott. *First-Century Slavery and 1 Corinthians 7:21*. Missoula, MT: University of Montana, 1973.

Beale, G. K. "The Old Testament Background of Reconciliation in 2 Corinthians 5–7 and Its Bearing on the Literary Problem of 2 Corinthians 6.14–7.1." *NTS* 35 (1989): 550–81.

Betz, Hans Dieter. *A Commentary on Paul's Letter to the Churches in Galatia*, Hermeneia—A Critical and Historical Commentary on the Bible. Philadelphia: Fortress, 1979.

Block, Daniel I. *Judges, Ruth*, NAC. Nashville, TN: Broadman, 1999.

Bright, John. *Jeremiah*. Edited by William Foxwell Albright and David Noel Freedman. 2d ed, AB. Garden City, NY: Doubleday, 1979.

Bruce, F. F. *The Epistle to the Galatians*. Edited by I. Howard Marshall and Donald A. Hagner, NIGTC. Grand Rapids, MI: Eerdmans, 1982.

———. *The Gospel of John*. Grand Rapids, MI: Eerdmans, 1983.

Buchanan, George Wesley. *The Book of Daniel*. Vol. 25, The Mellen Biblical Commentary Intertextual: Old Testament Series in Forty Volumes. Lewiston, NY: Edwin Mellen 1999.

Burke, D. G. "Eunuch." In *The International Standard Bible Encyclopedia*, edited by G. W. Bromiley, 200–202. Grand Rapids, MI: Eerdmans, 1982.

Bush, Frederick W. *Ruth, Esther*. Vol. 9, WBC. Dallas: Word, 1996.

Carson, Donald A. *The Gospel According to John*. Leicester, UK: Inter-Varsity, 1991.

Cartlidge, David R. "1 Cor. 7 as a Foundation for a Christian Sex Ethic." *JR* 55 (1975): 220–34.

"Celibacy." In *The New Encyclopedia of Judaism*, edited by Geoffrey Wigoder, 158–59. New York: New York University Press, 1989.

Charlesworth, James H., ed. *The Old Testament Pseudepigrapha*. 2 vols. New York: Doubleday, 1985.

Childs, Brevard S. *Isaiah*, The Old Testament Library. Louisville, KY: Westminster, 2001.

Collins, C. John. "Galatians 3:16: What Kind of an Exegete Was Paul?" *TynBul* 54.1 (2003): 75–86.

Collins, Raymond F. *First Corinthians*. Edited by Daniel J. Harrington, S.J., SP. Collegeville, MN: Liturgical Press, 1999.

Conzelmann, Hans. *1 Corinthians: A Commentary on the First Epistle to the Corinthians*, Hermeneia—A Critical and Historical Commentary on the Bible. Philadelphia: Fortress, 1975.

Danby, Herbert. *The Mishnah*. Oxford: Oxford University Press, 1933.

Danker, Frederick William, ed. *A Greek-English Lexicon of the New Testament*. 3d. ed. Chicago: University of Chicago Press, 2000.

Danylak, Barry. "Tiberius Claudius Dinippus and the Food Shortages in Corinth." *TynBul* 59.2 (2008): 231–70.

Davies, Eryl W. "Inheritance Rights and the Hebrew Levirate Marriage." *VT* 31.2 (1981): 138–44.

de Boer, Martinus C. "Paul's Quotation of Isaiah 54.1 in Galatians 4.27." *NTS* 50 (2004): 370–89.

Deming, Will. *Paul on Marriage and Celibacy: The Hellenistic Background of 1 Corinthians 7*. 2d ed. Grand Rapids, MI: Eerdmans, 2004.

Demosthenes. *Orations 50–59: Private Cases. In Neaeram*. Translated by A. T. Murray, LCL. Cambridge: Harvard University Press, 1939.

Dio Chrysostom: Discourses 12–30. Translated by J. H. Cohoon, LCL. Cambridge: Harvard University Press, 1939.

Dio's Roman History. Translated by Earnest Cary and Herbert Baldwin Foster. 9 vols. LCL. Cambridge: Harvard University Press, 1914-1927.

Dunn, James D. G. *The Epistle to the Galatians*. Peabody, MA: Hendrickson, 1993.

Eastman, Susan. *Recovering Paul's Mother Tongue*. Grand Rapids, MI: Eerdmans, 2007.

Emerton, J. A. "The Translation and Interpretation of Isaiah vi.13." In *Interpreting the*

Hebrew Bible: Essays in Honour of E. I. J. Rosenthal, edited by J. A. Emerton and S. C. Reif, 85–118. Cambridge: Cambridge University Press, 1982.

Engels, Donald W. *Roman Corinth: An Alternative Model for the Classical City*: Chicago: University of Chicago Press, 1990.

Epictetus. *The Discourses as Reported by Arrian, the Manual, and Fragments*. Translated by W. A. Oldfather. 2 vols. LCL. Cambridge: Harvard University Press, 1925–1928.

Epstein, I. *The Babylonian Talmud*. London: Soncino, 1952.

Fee, Gordon D. "1 Cor. 7:1 in the NIV." *JETS* 23 (1980): 307–14.

———. *The First Epistle to the Corinthians*, NICNT. Grand Rapids, MI: Eerdmans, 1987.

Fitzmyer, Joseph A. *First Corinthians: A New Translation with Introduction and Commentary*. Edited by William Foxwell Albright and David Noel Freedman, Anchor Yale Bible. New Haven, CT: Yale University Press, 2008.

Foerster, Werner. "κληρονόμος κτλ," *TDNT*. Edited by Gerhard Kittel and Freidrich Gerhard, 767–85. Grand Rapids, MI: Eerdmans, 1965.

Frost, Stanley Bruce. "The Memorial of the Childless Man." *Int* 25 (1972): 437–50.

Gundry-Volf, Judith M. "Celibate Pneumatics and Social Power: On the Motivations for Sexual Asceticism in Corinth." *USQR* 48, no. 3–4 (1994): 105–26.

Hasel, Gerhard F. *The Remnant*. Berrien Springs, MI: Andrews University Press, 1974.

Hayes, Richard B. *Echoes of Scripture in the Letters of Paul*. New Haven, CT: Yale University Press, 1989.

Héring, Jean. *The First Epistle of Saint Paul to the Corinthians*. London: Epworth, 1962.

Hesiod. *Theogony. Works and Days. Testimonia*. Translated by Glenn W. Most, Loeb Classical Library. Cambridge: Harvard University Press, 2006.

Holladay, William L., ed. *A Concise Hebrew and Aramaic Lexicon of the Old Testament*. Leiden: Brill, 1988.

House, Paul R. "Isaiah's Call and Its Context in Isaiah 1–6." *CTR* 6 (1993): 207–22.

Hunt, E. David. "Eunuch." In *The Oxford Classical Dictionary*. Edited by Simon Hornblower and Anthony Spawforth, 569. Oxford: Oxford University Press, 2003.

Instone-Brewer, David. *Divorce and Remarriage in the Bible: The Social and Literary Context*. Grand Rapids, MI: Eerdmans, 2002.

Josephus. *Jewish Antiquities, Books I–IV*. Translated by H. St. J. Thackeray, LCL. Cambridge: Harvard University Press, 1930.

———. *The Life Against Apion*. Translated by H. St. J. Thackeray, LCL. Cambridge: Harvard University Press, 1926.

Keil, C. F., and F. Delitzsch. *Biblical Commentary on the Prophecies of Isaiah*. Translated by James Martin. Vol. 1. Grand Rapids, MI: Eerdmans, 1950.

Bibliography

————. *The Pentateuch*. Translated by James Martin. Vol. 1, Commentary on the Old Testament in Ten Volumes. Grand Rapids: Eerdmans, 1973.

Kennedy, George A. *Progymnasmata: Greek Textbooks of Prose Composition and Rhetoric*. Leiden, UK: Brill, 2003.

Kistemaker, Simon J. *New Testament Commentary: 1 Corinthians*. Grand Rapids, MI: Baker, 1993.

Kitchen, K. A. *Ancient Orient and Old Testament*. Downers Grove, IL: InterVarsity, 1966.

Kline, Meredith G. *Treaty of the Great King: The Covenant Structure of Deuteronomy: Studies and Commentary*. Grand Rapids, MI: Eerdmans, 1963.

Knight, George A. *Servant Theology: A Commentary on the Book of Isaiah 40–55*, ITC. Edinburgh: Handsel, 1984.

Koole, Jan Leunis. *Isaiah Three*. 3 Vols. Historical Commentary on the Old Testament. Leuven: Peeters, 1997.

Lachs, Samuel Tobias. *A Rabbinic Commentary on the New Testament: The Gospels of Matthew, Mark and Luke*. Hoboken, NJ: Ktav, 1987.

Liddell, Henry George, and Robert Scott. *A Greek-English Lexicon with a Revised Supplement*. Oxford: Clarendon, 1996.

Lipiński, E. "נָחַל nāḥal נַחֲלָה nāḥalâ," *TDOT*. Edited by G. Johannes Botterweck, Helmer Ringgren and Heinz-Josef Fabry. Vol. 9, 319–35. Grand Rapids, MI: Eerdmans, 1998.

Livy. *History of Rome*. Translated by B. O. Foster, et al. 14 vols. LCL. Cambridge: Harvard University Press, 1919–59.

Loader, William. *Sexuality and the Jesus Tradition*. Grand Rapids, MI: Eerdmans, 2005.

Longenecker, Richard N. *Galatians*, WBC. Dallas: Word, 1990.

Love, Julian P. "Call of Isaiah: Exposition of Isaiah 6." *Int* 11.3 (1957): 282–96.

Lucian. Translated by A. M. Harmon, K. Kilburn, and M. D. MacLeod. 8 vols. LCL. Cambridge: Harvard University Press, 1913–1967.

Lutz, Cora, ed. *Musonius Rufus, "The Roman Socrates."* Vol. 10. Yale Classical Studies. New Haven, CT: Yale University Press, 1947.

Luz, Ulrich. *Matthew 8–20*. Translated by James E. Crouch, Hermeneia—A Critical and Historical Commentary on the Bible. Minneapolis: Fortress, 2001.

Malherbe, Abraham J. *Moral Exhortation: A Greco-Roman Sourcebook*. Philadelphia: Westminster Press, 1986.

Manor, Dale W. "A Brief History of Levirate Marriage as It Relates to the Bible." *ResQ* 27 (1984): 129–42.

Martínez, Florentino García. *The Dead Sea Scrolls Translated*. Translated by Wilfred G. E. Watson. 2d ed. Leiden, UK: Brill, 1992.

Martyn, J. Louis. *Galatians*. AB. New York: Doubleday, 1997.

————. *History and Theology in the Fourth Gospel*. Nashville, TN: Abingdon, 1979.

McConkie, Bruce R. *Mormon Doctrine.* Salt Lake City, UT: Bookcraft, 1966.

McKeown, James. *Genesis.* Grand Rapids, MI: Eerdmans, 2008.

Meeks, Wayne A. *The First Urban Christians: The Social World of the Apostle Paul.* 2d ed. New Haven, CT: Yale University Press, 2003.

———. "The Image of the Androgyne: Some Uses of a Symbol in Earliest Christianity." *HR* 13 (1974): 165–208.

Mendenhall, George. "Covenant Forms in Israelite Tradition." *The BA* 17 (1954): 50–76.

Motyer, Alec. *The Prophecy of Isaiah: An Introduction and Commentary.* Downers Grove, IL: InterVarsity, 1993.

Neusner, Jacob. *The Fathers According to Rabbi Nathan: An Analytical Translation and Explanation.* Atlanta: Scholars Press, 1986.

———, ed. *Genesis Rabbah: The Judaic Commentary to the Book of Genesis.* Atlanta: Scholars Press, 1986.

Nock, Arthur D. "Eunuchs in Ancient Religion." In *Essays on Religion and the Ancient World,* edited by Zeph Stewart, 7–15. Oxford: Clarendon, 1972.

Nolland, John *The Gospel of Matthew.* Edited by I. Howard Marshall and Donald A. Hagner, NIGTC. Grand Rapids, MI: Eerdmans, 2005.

Oswalt, John N. *The Book of Isaiah: Chapters 1–39,* NICOT. Grand Rapids, MI: Eerdmans, 1986.

———. *The Book of Isaiah, Chapters 40–66,* NICOT. Grand Rapids, MI: Eerdmans, 1998.

———. "Isaiah: Theology of." *NIDOTTE.* Edited by Willem VanGemeren. Vol. 4, 725–32. Grand Rapids, MI: Zondervan, 1997.

Parsons, Mikeal C. "Isaiah 53 in Acts 8: A Reply to Professor Morna Hooker." In *Jesus and the Suffering Servant: Isaiah 53 and Christian Origins.* Edited by William H. Bellinger Jr. and William R. Farmer, 104–19. Harrisburg, PA: Trinity Press International, 1998.

Pendrick, Gerard J., ed. *Antiphon the Sophist: The Fragments.* Cambridge: Cambridge University Press, 2002.

Philo. Translated by F. H. Colson and G. H. Whitaker. 10 vols. LCL. Cambridge: Harvard University Press, 1929–1962.

Phipps, William E. "Is Paul's Attitude toward Sexual Relations Contained in 1 Cor. 7:1?" *NTS* 28 (1982): 125–31.

———. *The Sexuality of Jesus.* Cleveland, OH: Pilgrim, 1996.

Pieper, August. *Isaiah II [Yesha'yah 2]: An Exposition of Isaiah 40–66.* Translated by Erwin E. Kowalke. Milwaukee, WI: Northwestern, 1979.

Piper, John. *This Momentary Marriage: A Parable of Permanence.* Wheaton, IL: Crossway, 2009.

Bibliography

Plato. *Laws: Books I–VI*. Translated by R. G. Bury. LCL. Cambridge, MA: Harvard University Press, 1926.

Plutarch. *Moralia*. Translated by Frank Cole Babbitt, et al. 16 vols. LCL. Cambridge: Harvard University Press, 1927–2004.

———. *Plutarch's Lives*. Translated by Bernadotte Perrin. 11 vols. LCL. Cambridge: Harvard University Press, 1914–1926.

Polybius. *The Histories*. Translated by W. R. Paton. 6 vols. LCL. Cambridge: Harvard University Press, 1922–1927.

Pritchard, James B., ed. *Ancient Near Eastern Texts Relating to the Old Testament*. 3d ed. with Supplement. Princeton, NJ: Princeton University Press, 1969.

Quesnell, Quentin. "'Made Themselves Eunuchs for the Kingdom of Heaven' (Mt 19,12)." *CBQ* 30 (1968): 335–58.

Ramsay, William M. "Historical Commentary on the Epistles to the Corinthians." *Expositor* 6.1 (1900): 19–31, 91–111, 203–17, 73–89, 380–87.

Reiterer, F. W. "שׁם šēm." *TDOT*. Edited by G. Johannes Botterweck, Helmer Ringgren, and Heinz-Josef Fabry. Vol. 15, 128–74. Grand Rapids, MI: Eerdmans, 2006.

Rizvi, Sayyid Muhammad. *Marriage and Morals in Islam*. Qum: Ansariyan, 1990.

Ross, Alan P. "#9005 שׁם." *NIDOTTE*. Edited by Willem VanGemeren. Vol. 4, 147–51. Grand Rapids, MI: Zondervan, 1996.

Scalise, Pamela J. "'I Have Produced a Man With the Lord': God as Provider of Offspring in Old Testament Theology." *RevExp* 91.4 (1994): 577–89.

Schmithals, Walter. *Gnosticism in Corinth*. Translated by John E. Steely. New York: Abingdon, 1971.

Schneider, Johannes. "εὐνοῦχος, εὐνουχίζω" *TDNT*. Edited by Gerhard Kittel and Freidrich Gerhard, 765–68. Grand Rapids, MI: Eerdmans, 1964.

Schoeps, H. J. *Paul: The Theology of the Apostle in the Light of Jewish Religious History*. Translated by Harold Knight. Philadelphia: Westminster, 1961.

Schrage, Wolfgang. *Der erste Brief an die Korinther 2. Teilband 1Kor 6,12–11,16*, Evangelisch-Katholischer Kommentar. Düsseldorf: Benziger Verlag, 1995.

———. "Zur Frontstellung der paulinischen Ehebewertung in 1 Kor 7 1–7." *ZNW* 67 (1976): 214–34.

Simpson, J. A., and E. S. C. Weiner, eds. *The Oxford English Dictionary*. 20 vols. Oxford: Clarendon, 1989.

Sipe, A. W. Richard. "Celibacy." *The Oxford Companion to Christian Thought*. Edited by Adrian Hastings, 104–5. Oxford: Oxford University Press, 2000.

Smith, P. A. *Rhetoric and Redaction in Trito-Isaiah: The Structure, Growth and Authorship of Isaiah 56-66* Leiden, UK: Brill, 1995.

Sobo, Elisa J., and Sandra Bell, eds. *Celibacy, Culture, and Society: The Anthropology of Sexual Abstinence*. Madison, WI: University of Wisconsin Press, 2001.

Talbert, Charles H. *Reading Corinthians: A Literary and Theological Commentary on I & II Corinthians*. Rev. ed. Reading the New Testament. London: SPCK, 1987.

Talmage, James E. *A Study of the Articles of Faith*. Salt Lake City, UT: Church of Jesus Christ of Latter-day Saints, 1974.

Taylor, C. C. W. *The Atomists Leucippus and Democritus*. Toronto: University of Toronto Press, 1999.

Thiselton, Anthony. *The First Epistle to the Corinthians: A Commentary on the Greek Text*. Edited by I. Howard Marshall and Donald A. Hagner, NIGTC. Grand Rapids, MI: Eerdmans, 2000.

Thompson, Thomas, and Dorothy Thompson. "Some Legal Problems in the Book of Ruth." *VT* 18 (1968): 79–99.

Tur-Sinai, N. H. "A Contribution to the Understanding of Isaiah i-xii." *ScrHier* 8 (1961): 145–88.

van der Woude, A. S. "שֵׁם šēm name." *TLOT*. Edited by Jenni Ernst and Claus Westermann. Vol. 3, 1348–67. Peabody, MA: Hendrickson, 1997.

Waltke, Bruce K. *Genesis: A Commentary*. Grand Rapids, MI: Zondervan, 2001.

Weinfeld, M. "The Covenant of Grant in the Old Testament and in the Ancient Near East." *JAOS* 90 (1970): 184–203.

———. "כְּרִ֫ית berîth." *TDOT*. Edited by G. Johannes Botterweck, Helmer Ringgren, and Heinz-Josef Fabry. Vol. 2, 253–79. Grand Rapids, MI: Eerdmans, 1975.

Wells, Roy D. "Isaiah as an Exponent of Torah." In *New Visions of Isaiah*, edited by R. F. Melugin and M. A. Sweeney, 140–55. Sheffield: Sheffield Academic Press, 1996.

Wenham, David. "Paul's Use of the Jesus Tradition." In *The Jesus Tradition outside the Gospels*, 7–37. Sheffield: JSOT, 1984.

Wenham, Gordon. *Genesis 1–15*, WBC. Waco, TX: Word, 1987.

———. *Genesis 16–50*, WBC. Waco, TX: Word, 1994.

Westermann, Claus. *Genesis 12–36*. Minneapolis: Augsburg, 1985.

Wilcox, Max. "The Promise of the 'Seed' in the New Testament and the Targumin." *JSNT* 5 (1979): 2–20.

Wilkinson, Bruce. *The Prayer of Jabez: Breaking Through to the Blessed Life*. Sisters, OR: Multnomah, 2000.

Winter, Bruce W. "Secular and Christian Responses to Corinthian Famines." *TynBul* 40 (1989): 86–106.

Wire, Antoinette Clark. *The Corinthian Woman Prophets: A Reconstruction through Paul's Rhetoric*. Minneapolis: Fortress, 1990.

Wright, Christopher J. H. "#5706 נחל." *NIDOTTE*. Edited by Willem VanGemeren. Vol. 3, 77–81. Grand Rapids, MI: Zondervan, 1996.

Wright, Tom. *Paul for Everyone: 1 Corinthians*. Louisville, KY: Westminster, 2004.

Bibliography

Xenophon. *Memorabilia. Oeconomicus. Symposium. Apology.* Translated by E. C. Marchant and O. J. Todd, LCL. Cambridge: Harvard University Press, 1923.

Yamauchi, Edwin M. "Was Nehemiah the Cupbearer a Eunuch?" *ZAW* 92.1 (1980): 132–42.

Young, Edward J. *The Book of Isaiah.* Vol. 3. Grand Rapids, MI: Eerdmans, 1972.

Notes

Introduction

1. One has only to read the description of Israel as the Lord's faithless bride in Ezek. 16:8–14 to catch a flavor of the cultural divide between the customs of Ezekiel's day and our own.

2. See *m. Yebam.* 6.6; *b. Yebam.* 63a–b; *'Abot R. Nat.* 3:4.6. The negative view toward celibate singleness persists to the modern period. The citation for "celibacy" in *The New Encyclopedia of Judaism* (1989) begins bluntly: "Marriage is a commandment in Jewish tradition and celibacy is deplored."

3. Koran 24:32; 30:21. See assessment of celibacy in Sayyid Muhammad Rizvi, *Marriage and Morals in Islam* (Qum: Ansariyan, 1990), 25–28 (http://www.rafed. net/english/books/ethics/marriage-and-morals-in-islam/), who details Mohammed's explicit rejection of celibate singleness.

4. Bruce R. McConkie, *Mormon Doctrine* (Salt Lake City, UT: Bookcraft, 1966), 117–19; James E. Talmage, *A Study of the Articles of Faith* (Salt Lake City, UT: Church of Jesus Christ of Latter-day Saints, 1974), 442–46; *Doctrine and Covenants* 131:1–4; 132:19–20.

5. U.S. Bureau of the Census, MS-1. "Marital Status of the Population 15 Years Old and Over, by Sex and Race: 1950 to Present"; Internet Release January 2010 (http://www.census.gov/population/socdemo/hh-fam/ms1.xls). The data from 1950 to 1960 also includes persons fourteen years old. Had these been excluded, the proportion of married individuals in these years would have been higher.

6. Office of National Statistics, *Population Trends,* Report No. 136 (Summer 2009), 82 Table 1.5, 114–5 Table 1 (http://www.statistics.gov.uk/downloads/theme_ population/Popular-Trends136.pdf). This data excludes persons 15 years old, included in the U.S. data in Fig. 1.1. Had this data been included, the proportion of married persons would have been lower than depicted.

7. George Barna, *Single Focus: Understanding Single Adults* (Ventura: Regal, 2003).

8. Ibid., 86, 89.

9. Ibid. On average 49 percent of the widowed attend and 37 percent of the divorced, but only 29 percent of never-married adults.

10. Barna, *Single Focus,* 88–89.

11. Ibid., 92.

12. Ibid.

13. Deut. 23:1. See also 2 Kings 20:18.

14. See definition 4 for "testament" in J. A. Simpson and E. S. C. Weiner, eds., *The Oxford English Dictionary*, 20 vols. (Oxford: Clarendon,1989).

Chapter 1: Begetting from the Beginning

1. *m. Yebam.* 6:6.

2. Though Ishmael is not given the imperative to be fruitful, he is given fruitfulness by God. The parallel with Jacob is apparent. Ishmael also begets twelve sons who become twelve tribes (Gen. 25:16).

3. Maimonides, *Mishneh Torah*, Positive Commandment 212.

4. See also Matt. 19:3–6; Mark 10:5–9.

5. Maimonides, *Mishneh Torah*, Positive Commandment 213.

6. ʾAbot R. Nat. 3:4.6, in *The Fathers According to Rabbi Nathan: An Analytical Translation and Explanation*, trans. Jacob Neusner (Atlanta: Scholar's Press, 1986), 33.

7. See Plato, *Laws* 4.721A. Plato's *Laws* is his more mature treatise on political theory in comparison with his earlier more avant-garde work in *The Republic*.

8. Gordon Wenham, *Genesis 1–15*, WBC (Waco, TX: Word, 1987), 80.

9. Ibid., 81; Justin, *Dial.* 102; Irenaeus, *Haer.* 4.40; 5.21.

10. Pamela J. Scalise, "'I Have Produced a Man with the Lord': God as Provider of Offspring in Old Testament Theology," *RevExp* 91.4 (1994): 577–79.

11. I am indebted in this section to the observations of Max Wilcox, "The Promise of the 'Seed' in the New Testament and the Targumin," *JSNT* 5 (1979): 14–15.

12. Translations of the Pseudepigrapha are from James H. Charlesworth, ed., *The Old Testament Pseudepigrapha*, 2 vols. (New York: Doubleday, 1985).

13. *Genesis Rabbah* 23.5.2, in *Genesis Rabbah: The Judaic Commentary to the Book of Genesis*, ed. Jacob Neusner (Atlanta: Scholars Press, 1986), 259.

14. Cf. Acts 7:5; Heb. 11:13.

15. James McKeown, *Genesis* (Grand Rapids, MI: Eerdmans, 2008), 85.

16. Claus Westermann, *Genesis 12–36* (Minneapolis: Augsburg, 1985), 230.

17. M. Weinfeld, "כְּרִ״ח *berîth*," *TDOT*, ed. G. Johannes Botterweck, Helmer Ringgren, and Heinz-Josef Fabry (Grand Rapids, MI: Eerdmans, 1975), 2:255.

18. M. Weinfeld, "The Covenant of Grant in the Old Testament and in the Ancient Near East," *JAOS* 90 (1970): 184. Work on ancient Near Eastern parallels for the Sinai covenant was done by George Mendenhall, "Covenant Forms in Israelite Tradition," *BA* 17 (1954). Weinfeld, "The Covenant of Grant in the Old Testament and in the Ancient Near East," extended this work to examine the Abrahamic and Davidic covenants.

19. Weinfeld, "Covenant of Grant," 184–85.

20. Ibid., 185.

21. Ibid., 199–200; 189–90. E.g., the expression "on that day" in 15:18, and the specific boundaries of the land granted in 15:18–21.

22. See Gordon Wenham, *Genesis 16–50*, WBC (Waco, TX: Word, 1994), 8, for analysis of the parallels.

23. Bruce K. Waltke, *Genesis: A Commentary* (Grand Rapids, MI: Zondervan, 2001), 258.

24. Wenham, *Genesis 16–50*, 20. Cf. 28:3; 35:11; 48:3; 49:25.

25. McKeown, *Genesis*, 99–100.

26. Although the etymology is disputed, this explanation seems to make the best sense. See Waltke, *Genesis*, 259–60.

27. The Hebrew precedes the main conjugated verb with an infinitive absolute to convey added emphasis.

28. Again the infinite absolute is present in the verb "multiply" (*rabah*).

Chapter 2: Living in the Land

1. Bruce Wilkinson, *The Prayer of Jabez: Breaking Through to the Blessed Life* (Sisters, OR: Multnomah, 2000).

2. M. Weinfeld, "The Covenant of Grant in the Old Testament and in the Ancient Near East," *JAOS* 90 (1990): 184–85.

3. Meredith G. Kline, *Treaty of the Great King: The Covenant Structure of Deuteronomy: Studies and Commentary* (Grand Rapids, MI: Eerdmans, 1963); K. A. Kitchen, *Ancient Orient and Old Testament* (Downers Grove, IL: InterVarsity, 1966), 90–102.

4. Following Kitchen, *Ancient Orient and Old Testament*, 96–97.

5. See below on the significance of having one's name "blotted out."

6. E. Lipiński, "נָחַל nāḥal נַחֲלָה nāḥalâ," *TDOT*, ed. G. Johannes Botterweck, Helmer Ringgren, and Heinz-Josef Fabry (Grand Rapids, MI: Eerdmans, 1998), 9:320.

7. Cf. Num. 33:50–56.

8. This section is indebted to Christopher J. H. Wright, "#5706 נחל," *NIDOTTE*, ed. Willem VanGemeren (Grand Rapids, MI: Zondervan, 1996), 3:77.

9. A. S. van der Woude, "שֵׁם šēm name," *TLOT*, ed. Jenni Ernst and Claus Westermann (Peabody, MA: Hendrickson, 1997), 3:1357.

10. Alan P. Ross, "#9005 שֵׁם," *NIDOTTE*, 4:147.

11. Bill T. Arnold and Bryan E. Beyer, eds., *Readings from the Ancient Near East: Primary Sources for Old Testament Study* (Grand Rapids, MI: Baker, 2002), 32; for full text see James B. Pritchard, ed., *Ancient Near Eastern Texts Relating to the Old Testament*, 3d ed. with sup. (Princeton, NJ: Princeton University Press, 1969), 60–72, 501–3.

12. On this topic generally see Stanley Bruce Frost, "The Memorial of the Childless Man," *Int* 25 (1972). C. F. Keil and F. Delitzsch, *The Pentateuch*, trans. James Martin, vol. 1, Commentary on the Old Testament in Ten Volumes (Grand Rapids, MI: Eerdmans, 1973), 422–23, describe this preoccupation of the ancients as "the desire inherent in man, who is formed for immortality, and connected with the hitherto undeveloped belief in an eternal life, to secure a continued personal existence for himself and immortality for his name, through the perpetuation of his family and in the son who took his place."

13. F. W. Reiterer, "שׁם šēm," *TDOT*, ed. G. Johannes Botterweck, Helmer Ringgren, and Heinz-Josef Fabry (Grand Rapids, MI: Eerdmans, 2006), 15:161.

14. Thomas Thompson and Dorothy Thompson, "Some Legal Problems in the Book of Ruth," *VT* 18 (1968): 87.

15. Cf. 2 Kings 14:27; Josh. 7:9.

16. Of kings and nations see also Deut. 7:24; Ps. 9:5; Nah. 1:14. Of destroying other gods see Deut. 12:3; Zech. 13:2.

17. The only clear examples of the practice in the OT are Tamar (Genesis 38) and Ruth, although the latter is not strictly a case of levirate marriage. By the Rabbinic era the practice was generally avoided in favor of the ritual of humiliation. See Dale W. Manor, "A Brief History of Levirate Marriage as It Relates to the Bible," *ResQ* 27(1984): 129–42.

18. Cf. Eryl W. Davies, "Inheritance Rights and the Hebrew Levirate Marriage," *VT* 31.2 (1981): 138–44, who argues the provision was principally for the benefit of the widow.

19. Also referred to in some countries as *compulsory purchase* or *expropriation*.

20. Following Daniel I. Block, *Judges, Ruth*, NAC (Nashville: Broadman, 1999), 710.

21. Ibid., 709.

22. Following Frederick W. Bush, *Ruth, Esther*, WBC (Dallas: Word, 1996), 9:211–15, 232.

23. Ibid., 232.

24. As Bush (ibid., 232–33) points out, he could have also bought the land and then ignored his pledge to marry Ruth, but this would have resulted in him losing face (as greedy) before the elders. On the other hand, if he agreed to take the land but allowed Boaz to marry Ruth, then once again he would stand to lose the land to the heir raised by Boaz.

25. The verb is a hiphil form. William L. Holladay, ed., *A Concise Hebrew and Aramaic Lexicon of the Old Testament* (Leiden, UK: Brill,1988), 316.

26. See esp. Lev. 24:22; but also Ex. 12:19, 48–49; Lev. 16:29; 17:15; 18:26; 19:34; 24:16; Num. 9:14; 15:29–30.

27. Weinfeld, "Covenant of Grant in the Old Testament," 185.

Chapter 3: Prophetic Paradox

1. Cf. Isa. 30:1, 9 where they are "stubborn" and "lying" children.

2. Jeroboam (1 Kings 15:29), Baasha (1 Kings 16:12), and Omri/Ahab (1 Kings 21:22; 2 Kings 10:17) each have their houses "cut-off."

3. Coniah is short for Jeconiah, the personal name of Jehoiachin. See John Bright, *Jeremiah*, ed. William Foxwell Albright and David Noel Freedman, 2d ed., AB (Garden City, NY: Doubleday, 1979), 143.

4. I.e., hiphil forms of the three verbs, *shamen, kaved,* and *sha'a'*.

5. Paul R. House, "Isaiah's Call and Its Context in Isaiah 1–6," *CTR* 6 (1993): 220.

6. Ibid., 221.

7. See J. A. Emerton, "The Translation and Interpretation of Isaiah vi.13," in *Interpreting the Hebrew Bible: Essays in Honour of E. I. J. Rosenthal*, ed. J. A. Emerton and S. C. Reif (Cambridge: Cambridge University Press, 1982), 85–118, on the difficulties in this verse. Brevard S. Childs, *Isaiah*, OTL (Louisville, KY: Westminster, 2001), 58, writes: "The force of the entire narrative of chapter 6, particularly in the larger context of chapters 1-12, strove for an exposition of the meaning of v. 13."

8. Emerton, "The Translation and Interpretation of Isaiah vi.13," 108.

9. G. K. Beale, "The Old Testament Background of Reconciliation in 2 Corinthians 5–7 and Its Bearing on the Literary Problem of 2 Corinthians 6.14–7.1," *NTS* 35 (1989): 263.

10. N. H. Tur-Sinai, "A Contribution to the Understanding of Isaiah i-xii," Scri Hier 8 (1961): 145–88.

11. E.g., Gerhard F. Hasel, *The Remnant* (Berrien Springs, MI: Andrews University Press, 1974), 247. Similarly C. F. Keil and F. Delitzsch, *Biblical Commentary on the Prophecies of Isaiah*, trans. James Martin, vol. 1 (Grand Rapids, MI: Eerdmans, 1950), a "root-stump."

12. In 4:3 and 62:12 the eschatological focus is evident. 63:18 has a prototypical ideal in view.

13. Hasel, *The Remnant*, 238.

14. Childs, *Isaiah*, 58.

15. Alec Motyer, *The Prophecy of Isaiah: An Introduction and Commentary* (Downers Grove, IL: InterVarsity, 1993), 80, suggests both an individual and a people are in view. A parallel arises in the pseudepigraphic book of *Jubilees* where the writer uses the expression "holy seed" to refer to both the individual Jacob (*Jub.* 16:17; 25:12) and his offspring (*Jub.* 25:3, 18).

16. Julian P. Love, "Call of Isaiah: Exposition of Isaiah 6," *Int* 11.3 (1957): 296, writes, "Always it is a child that is an emblem of his hope."

17. John N. Oswalt, *The Book of Isaiah: Chapters 1–39*, NICOT (Grand Rapids, MI: Eerdmans, 1986), 227.

18. Ibid., 246.

19. Motyer, *The Prophecy of Isaiah*, 104.

20. Oswalt, *The Book of Isaiah*, 247.

21. Motyer, *The Prophecy of Isaiah*, 121.

22. This is not to dismiss Isaiah's depiction of the gathered remnant of physical Israel in 11:11ff. But this is a secondary increase that adds to the already existing worldwide eschatological people described in 11:10. Seeing the Jewish remnant as a secondary rather than primary work of God fits with Paul's description of the "partial hardening" and salvation of Israel in Rom. 11:25–26.

23. I.e., Isa. 54:17; 56:6; 63:17; 65:8, 9, 13 (3x); 14, 15, 66:14.

24. I.e., Isa. 41:8, 9; 42:1, 19 (2x); 43:10; 44:1, 2, 21 (2x), 26; 45:4; 48:20; 49:3, 5, 6, 7; 50:10, 52:13; 53:11.

25. George A. Knight, *Servant Theology: A Commentary on the Book of Isaiah 40–55*, ITC (Edinburgh: Handsel, 1984), 169.

26. Jan Leunis Koole, *Isaiah Three*, 3 vols., Historical Commentary on the Old Testament (Leuven: Peeters, 1997), 2:321. John N. Oswalt, *The Book of Isaiah, Chapters 40–66*, NICOT (Grand Rapids, MI: Eerdmans, 1998), 402, comments, "The meaning of the Servant's suffering is to be found in God's intention that he should become an atoning sacrifice for sin."

27. Motyer, *The Prophecy of Isaiah*, 440; Oswalt, *Book of Isaiah, Chapters 40–66*, 402; Edward J. Young, *The Book of Isaiah*, vol. 3 (Grand Rapids, MI: Eerdmans, 1972), 3:355; Koole, *Isaiah Three*, 324; August Pieper, *Isaiah II [Yesha`yah 2]: An Exposition of Isaiah 40–66*, trans. Erwin E. Kowalke (Milwaukee, WI: Northwestern, 1979), 450–51. See Koole, *Isaiah Three*, 324, for others.

28. Koole, *Isaiah Three*, 2:324.

29. Oswalt, *Book of Isaiah, Chapters 40–66*, 402.

30. Earlier in 49:21, Isaiah speaks of a "barren" Zion with unexpected children who asks, "Who has borne me these?" The answer comes in 53:10 in the offspring of the suffering servant. See Motyer, *The Prophecy of Isaiah*, 395, 440.

31. Oswalt, *The Book of Isaiah, Chapters 40–66*, 413.

32. Motyer, *The Prophecy of Isaiah*, 445.

33. The text of Isa. 53:12 uses the (piel) verb *khalaq*, which also is used of allocation of the land by Joshua (Josh. 13:7).

34. Motyer, *The Prophecy of Isaiah*, 440.

35. See John N. Oswalt, "Isaiah: Theology of," *NIDOTTE*, 4:725–26; P. A. Smith, *Rhetoric and Redaction in Trito-Isaiah: The Structure, Growth and Authorship of Isaiah 56–66* (Leiden, UK: Brill, 1995), 54–60.

36. The Talmud (*b. Yebam.* 24a) makes it explicit that the eunuch's name is "blotted out."

37. Roy D. Wells, "Isaiah as an Exponent of Torah," in *New Visions of Isaiah*, ed. R. F. Melugin and M. A. Sweeney (Sheffield: Sheffield Academic Press, 1996), 144. Ex. 31:16 refers to observing the Sabbath as covenant.

38. A similar blessing to the eunuch appears in Wis 3:14, where he is given a "lot" (*klēros*) in the temple of the Lord. *Klēros* is the root for the Greek word "inheritance" (*klēronomia*).

39. Compare NASB: "nor from the mouth of your offspring, nor from the mouth of your offspring's offspring."

40. The ESV follows the Hebrew grammar in translating "offspring *of* the blessed of the LORD." The LXX renders the less awkward "offspring blessed of the LORD." In light of the conceptual parallel with 61:9 we also follow the simpler LXX rendering (so also NIV, NRSV).

41. Isa. 44:3; 48:19; 61:9. Cf. Job 5:25; 21:8.

42. Motyer, *The Prophecy of Isaiah*, 543.

43. Ammianus Marcellinus, *Rerum gestarum libri* 14.6.17. D. G. Burke, "Eunuch," in *ISBE*, ed. G. W. Bromiley (Grand Rapids, MI: Eerdmans, 1982), 200.

44. Ibid., 200.

45. See Frost, "The Memorial of the Childless Man," 444–45, and George Wesley Buchanan, *The Book of Daniel*, vol. 25, The Mellen Biblical Commentary Intertextual: Old Testament Series in Forty Volumes (Lewiston, NY: Edwin Mellen 1999), 22, who argue he was a eunuch. Edwin M. Yamauchi, "Was Nehemiah the Cupbearer a Eunuch?" *ZAW* 92.1(1980): 142, is less convinced.

46. See *b. San 93b*; *Pirqe R. El.* Isa. 39:7, 56:4–5.

47. *b. San 93b*.

Chapter 4: Good News for the Gentiles

1. Though it is sometimes tempting to see all the OT covenants as a unified whole, Paul recognized multiple OT *covenants* (Rom. 9:4), and sometimes distinguishes between them.

2. See C. John Collins, "Galatians 3:16: What Kind of an Exegete Was Paul?" *TynBul* 54.1 (2003): 76–79, for a summary of ways scholars have reconciled Paul's exegesis in this verse. Some, e.g., H. J. Schoeps, *Paul: The Theology of the Apostle in the Light of Jewish Religious History*, trans. Harold Knight (Philadelphia: Westminster, 1961), 181, 234, see no justification for Paul's exegetical move.

3. Elsewhere he uses the term as a reference to Abraham's collective "seed" (Rom. 4:18; 9:8; 2 Cor. 11:22).

4. See C. K. Barrett, "The Allegory of Abraham, Sarah, and Hagar in the Argument of Galatians," in *Essays on Paul* (Philadelphia: Westminster, 1982), 158–68.

5. Ibid., 160. Abraham himself was also viewed (anachronistically) as an exemplar of obedience to the law in Jewish tradition as illustrated in Sir 44:19:

"Abraham was the great father of a multitude of nations, and no one has been found like him in glory; he kept the law of the Most High, and was taken into covenant with him."

6. Also Ps. 89:3–4, 29, 36.

7. See Max Wilcox, "The Promise of the 'Seed' in the New Testament and the Targumin," 2–20.

8. 4QFlor 1:10–11 cites 2 Sam. 7:12 and comments, "This [refers to the] «branch of David»." Florentino García Martínez, *The Dead Sea Scrolls Translated*, trans. Wilfred G. E. Watson, 2d ed. (Leiden, UK: Brill, 1992), 136.

9. The term "offspring of David" also appears in 2 Tim. 2:8, while the closely related expression "Son of David" is a recurring title for Jesus in the Synoptic Gospels.

10. See Wilcox, "The Promise of the 'Seed' in the New Testament and the Targumin," 5, who attributes the observation to Otto Betz.

11. I.e., 3:16: "to your offspring" (*tō spermati sou*); 3:19: "to whom" (*hō*).

12. F. F. Bruce, *The Epistle to the Galatians*, ed. I. Howard Marshall and Donald A. Hagner, NIGTC (Grand Rapids, MI: Eerdmans, 1982), 171–72.

13. Cf. the similar expression regarding Abraham but in the third person in 18:18: "All the nations of the earth shall be blessed in him."

14. Cf. the similar expression also given to Isaac in 26:1 where identical wording regarding his offspring appears in the Hebrew MT and in the Greek LXX.

15. The Greek word *klēronomia* translates the Hebrew *nakhalah,* a word commonly used in reference to God's provision of the land. The association of the cognate verb appears in Gen. 15:7 (LXX) in direct reference to the land promise: "I am God that brought you out of the land of the Chaldeans, so as to give to you this land to inherit" (AT). The same verb appears in Gen. 21:10, which Paul cites in Gal. 4:30.

16. The Greek nouns "inheritance" (*klēronomia*) and "heir" (*klēronomos*) relate etymologically to the underlying term "lot" or *klēros*. As in the English word "lot," *klēros* divides into two main senses: the "lot which is drawn" and the "lot of the land," a duality linked to the ancient system of economic settlement. The link between the two senses of "lot" meant that *klēros* naturally assumed the specific meaning of "the portion (lot) of land which is assigned by lot." Both *klēros* (49x) and *klēronomia* (143x) are used to translate the Hebrew term *nakhalah* ("inheritance") in the LXX. See Werner Foerster, "κληρονόμος κτλ," TDNT, ed. Gerhard Kittel and Freidrich Gerhard (Grand Rapids, MI: Eerdmans, 1965), 3:758, 769.

17. Werner Foerster, "κληρονόμος κτλ," TDNT, 3:779–81.

18. E.g., *Jub.* 17:3; 22:14; 32:19.

19. *1 Enoch* 5:7.

20. *1 Enoch* 40:9; *2 Enoch* 50:2; *4 Ezra* 7:9; 17, 96; *Pirke Aboth* 5:22.

21. Barrett, "The Allegory of Abraham, Sarah, and Hagar in the Argument of Galatians," 167.

22. Richard B. Hayes, *Echoes of Scripture in the Letters of Paul* (New Haven, CT: Yale University Press, 1989), 112.

23. Comparisons not explicitly stated are in brackets.

24. J. Louis Martyn, *Galatians*, AB, 434, 451–54, has been influential in arguing that Paul uses the Greek verb "beget" (*gennaō*) in these verses not in a physical sense but only in a special "missioning" sense of begetting churches. Martyn argues his point by observing Paul's substitution of the verb "beget" (*gennaō*) for "bear" (*tiktō*) that is consistently used in the Genesis account. According to Martyn, Paul's special "missioning" sense for the verb is confirmed by the fact that Paul "employs the verb 'to beget,' linking it with the noun 'child/children,' only in speaking of the genesis of Christians and Christian churches through the power of the gospel." But the evidence is too scant to warrant Martyn's conclusions. There is only one clear instance where Paul uses *gennaō* in reference to begetting a church (1 Cor. 4:14–15), and he uses it of conventional birth in Rom. 9:11. If Paul habitually used *tiktō* to refer to the natural process of giving birth and used *gennaō* only in the special sense Martyn claims, then his case would be plausible. But Paul *never* uses *tiktō* (save his LXX citation in Gal. 4:27). While the LXX writer of Genesis tends to reserve "beget" (*gennaō*) for males and "bear" (*tiktō*) for females, Paul uses *gennaō* for both males and females and never uses *tiktō*. Moreover, all Paul's other uses of "according to the flesh" (*kata sarka*) confirm that he is speaking of *physical* birth (Rom. 1:3; 4:1; 9:3–5; 2 Cor. 11:18-22).

25. E.g., Bruce, *The Epistle to the Galatians*, 218; Hayes, *Echoes of Scripture*, 114–15; James D. G. Dunn, *The Epistle to the Galatians* (Peabody, MA: Hendrickson, 1993), 248–49.

26. E.g., Hans Dieter Betz, *A Commentary on Paul's Letter to the Churches in Galatia*, Hermeneia: A Critical and Historical Commentary on the Bible (Philadelphia: Fortress, 1979), 243; Richard N. Longenecker, *Galatians*, WBC (Dallas: Word, 1990), 211.

27. E.g., Martyn, *Galatians*, 436–37; Susan Eastman, *Recovering Paul's Mother Tongue* (Grand Rapids, MI: Eerdmans, 2007), 131–32.

28. Barrett, "The Allegory of Abraham, Sarah, and Hagar in the Argument of Galatians," 167.

29. Hayes, *Echoes of Scripture*, 118; similarly Eastman, *Recovering Paul's Mother Tongue*, 141.

30. Martyn, *Galatians*, 442.

31. E.g., Martinus C. de Boer, "Paul's Quotation of Isaiah 54.1 in Galatians 4.27," *NTS* 50 (2004): 389, who concludes that Paul chose to cite Isa. 54:1 "because the passage mentions two women, corresponding to Sarah and Hagar."

32. Hayes, *Echoes of Scripture*, 118–21.

33. A critique also raised by Eastman, *Recovering Paul's Mother Tongue*, 144.

34. E.g., Isa. 54:11–12; *Tob.* 13:16–17; 4Q164; Rev. 21:10–21; see ibid., 148–9.

35. Versus the NLT: "You who have never given birth . . . you who have never been in labor."

36. See discussion in chap. 5.

37. Cf. Phil. 2:22; 1 Tim. 1:18.

Chapter 5: The King and the Kingdom

1. I translate these to highlight the birth imagery present.

2. Contrary to J. Louis Martyn, *History and Theology in the Fourth Gospel* (Nashville, TN: Abingdon, 1979), 161–63, who suggests that Nicodemus is a symbolic figure representing a local Jewish leader at the time John was writing.

3. The word order in the Greek appears to emphasize his status as "come from God."

4. F. F. Bruce, *The Gospel of John* (Grand Rapids, MI: Eerdmans, 1983), 83.

5. Such "exclusions" in *m. Sanh.* 10:1 include those who deny the resurrection, those that deny the divine origin of the Law, Epicureans, those who read heretical books, users of charms, and those who utter the divine name.

6. *m. Sanh.* 10:1, Herbert Danby, *The Mishnah* (Oxford: Oxford University Press, 1933), 397.

7. John 3:31; 19:11, 23.

8. As C. K. Barrett, *The Gospel According to St. John: An Introduction with Commentary and Notes on the Greek Text*, 2d ed. (Philadelphia: Westminster, 1978), 207, explains, the notion of divine begetting and rebirth was already present in first-century Hellenistic religious terminology but was rigidly avoided in Judaism because it spoke in direct terms of the invasion of the present life by the power of God and thus eliminated the distinction between the present life and the age to come. For a discussion between Jewish teachers, Jesus' claim is remarkable indeed!

9. So D. A. Carson, *The Gospel According to John* (Leicester, UK: Inter-Varsity, 1991), 190–91.

10. The ESV's translation of the anarthrous *pneumatos* as "the Spirit" is probably unwarranted in favor of the NET's "spirit." See ibid., 195.

11. Cf. Matt. 3:11; Luke 3:16; John 1:33.

12. The same verb *pisteuō* is used to convey both "to have faith" and "to believe." Thus, Paul describes Abraham's quintessential act of "faith" in Gal. 3:6 as "Abraham believed (*pisteuō*) God, and it was counted to him as righteousness."

13. E.g., Rom. 8:15: "You have received the Spirit of adoption as sons"; Rom. 8:23; Gal. 4:5; Eph. 1:5.

14. *m. Yebam.* 6:6; *b. Yebam.* 63a-b; *'Abot R. Nat.* III:IV.6.

15. Ulrich Luz, *Matthew 8–20*, trans. James E. Crouch, Hermeneia: A Critical and Historical Commentary on the Bible (Minneapolis: Fortress, 2001), 497, writes bluntly, "Protestant interpreters show an amazing lack of interest in this text."

16. For further discussion of this debate and its relevance to the present pericope see David Instone-Brewer, *Divorce and Remarriage in the Bible: The Social and Literary Context* (Grand Rapids, MI: Eerdmans, 2002), 110–14; 133–36.

17. The interaction described in Mark's account (Mark 10:2–12) is slightly different, but the point is the same.

18. John Nolland, *The Gospel of Matthew*, ed. I. Howard Marshall and Donald A. Hagner, NIGTC (Grand Rapids, MI: Eerdmans, 2005), 773.

19. Although Matthew includes the exception clause for sexual immorality, the parallel accounts given by Mark 10:11b–12 and Luke 16:18 do not.

20. There is a verbal tie between the Pharisees' question concerning any "cause/case" (*aitia*) for divorce allowed by Moses, and the only permissible "case" (*aitia*) for divorce that Jesus allows.

21. E.g., Dale Allison, *Matthew: A Shorter Commentary* (London: T&T Clark, 2004), 315, who suggests that they are reaching "a conclusion also reached by certain Essenes and Greek and Roman philosophers that it is better not to marry." William Loader, *Sexuality and the Jesus Tradition* (Grand Rapids, MI: Eerdmans, 2005), 128, proposes that it is the assumption of the disciples' question that women are the cause of sexual immorality.

22. Will Deming, *Paul on Marriage and Celibacy: The Hellenistic Background of 1 Corinthians 7*, 2d ed. (Grand Rapids, MI: Eerdmans, 2004), 95, has also recognized the connection here with the Greek marriage debate. The language arises, e.g., in the Stoic philosopher Hierocles, who asserts, "I affirm, therefore, that marriage is also advantageous (*sympheron*), in the first place, because it bears a truly divine fruit in the procreation of children" (*Stob.* 4.22.24; Abraham J. Malherbe, *Moral Exhortation: A Greco-Roman Sourcebook* [Philadelphia: Westminster, 1986], 101). Epicureans and Cynics, on the other hand, generally advised against marriage (e.g., Diogenes Laertius 10.119). First-century rhetoricians such as Aelius Theon (*Progymnasmata* 125.9–20) used the marriage question as a rhetorical exercise for debate. It was an exercise for the debater to demonstrate that marriage was something indeed "good" (*kala*) and "beneficial" (*sympheronta*). See chap. 6.

23. *b. Yebam.* 63a; I. Epstein, *The Babylonian Talmud* (London: Soncino, 1952).

24. *'Abot R. Nat.* 3:4.6.B; Jacob Neusner, *The Fathers According to Rabbi Nathan: An Analytical Translation and Explanation.* (Atlanta: Scholars Press, 1986)

25. *m. Yebam.* 6:6; *b. Yebam.* 63b; *b. Yebam.* 64a; *Gen. Rab.* 34:14.

26. *m. Yebam.* 6:6; *b. Yebam.* 64a. See also discussion in Instone-Brewer, *Divorce and Remarriage in the Bible*, 91–93.

27. As Sir 25:16–26 describes.

28. As rabbinic scholar Instone-Brewer, *Divorce and Remarriage in the Bible*, 170, can also appreciate.

29. *b. Sanh.* 57a.

30. *b. Šabb.* 111a. Here Gen. 1:28 is also in view.

31. *b. Sanh.* 56b.

32. Josephus, *C. Ap.* 2:270–71. Ps.-Phoc. 187; Eusebius, *Praep. ev.* 8.7.7 citing Philo.

33. *m. Yebam.* 8:4-6; *b. Yebam.* 79b-80b. Instone-Brewer, *Divorce and Remarriage in the Bible*, 169–70, deems the sources as NT era.

34. *b. Sbb.* 152a, in Epstein, *The Babylonian Talmud* (1952).

35. *b. Yebam.* 24a.

36. *b. Sanh.* 36b.

37. Sir 30:19–20.

38. *T. Jud.* 23:1-5.

39. Josephus, *Ant.* 4.290–91; LCL, H. S. J. Thackeray, with "You" for "Ye" in final sentence.

40. Henry George Liddell and Robert Scott, *A Greek-English Lexicon with a Revised Supplement* (Oxford: Clarendon, 1996), 337.

41. The example of Genucius is given by Valerius Maximus (7.7.6), who, as a eunuch priest of Cybele, had his genitalia amputated.

42. Philo, *Spec. Laws* 1.325; *Philo*, trans. F. H. Colson and G. H. Whitaker, 10 vols., LCL (Cambridge: Harvard University Press, 1929–1962), 7:289.

43. Johannes Schneider, "εὐνοῦχος, εὐνουχίζω," *TDNT*, 2:765.

44. E. David Hunt, "Eunuch," in *OCD*, 3d ed., ed. S. Hornblower and A. Spawforth (Oxford, 1996), 569.

45. Herodotus, 8.104–6.

46. Lucian, *Eunuch.* 6; *Lucian*, trans. A. M. Harmon, K. Kilburn, and M. D. MacLeod, 8 vols., LCL (Cambridge: Harvard University Press, 1913–1967), 5:337.

47. Lucian, *Eunuch.* 6.

48. Arthur D. Nock, "Eunuchs in Ancient Religion," in *Essays on Religion and the Ancient World*, ed. Zeph Stewart (Oxford: Clarendon Press, 1972), 7.

49. Ibid., 14.

50. Hunt, "Eunuch," 569.

51. Suetonius, *Claud.* 28; *Ner.* 28; Dio Cassius 67.2.3.

52. Josephus, *Ant.* 16.230; 17.44.

53. Josephus, *Vit.* 1.429.

54. Dio Cassius 67.2.3; Philostratus, *Vit. Apoll.* 6.42; Dio Cassius 68.2.4.

55. Schneider, "εὐνοῦχος, εὐνουχίζω" *TDNT,* 2:765.

56. Liddell and Scott, *Greek-English Lexicon*, 724.

57. Something Paul references in 1 Cor. 7:28.

58. See further discussion in chap. 6.

59. See discussion in chap. 3.

60. Burke, "Eunuch," 200.

61. Mikeal C. Parsons, "Isaiah 53 in Acts 8: *A Reply to Professor Morna Hooker*," in *Jesus and the Suffering Servant: Isaiah 53 and Christian Origins*, ed. William H. Bellinger Jr. and William R. Farmer (Harrisburg, PA: Trinity Press International, 1998), 108n6.

62. As discussed in chap. 3, Daniel's status as eunuch is not explicitly stated, but the evidence points this direction. Even if he wasn't physically castrated, he was a model eunuch in his service to the court.

63. Philo, *Alleg. Interp.* 3.236–42.

64. Exegetes have disagreed whether "this saying" refers to the disciples' statement in v. 10 or to Jesus' earlier pronouncement in v. 9. See Luz, *Matthew 8–20*, 496–501, and Quentin Quesnell, "'Made Themselves Eunuchs for the Kingdom of Heaven' (Mt 19,12)," *CBQ* 30 (1968). The latter option is unlikely on two accounts. (1) It would imply that Jesus' pronouncement on divorce in 19:9 was only for some and not for others—an unlikely possibility since his argument on divorce is rooted in creation. (2) The introductory "for" in 19:12 most probably indicates that what follows explains what precedes. It seems much more likely that the eunuch discussion explains cases where it is "better not to marry" than the situation of a divorced person.

65. Plutarch, *Cat. min.* 64.3; Plutarch, *Plutarch's Lives*, trans. Bernadotte Perrin, 11 vols., LCL (Cambridge: Harvard University Press, 1914–1926), 8:393.

66. Ps.-Phoc. 89.

67. Josephus, *C. Ap.* 1.225; Josephus, *The Life Against Apion*, trans. H. St. J. Thackeray, LCL (Cambridge: Harvard University Press, 1926), 225.

68. I am not persuaded that Jesus' statement necessarily implies a lifetime renouncement of marriage, although for some it will.

69. *b. Ber.* 17a.

70. Mormonism, e.g., heightens emphasis on the importance of marriage and family both in this age and in "worlds" to come.

71. The "question" is merely for sake of argument, since in the tannaitic period (AD 0–200) a Jewish woman who had been widowed several times was not permitted to remarry, since she was considered to be dangerous and was called a *qatlanit* or "killer." See Samuel Tobias Lachs, *A Rabbinic Commentary on the New Testament: The Gospels of Matthew, Mark and Luke* (Hoboken, NJ: Ktav, 1987), 360–61.

72. Language common to all three Gospels is in boldface (English follows Greek wording closely).

73. The expression "sons of this age" also appears in 16:8 where Luke is contrasting the unregenerate "sons of this age" with the regenerate "sons of light." But here the contrast appears to parallel the contrast of ages he also makes in 18:30.

74. Cf. the obscure text in Gen. 6:2-4 where the supernatural "sons of God" *do* have relations with women.

75. The Talmud (*b. Ber.* 17a) suggests that the afterlife will be devoid not only of procreation but also of physical eating and drinking, business, and competition.

76. Paul later alludes to Peter taking along a "sister /[believing] wife" with him in his ministry (1 Cor. 9:5).

77. John 13:23; 19:26; 20:2; 21:7, 20.

78. However, faithfulness to following Jesus takes precedence over traditional family demands if the two should directly conflict.

Chapter 6: A *Charisma* in Corinth

1. Jean Héring, *The First Epistle of Saint Paul to the Corinthians* (London: Epworth, 1962), 48.

2. William M. Ramsay, "Historical Commentary on the Epistles to the Corinthians," *The Expositor* 6.1 (1900): 283.

3. Compare the original NIV translation of 7:1b: "It is good for a man not to marry."

4. E.g., Elisa J. Sobo and Sandra Bell, eds., *Celibacy, Culture, and Society: The Anthropology of Sexual Abstinence* (Madison, WI: University of Wisconsin Press, 2001), 11.

5. A. W. Richard Sipe, "Celibacy," in *The Oxford Companion to Christian Thought*, ed. Adrian Hastings (Oxford: Oxford University Press, 2000), 104.

6. Tom Wright, *Paul for Everyone: 1 Corinthians* (Louisville, KY: Westminster, 2004), 77.

7. Wolfgang Schrage, "Zur Frontstellung der paulinischen Ehebewertung in 1 Kor 7 1–7," *ZNW* 67 (1976): 220.

8. Gordon D. Fee, *The First Epistle to the Corinthians*, NICNT (Grand Rapids: Eerdmans, 1987), 269.

9. Raymond F. Collins, *First Corinthians*, ed. Daniel J. Harrington, S. J., SP (Collegeville, MN: Liturgical Press, 1999), 253.

10. E.g., Fee, *First Corinthians*, 269; S. Scott Bartchy, *First-Century Slavery and 1 Corinthians 7:21* (Missoula, MO: University of Montana, 1973), 149; Wayne A. Meeks, "The Image of the Androgyne: Some Uses of a Symbol in Earliest Christianity," *HR* 13 (1974): 202; David R. Cartlidge, "1 Cor. 7 as a Foundation for a Christian Sex Ethic," *JR* 55 (1975): 229–30; Antoinette Clark Wire, *The Corinthian Woman Prophets: A Reconstruction through Paul's Rhetoric* (Minneapolis: Fortress, 1990), 127;

Judith M. Gundry-Volf, "Celibate Pneumatics and Social Power: On the Motivations for Sexual Asceticism in Corinth," *USQR* 48 (1994): 105–26.

11. E.g., the Corinthians' apparent disposition against marriage (7:10) may be for other reasons, as also their apparent neglect of marital relations (7:3–5).

12. Gordon D. Fee, "1 Cor. 7:1 in the NIV," *JETS* 23 (1980) has argued strongly that the verb "touch" (*haptō*) must be understood as a euphemism for sexual relations rather than for marriage.

13. Simon J. Kistemaker, *New Testament Commentary: 1 Corinthians* (Grand Rapids: Baker, 1993), 209.

14. Charles H. Talbert, *Reading Corinthians: A Literary and Theological Commentary on I and II Corinthians*, rev. ed., Reading the New Testament (London: SPCK, 1987), 37.

15. William E. Phipps, "Is Paul's Attitude toward Sexual Relations Contained in 1 Cor. 7:1?" *NTS* 28 (1982): 128.

16. Fee, *First Corinthians*, 276.

17. The term "effeminate" (*malakoi*) is also in reference to homosexual coitus.

18. *1 Clem.* 30.1.

19. A possibility highly criticized by Walter Schmithals, *Gnosticism in Corinth*, trans. John E. Steely (New York: Abingdon, 1971), 338.

20. E.g., Fee, "1 Cor. 7:1 in the NIV," 314; Wire, *Women Prophets*, 72–97, 113–15.

21. In 7:28 Paul uses the second person "you" to refer to direct address to males and switches to the third person when he speaks of just the women. The response comes as part of the reply he gives to their main question being referenced in 7:25, which suggests those responsible for the correspondence are male. If this is the case, then the ones purported to be positing the ascetic statement in 7:1, the "you" who wrote the letter, are also surely male rather than female.

22. Joseph A. Fitzmyer, *First Corinthians: A New Translation with Introduction and Commentary*, ed. William Foxwell Albright and David Noel Freedman, Anchor Yale Bible (New Haven, CT: Yale University Press, 2008), 21; Donald W. Engels, *Roman Corinth : An Alternative Model for the Classical City* (Chicago: University of Chicago Press, 1990), 84, estimates the size of the city and environs to be about 100,000.

23. Wayne A. Meeks, *The First Urban Christians: The Social World of the Apostle Paul*, 2d ed. (New Haven, CT: Yale University Press, 2003), 212n264. Names are no guarantee of the ethnic identification of particular individuals, but the mix of different types of names probably reflects the amalgamation of ethnicities present in the city.

24. Cf. also Acts 18:6.

25. John M. G. Barclay, "Thessalonica and Corinth: Social Contrasts in Pauline Christianity," *JBL* 47 (1992): 49–74. The observations of this paragraph are largely indebted to Barclay's article.

26. Demosthenes, *Neaer.* 1386.122; Demosthenes, *Orations 50–59: Private Cases*. In *Neaeram*, trans. A. T. Murray, LCL (Cambridge: Harvard University Press, 1939), 445–47.

27. Xenophon, *Mem.* 2.2.4; Xenophon, *Memorabilia. Oeconomicus. Symposium. Apology*, trans. E. C. Marchant and O. J. Todd, LCL (Cambridge: Harvard University Press, 1923), 105–7.

28. Plutarch, *Conj. praec.* 16; Plutarch, *Moralia*, trans. Frank Cole Babbitt, et al., 16 vols., LCL (Cambridge: Harvard University Press, 1927–2004), 2:309.

29. Polybius, 36.17.5–7; Polybius, *The Histories*, trans. W. R. Paton, 6 vols., LCL (Cambridge: Harvard University Press, 1922–27), 6:385.

30. Antipater of Tarsus 39–44; Deming, *Celibacy*, 227.

31. Livy, *Praef.* 9; Livy, *History of Rome*, trans. B. O. Foster, et al., 14 vols., LCL (Cambridge: Harvard University Press, 1919–1959), 1:7.

32. Sallust, *Bell. Cat.* 10.1–3; 13.3; Horace, *Od.* 3.6.17; Cicero, *Marcell.* 23; Quintillian *Inst.* 1.6.36.

33. Hierocles from Stobaeus 4.22.22; Malherbe, *Moral Exhortation: A Greco-Roman Sourcebook* , 100. Musonius Rufus 12, 13a; Cora Lutz, ed. *Musonius Rufus "The Roman Socrates,"* vol. 10, Yale Classical Studies (New Haven, CT: Yale University Press, 1947), 86–89.

34. Augustus describes himself as "supervisor of laws and morals" (*Res Gestae* 6.1).

35. Horace extols Augustus's measures of moral reform in his famous "Secular Hymn" (*Carmen saeculare*) on occasion of the secular games in 17 BC.

36. Dio Cassius 56.1.1–2.

37. Dio Cassius 56.4–9.

38. Dio Cassius 56.10.3; *Dio's Roman History*, trans. Earnest Cary and Herbert Baldwin Foster, 9 vols., LCL (Cambridge: Harvard University Press, 1914–1927), 7:25.

39. Hesiod, *Theog.* 565–67.

40. Hesiod, *Theog.* 570; Hesiod, *Theogony. Works and Days. Testimonia*, trans. Glenn W. Most, LCL (Cambridge: Harvard University Press, 2006), 49.

41. Hesiod, *Theog.* 571–7.

42. Hesiod, *Theog.* 585–93; Hesiod, *Theogony. Works and Days. Testimonia*, 51.

43. Hesiod, *Theog.* 600–605.

44. Hesiod, *Theog.* 607–12; Hesiod, *Theogony. Works and Days. Testimonia*, 53.

45. Hesiod, *Op.* 403–9; ibid., 121.

46. *Op.* 373–75. Hesiod warns, "Do not let an arse-fancy woman deceive your mind by guilefully cajoling you while she pokes into your granary: whoever trusts a woman [i.e., wife], trusts swindlers"; Hesiod, *Theogony. Works and Days. Testimonia*, 117–19.

47. Hesiod, *Op.* 696–705; Hesiod, *Theogony. Works and Days. Testimonia*, 143.

48. Thales Stob. 4.22.65]. Anaxagoras also gave up his responsibilities of patrimony for sake of pursing his other intellectual pursuits (Diogenes Laertius, 2.7).

49. Antiphon fr. 49.1–8. See Gerard J. Pendrick, ed. *Antiphon the Sophist: The Fragments* (Cambridge: Cambridge University Press, 2002), 193–5.

50. Antiphon fr. 49.9–29.

51. Democritus [Stob. 4.24.31]; C. C. W. Taylor, *The Atomists Leucippus and Democritus* (Toronto: University of Toronto Press, 1999), D140.

52. Xenophon, *Oeconomicus* 7.18–22; Xenophon, *Memorabilia. Oeconomicus. Symposium. Apology*, 419. Xenophon also observes that humans require shelter and the wife is better suited for managing indoor domestic affairs.

53. Implied by *Oeconomicus* 7.1. See Deming, *Celibacy*, 59–60.

54. Diogenes Laertius 3.78.

55. Plato, *Leg.* 4.720F–721D; Plato, *Laws: Books I–VI*, trans. R. G. Bury, LCL (Cambridge: Harvard University Press, 1926), 313. Plato also argues that marriage and procreation is by nature's ordinance the way he shares in immortality.

56. Aristotle, *Nic.* 1.7.15; 1.8.15–16.

57. Musonius Rufus 14; Lutz, ed. *Musonius Rufus "The Roman Socrates,"* 92–95. Conversely, Epictetus 3.7.19 accuses the Epicureans of destroying the state by not marrying. See also Deming, *Celibacy*, 51–52.

58. Hierocles, *On Duties* [Stob. 4.22.24]; Malherbe, *Moral Exhortation: A Greco-Roman Sourcebook*, 101–2.

59. The Cynic perspective is articulated by Theophrastus, recorded by Jerome *Jov.* 1.47. See also Deming, *Celibacy*, 51–52. Deming frames the marriage question as a "Stoic-Cynic" debate, while in actuality the discussion was broader and more pervasive.

60. Diogenes Laertius, 10.119.

61. Epicurus, *Ep. Men.* 131–2; Diogenes Laertius 10.136; Seneca, *Ep.* 66.45.

62. Jerome, *Jov.* 1.48; Theodoret *Graec. aff.* 12.74; Epictetus, *Diatr.* 3.7.19.

63. Dio Chrysostom, *De Pace* (*Or.* 22) 2–3; *Dio Chrysostom: Discourses 12–30*, trans. J. H. Cohoon, LCL (Cambridge: Harvard University Press, 1939), 293.

64. Theon, *Progymn.* 120, 121.6–17; Quintillian, *Inst.* 2.4.24–25; Hermogenes, *Progymn.* 24–25; Aphthonius, *Progymn.* 41; Nicolaus *Progynm.* 71–72. On the *Progymnasmata* see George A. Kennedy, *Progymnasmata: Greek Textbooks of Prose Composition and Rhetoric* (Leiden, UK: Brill, 2003).

65. See David Wenham, "Paul's Use of the Jesus Tradition," in *The Jesus Tradition outside the Gospels* (Sheffield: JSOT, 1984), 7–15, on the Synoptic issues involved. He concludes there is "some reason to believe" that Paul is drawing upon the whole tradition in Matthew 19 including the eunuch *logion*.

66. Menander, *Thais* fr. 218.

67. The verbs are not identical, but the concept is the same.

68. Frederick William Danker, ed., *A Greek-English Lexicon of the New Testament*, 3d. ed. (Chicago: University of Chicago Press, 2000), 732.

69. For further exegetical details on 1 Corinthians 7 see the author's University of Cambridge PhD thesis.

70. Where Paul speaks of either a particular case of *porneia* (1 Cor. 5:1) or of immorality in abstract generality (1 Cor. 6:13, 18), he uses the singular. This is the only instance where he uses the plural.

71. Some scholars, e.g., Fee, *First Corinthians*, 283, look for the antecedent of "this" to be a previously stated concession rather than a command, but Paul's need to clarify that "this" is *not* a command but a concession suggests that the antecedent reads as a stated command.

72. The Jews recognized the wife's right to marital relations from Ex. 21:10.

73. Aristotle, *Eth. nic.* 1145A lists "lack of self-control" (*akrasia*) with "vice" (*kakia*) and "bestiality" *thēriotēs* as one of three states of moral character to be avoided. The only other NT occurrence of *akrasia* is Matt. 23:35, among the *woes* condemning the Pharisees.

74. To express an unattainable wish he uses the imperfect tense. C. K. Barrett, *A Commentary on the First Epistle to the Corinthians*, 2d ed. (London: A & C Black, 1971), 158; so also Fitzmyer, *First Corinthians: A New Translation with Introduction and Commentary*, 282. Cf. the present in 1 Cor. 11:3; 10:1; 11:3; 12:1 with the imperfect in Gal. 5:20; Rom. 9:3.

75. Liddell and Scott, *Greek-English Lexicon*, 1915.

76. E.g., Kistemaker, *1 Corinthians*, 209–10; Fee, *First Corinthians*, 275–76; Anthony Thiselton, *The First Epistle to the Corinthians: A Commentary on the Greek Text*, ed. I. Howard Marshall and Donald A. Hagner, NIGTC (Grand Rapids, MI: Eerdmans, 2000), 499.

77. Kistemaker, *1 Corinthians*, 209.

78. Paul spent three years in Arabia before going to Jerusalem and another fourteen years in Syria and Cilicia before returning to Jerusalem with Barnabas and Titus (Gal. 1:17–2:1). What he did in these early years is uncertain.

79. E.g., Barnabas (1 Cor. 9:6), Silas/Silvanus (1 Thess. 1:1), Luke (2 Tim. 4:11), Mark (2 Tim. 4:11), Priscilla and Aquila (Acts 18:18), Timothy (Acts 19:22), Titus (2 Cor. 8:23), Epaphroditus (Phil. 2:25), Erastus (Acts 19:22), Euodia and Syntyche (Phil. 4:2), Clement (Phil. 4:3), Urbanus (Rom. 16:9), Tychicus (Col. 4:7).

80. Contra Fee, *First Corinthians*, 322–27, who proposes that the term be consistently applied throughout the passage.

81. Contra ibid., 327n19, the NT never uses *parthenos* to refer to a betrothed woman without additional qualification (e.g., Luke 1:27; Matt. 1:18). Neither Liddell and Scott, *Greek-English Lexicon*, 1339, nor Danker, *Greek-English Lexicon*, 777, point to any examples where the term by itself designates a "betrothed" woman.

82. There is a parallel here in the use of "woman" (*gynē*) in Greek where the same term modified by a possessive pronoun designates "wife" rather than the generic "woman" (e.g., 1 Cor. 7:2).

83. *Parthenos* was seldom used of males, since, for the Greeks, only the woman's virginity was deemed important for marriage (Hesiod, *Op.* 699). But Rev. 14:4 also uses the term for males suggesting that the biblical authors take a different view!

84. E.g., Hans Conzelmann, *1 Corinthians: A Commentary on the First Epistle to the Corinthians*, Hermeneia: A Critical and Historical Commentary on the Bible (Philadelphia: Fortress, 1975), 132; see esp. n. 13. Wolfgang Schrage, *Der erste Brief an die Korinther 2. Teilband 1Kor 6,12–11, 16*, Evangelisch-Katholischer Kommentar (Düsseldorf: Benziger Verlag, 1995), 156–57; Collins, *First Corinthians*, 293.

85. E.g. Bruce W. Winter, "Secular and Christian Responses to Corinthian Famines," *TynBul* 40 (1989): 91–100.

86. And does this imply the apostle was "in error" as W. E. Phipps, *The Sexuality of Jesus* (Cleveland, OH: Pilgrim, 1996), 99, suggests?

87. Rom. 13:5; 1 Cor. 7:37; 9:16; 2 Cor. 6:4; 9:7; 12:10; 1 Thess. 3:7; Philem. 14.

88. See author's PhD thesis.

89. The likelihood of a food shortage in Corinth at this time is also supported by other sources. See Barry Danylak, "Tiberius Claudius Dinippus and the Food Shortages in Corinth," *TynBul* 59.2 (2008): 231–70.

90. Epictetus, *Diatr.* 3.22.70–72; Epictetus, *The Discourses as Reported by Arrian, the Manual, and Fragments*, trans. W. A. Oldfather, 2 vols., LCL (Cambridge: Harvard University Press, 1925–1928), 2:155.

91. Musonius Rufus 14; Lutz, ed., *Musonius Rufus "The Roman Socrates,"* 92–95; Epictetus 3.7.19; Deming, *Celibacy*, 51–52.

92. The connection with the classic Greek marriage question is apparent in the vocabulary of "concern," the concluding adverb "without distraction," and the adjective "benefit," the verbal form of which we encountered in the disciples' question on marriage in Matt. 19:10. See further discussion in David L. Balch, "1 Corinthians 7:32–35 and Stoic Debates about Marriage, Anxiety, and Distraction," *JBL* 102 (1983): 429–39; and Deming, *Celibacy*, 193–201.

93. Menander [*Stobaeus*] 4.22.44; see also Plato the Comic in *Anthologia Graeca* 9.35; Theophrastus cited in Jerome, *Jov.* 1.47.

94. Horst Balz and Gerhard Schneider, eds., *Exegetical Dictionary of the New Testament*, 3 vols. (Edinburgh: T & T Clark,1990–1993), 2:81.

95. Liddell and Scott, *Greek-English Lexicon*. See esp. *Sent. Sextus* 230a; also Wis 6:14; 9:4; Heroditus, *Hist.* 5.18.

Epilogue

1. John Piper, *This Momentary Marriage: A Parable of Permanence* (Wheaton, IL: Crossway, 2009), 41–48, describes marriage as "God's showcase of covenant-keeping grace."

Subject Index

Scripture Index

251

Scripture Index

3:20–21	166	20:34	148
3:31–35	166	20:34–36	144, 150, 164
3:34–35	167	20:35	109
6:3	169	20:35–36	52
7: 5	166	20:39	163
7: 10	173	21:23	206
7: 13	166	22:20	40, 136
10:2–12	150, 233n17	23:27	171
10:5–9	226n4	23:56	171
10:11–12	191, 233n19	24:1–11	171
10:17	124	24:31	22
10:19	173		
10:25	152	**John**	
10:28–30	167	1:12–13	147
12:18–27	163	1:33	233n11
12:25	164	2:6	161
15:40	171	3:1	144
15:43	209	3:3–8	145
19:19	166	3:4	146
		3:5	146
Luke		3:6	147
1:27	205, 240n81	3:8	147
3:16	233n11	3:10	144, 146–47
4:17–19	108	3:12	146
8:1–3	170	3:16	147
8:19–21	166	3:27	161
9:21–56	143	3:31	233n7
9:61–62	168	7: 5	166
10:1	170	7: 42	120
10:1–2	149	12:2	171
10:25	124	12:39–41	91
10:25–37	143	13:23	236n77
10:38	171	14:2	106
10:38–42	169	14:2–3	165
11:27–28	168	16:13	22
12:15	55	19:11	233n7
12:51–53	168	19:23	233n7
14:15–24	168	19:26	169, 236n77
14:20	168	20:2	236n77
14:26	168	20:31	149
16:8	236n73	21:7	236n77
16:18	191, 233n19	21:20	236n77
18:18	124	21:25	161
18:20	166, 173		
18:28	168	**Acts**	
18:29–30	167	1:8	149
18:30	236n73	7: 5	226n14
18:31	170	8:26–40	107
19:5	171	13:50	209
20:27–40	163	15:7	149

253